THE PSALMS

The Bible & Liberation

An Orbis Series in Biblical Studies

Norman K. Gottwald and Richard A. Horsley,
General Editors

The Bible & Liberation Series focuses on the emerging range of political, social, and contextual hermeneutics that are changing the face of biblical interpretation today. It brings to light the social struggles behind the biblical texts. At the same time it explores the ways that a "liberated Bible" may offer resources in the contemporary struggle for a more human world.

Already published:

The Bible and Liberation: Political and Social Hermeneutics (Revised edition), Norman K. Gottwald and Richard A. Horsley, Editors

Josiah's Passover: Sociology and the Liberating Bible, Shigeyuki Nakanose

THE PSALMS

*Songs of Tragedy, Hope,
and Justice*

J. David Pleins

ORBIS BOOKS

Maryknoll, New York 10545

The Catholic Foreign Mission Society of America (Maryknoll) recruits and trains people for overseas missionary service. Through Orbis Books, Maryknoll aims to foster the international dialogue that is essential to mission. The books published, however, reflect the opinions of their authors and are not meant to represent the official position of the society.

Copyright © 1993 by J. David Pleins

Published by Orbis Books, Maryknoll, NY 10545

Acknowledgment: *From Collected Poems of W. H. Auden* by W. H. Auden, copyright © 1979 by Edward Mendelson, William Meredith and Monroe K. Spears, Executors of the Estate of W. H. Auden. Reprinted by persmission of Random House, Inc.

Manufactured in the United States of America

Library of Congress Cataloging-in-Publication Data

Pleins, J. David.
    The Psalms : songs of tragedy, hope, and justice / J. David Pleins.
        p.   cm. — (Bible and liberation series)
    Includes bibliographical references and index.
    ISBN 0-88344-928-5
    1. Bible. O.T. Psalms—Criticism, interpretation, etc.
I. Title.   II. Series.
BS1430.2.P53   1993
223'.206—dc20   93-17541
                                                              CIP

May I, composed like them
Of Eros and of dust,
Beleaguered by the same
Negation and despair,
Show an affirming flame.

W. H. Auden,
September 1, 1939

Contents

PART III
HISTORY, WISDOM, PROPHECY

Preface

The need for a biblical historian to write a book on social justice and liberation was pressed home to me several years ago by Gustavo Gutiérrez. This book represents a partial answer to questions raised in our conversations concerning the use of scripture in modern contexts of oppression and injustice. In the pursuit of a biblical theology of poverty I have found the need to grapple with matters of justice, not merely in abstract sociological terms, but to tackle the question of suffering in *human* terms. This book attempts to give a coherent reading of the psalms, taking into account *both* the individual and communal dimensions of the texts. It is my conviction that a spirituality that refuses to splinter off personal questions from global concerns constitutes the matrix for a worship *praxis* that can foster liberation.

Many friends and colleagues have nurtured and jarred my thinking about the Psalter over the last several years. While space does not permit a full description of their contribution, I hope that this listing of names will remind them of the fruitful conversations we have had that have ultimately shaped this book: Ed Almazol, Astrid Beck, Fran Bohan, Greg Beshouri, Scott and Mary Crickmore, Ruth Dunn, David F. Graf, Tom Hanks, Gary Herion, Rev. Jonathan Hevita, Rev. Galen Hora, Wendy Kaufman, Hoy Ledbetter, Patricia Narciso, Beth Petro, George Pickering, Lou Poulain, Scott Rains, Robyn Ramsey, Rev. Leo Rooney, Scott and Judie Shalkowski, Rev. Herb Schmidt, Steve and Becky Spina, Craig Watts, Jeff Wild, and Lee Wyatt. Friends like these remind us of the need for biblical scholars to address the pressing issues of our day. A special thanks to my mentors: David Noel Freedman, David P. Himle, Charles R. Krahmalkov, and George E. Mendenhall. I would also like to offer a word of thanks to the support of these efforts given by the Department of Religious Studies at Santa Clara University, especially my colleagues Sr. Rita Claire Dorner, Joseph Grassi, Sr. Anne Marie Mongoven, Steve Privett, S.J., Sal Tassone, S.J., and our department Chair, James W. Reites, S.J. I am also thankful to the many students in our undergraduate department and our graduate program in parish ministry. The tone and direction of this book have been indelibly impressed by the questions raised in our class discussions.

Additional words of thanks go to James Hansen and Tom Conry, who invited me to present this material at two sessions of the School for Cantor and Lectors of the National Association of Pastoral Musicians. Their enthusiasm helped to bring this book to its completion. I am grateful as well to Walter Brueggemann for his insightful comments on the draft chapters of this work. I, of course, assume responsibility for the drawbacks of such a project, but I hope that any limitations will serve to stimulate further reflection and action.

My thanks to Cynthia Bradley of our Orradre library, whose unflagging assistance permitted me to secure numerous research materials for this book. Thanks also to our department administrative assistant Bernadette Proulx for her timely technical assistance in preparing this manuscript for publication.

I am particularly grateful to Robert Ellsberg and Robert Gormley of Orbis Books for their spirited support of this project.

This book is dedicated to my wife, Teresa, and our children, Shannon, Sarah, and Christopher. They have truly made this a labor of love.

DAVID PLEINS
Feast of St. Charles Lwanga and Companions, 1992

Introduction

A Poetry of Justice

Personal suffering and national disaster, individual hope and collective aspiration constitute the human spiritual terrain out of which the Psalms arise. These 150 sacred hymns and prayers represent Israel's way of speaking to God in a world of individual pain, political oppression, and communal distress. To this day in our worship, the poets' vocabulary of justice continues to draw out of us a response to suffering and injustice. The Psalms give voice to a variety of emotions that are all part of the struggle to build God's world of justice. Anger at oppression stands side by side hope for human history. Despair over war finds its place next to joy for God's creation. Underlying all the issues, however, are still more basic concerns that form the heartbeat of this book, namely the question of "suffering, social justice, and worship" in the Psalter. Wrestling with these questions we, as individuals and as community, come face-to-face with Israel's God of justice in a world touched by both eros and dust.

In this Introduction, I want to set out the overarching scholarly matrix of this poetic tapestry. How does the modern study of the Psalms reshape the kinds of questions we as a community need to ask as we seek to appropriate the Psalter in an era of global change? Can we find in the Psalter a vital expression of the justice question? If the Psalter is the poetry of suffering and justice, how shall we enter into its particular literary mode of expression so as to recapture its vibrant tones in our worship today? These are the questions that shall spark our exploration.

THE PSALTER: STRUCTURE AND TEXTURE

By and large, the modern study of the psalms takes place within the framework established by H. Gunkel.[1] Gunkel, in particular, is credited with dividing the psalms into recognizable literary genres — a pattern followed in this book. Not content with literary classification alone, Gunkel's student S. Mowinckel sought to establish the cultic background of the Psalter.[2] While much of what Gunkel and Mowinckel advocated has been subject to refinement and debate, the lively cultic and literary framework developed by these and other scholars endures.[3]

The Psalter is the product of a complex history of writing and compilation.[4] The Psalter's division into five books (I = Pss. 1–41; II = 42–72; III = 73–89; IV = 90–106; V = 107–150) represents an artificial construction, modeled on the five books of the Torah — a construction that obscures the presence of earlier collections in the Psalter. These earlier collections reveal the complex layering of the Psalter's historical development that took shape over several centuries.[5]

Presumably the oldest collection is found in book one and consists of a number of psalms attributed to King David (Pss. 3–41). Individual laments dominate this collection. Another collection of psalms attributed to David can be found in Psalms 51–72. Surrounding this latter collection are the so-called guild collections of Korah (42–49) and Asaph (73–83) — psalms in which the "we" collective form predominates. Strikingly, the overall group extending from 42–83 shows a notable preference for using the Hebrew term *'ĕlohîm* when referring to God, rather than YHWH — the divine name that is most frequent in the first David collection (cf. Pss. 14 and 53 for this linguistic alteration).[6] It is unclear at what point in time these texts were grouped together, but the marked use of the word *'ĕlohîm* would seem to indicate that 42–83 once formed a separate collection to which the non-Elohistic Korah psalms (Pss. 84–85, 87–88) were added "as a kind of appendix."[7]

Other developments are less clear, but it is logical to suppose that Psalms 3–41 and 42–88 were joined together as a single unit sandwiched between the messianic/royal texts of Psalms 2 and 89 — texts that would have functioned as fitting introductions and conclusions to such a collection. It is also reasonable to suppose that Psalms 1 and 119 — texts that emphasize the notion of instruction or torah — at one point enclosed a still larger collection of psalms, bringing together the David collections with other texts and giving this new collection a wisdom/meditation cast. As the full 150 psalms are joined — drawing together additional smaller collections such as the psalms of ascent (Pss. 120–134), another David collection (Pss. 138–145), and the hallelujah psalms (Pss. 106, 111–113, 135, 146–150) — we begin to notice a new, overall pulse to the work: The movement is from lament, which dominates the first part of the Psalter, to praise, which dominates the latter half, as Westermann has argued.[8] The emergent emphasis on praise is reflected in the Jewish title for the Psalter, *tĕhillîm*, which means "praises."

What are the psalms? Are they prayers or hymns? What is the ritual function of the Psalter? At one level, Bonhoeffer was justified in titling his book on the psalms *Das Gebetbuch der Bibel* ("The prayer book of the Bible"), because the Psalter is indeed *a prayer book* or, shall we say, it is a collection that contains a number of texts that find their origins in the prayers of individuals in need.[9] The superscription of Psalm 102, "a prayer of the oppressed," is indicative of this dimension of the Psalter. Yet, Seybold is correct in saying that the recurrent use of "hallelujah" in the latter part of the Psalter "made the texts available for general use in the congregation."[10] Likewise, the Greek and Latin titles for the collection, namely the Latin *psalmus/psalmi* and Greek *psalmoi/psalterion*, referring as they do to "stringed instruments," "appear to conceive of the Psalter from the musical point of view, as *a song-book*, while they fail to take account of the large number of prayer texts which it contains."[11] Beyond prayer and music, the Psalter also presents itself, through its wisdom psalms, as a body of texts useful for *meditation and reflection* (Ps. 1:1). From this latter perspective, the Psalter is a vast body of instruction governing life and human action.[12] We see, therefore, in the overall development of the Psalter, a checkered history that incorporates prayer, hymnody, and meditative reflection.

TOWARD A JUSTICE METHODOLOGY

Ultimately for the Jewish and Christian traditions, it is the Psalter's hymnodic, cultic character that has come to dominate. The community's embrace of the tradition engulfs and adapts the individuated origins of the texts, thereby allowing the tradition to carry the psalms into successive eras of questioning, doubt, struggle, sorrow, and injustice.[13] In light of this reception and use of the Psalter as scripture, B. Childs, the preeminent architect of the canonical criticism of the Hebrew Bible, is correct to assert that we need to go beyond discussions of the original sociological context of the psalms and begin to pay attention to the changing usage of the psalms in religious communities over the centuries.

Childs's approach has important implications for a political reading of the Psalter. Where a materialist or sociological analysis might emphasize that the royal psalms, for example, originated in the royal sphere of the ancient monarchies, Childs will point out that these texts were preserved and "treasured" in light of their messianic *reinterpretation*.[14] This reinterpretation elicits from these texts a markedly different reading than that discerned through socioeconomic and historical analysis.[15] For Childs this "shifting" is indicative of the removal of the psalms from their original cultic or sociological context to a revitalized status as sacred scripture within the broader religious tradition. According to Childs's analysis, this later reshaping of the text is as integral to its interpretation as is the discovery of the text's original setting and use. In our approach to the Psalter, therefore, we must not ignore the fact that the ancient hymns and prayers addressed to God have now become God's word to God's people — i.e., they have become authoritative documents for communities existing long after the time of the original writing of the texts.[16]

Certainly there is great merit in Childs's thesis. The changing needs of the community have left their stamp on the psalms. The community has preserved these texts beyond their original context and we can learn a great deal from listening to the powerful messages the carriers of the tradition found while collecting and adapting the psalms.[17] In this way, we can argue that we too are justified in bringing our own needs to the text in order to read them with new eyes in the modern worship context.[18] And yet, I would argue that in appreciating the final layers of the canon, i.e., entertaining the issues and concerns of the later stages of the tradition, we should not overlook—to the extent that we are able to discern them—the initial questions and contexts that gave birth to the psalms. Unearthing the royal dimension of some psalms, for example, makes clear to us the political questions that were alive at the earliest stages of the tradition and reopens us to the political dimension of the received tradition. In this way, a recovery of the royal side of the Psalter helps to define a practical way in which the psalms can continue to be received today in relation to matters of social justice.

When read with both canon and context in mind, the Psalter is found to contain a richly textured language of human experience before God. Psalms that were originally individual prayers can now be received by the community as its expression of collective grief or hope. We can immerse ourselves at the beginnings of the tradition to wrestle with the sociopolitical context and questions of the text. We can locate ourselves at another stage of the tradition and meditate on these texts as documents imparting spiritual instruction. Or we can place ourselves in yet another stage of the tradition to be moved by the psalms to sing songs of tragedy and trust, lament and praise. However, no matter what our port of entry, the issues of suffering, social justice, and worship continually confront us in our engagement of the texts. These questions are critical to our continued appropriation of the psalms as living documents in church and synagogue today.

It is my belief that a vigorous interaction between ancient text and modern context will spawn new insights into our communal relation to the God of justice. This book should be read as an essay in constructive theology. While there is ample discussion and reference to previous scholarly discussion of the Psalter, what I have found dissatisfying with the bulk of these studies is their often tangential approach to justice and liberation questions.[19] By placing questions of suffering and social justice at the center of our discussion, we can tap the scholarly discussions to underscore the vitality of the Psalter's theological outlook for a modern worship that wishes to grapple with contemporary issues of oppression and liberation.

To this end, I offer thoughout the book my own translation of the Psalms and other biblical materials. A fresh translation of these texts helps to bring out the language of poverty, oppression, and justice so often obscured in other translations of the biblical text. I have also chosen to employ inclusive language with respect to persons and nonsexist wording in relation to God throughout this book, reflecting my belief in the enduring character of the psalms for contemporary worship. Of course, this is a complex, much debated endeavor, but I believe that the sensitive translator must respect both the historical context of the biblical record and the continued use of those writings as part of a living religious tradition. As an aside, I should also note here that the verse numbering followed in this book is that of the Hebrew Bible. In many cases, this verse numbering is one verse off from the system employed in the standard English translations of the Hebrew Bible. Thus, for example, the Hebrew Bible's Psalm 68:2 is numbered 68:1 in typical English translations. The goal of the translations presented in this book is to make clear the Hebrew Bible's abiding commitment to those who suffer and are oppressed. The notion of inclusive language will be addressed more specifically in chapter 6.

READING THE POETRY OF THE PSALTER

Seybold is correct to point out that some of the psalms at least were "composed as a work of art, and it is as a work of art that it is to be read and heard."[20] He bases his consideration in part on Psalm 45, which presents itself as the composition of a "skillful scribe." In some sense this observation can be applied to Psalms as a whole because it contains works of poetry of unparalleled skill in the Hebrew scriptures. For a fuller appreciation of the Psalter, I would like to outline here some of the basic principles of Hebrew poetry.

Hebrew poetic texts are often written using bicola or couplets, i.e., paired lines that bear close relation to each other.[21] Quite often this relationship is synonymous, that is, the word order and vocabulary of the second half of the couplet mirrors that of the first half:

> *Many bulls surround me.*
> *Mighty ones of Bashan encircle me* (Ps. 22:13).

> *My throat thirsts for you,*
> *My body aches for you* (Ps. 63:2b).

In many cases, the second colon (or balancing line in the couplet) is not "synonymous" in the sense that it simply replaces the initial colon word by word; rather, the second colon frequently intensifies, heightens, or makes the meaning of the first colon more specific:

> *They have set your sanctuary on fire.*
> *They have profaned the place where your name dwells*
>   (Ps. 74:7).[22]

At times the second colon (or the balancing line in the couplet) offers a negative or contrasting counterpart to the first:

> Positive: *I told you of my sin;*
> Contrast: *I did not cover up my iniquity* (Ps. 32:5a).

A number of common variations in arrangement occur. Commonly, the bicolon is arranged chiastically, i.e., the second colon reverses or crisscrosses the word order of the first half of the couplet — a phenomenon that is often obscured in English translation:

> *Who lifts (a) — out of the dust (b) — the poor (c).*
> *Out of the garbage pile (b') — raises (a') — the poor (c)*
>   (Ps. 113:7).

While the couplet form is undoubtedly the most frequent line type, there are occasionally examples of tricola (three colons or lines) and, less commonly, quatrains (four colons or lines in a group):

> Tricolon:
> *They [the wicked] set an ambush in a hidden place like*
>   *the lion in his lair.*
> *They set an ambush to catch the oppressed person.*
> *They catch the oppressed by drawing them in with their*
>   *net* (Ps. 10:9).

> Quatrain:
> *They conspire secretly against your people.*
> *They counsel together against those you treasure.*
> *They have said, "Let's cut them off as a nation.*
> *The name of Israel will not be mentioned ever again"*
>   (Ps. 83:4–5).

Apart from the rather significant absence of a discernible meter pattern, biblical Hebrew poetry makes uses of poetic devices common in western poetry, namely assonance, alliteration, metaphor, simile, repeated words, word plays, refrains, and so forth.[23] The acrostic form is found in Psalms 25, 34, 37, 111, 112, 119, 145, and presumably represents the original structuring behind Psalms 9–10. In an acrostic, each poem is organized according to the letters of the Hebrew alphabet.

These comments, though brief, should permit the reader a greater degree of appreciation for the craft behind the composition of the Psalter. Poetry is more than form, of course. Poetry's images and vocabulary derive their power from their ability to retrace new lines over the human condition. The repetitive and intensifying style of Hebrew poetry surrounds and continually immerses the hearer or singer in the issues of the text, as Bonhoeffer notes:

> This form . . . encourages us not to allow the prayer to be cut off prematurely, and it invites us to pray together with one another. That which seems to be unnecessary repetition to us, who are inclined to pray too hurriedly, is actually proper immersion and concentration in prayer. It is at the

same time the sign that many, indeed all believers, pray with different words yet with one and the same word. Therefore the verse form in particular summons us to pray the Psalms together.[24]

As we know from Bonhoeffer's life and death, this immersion in biblical experience translated into a heightened sensitivity toward the injustices that beset his homeland under Nazi rule. We are reminded therefore that the study of the Psalter's poetry requires not simply a technical appreciation of its literary devices but also a command of the contexts and questions that give birth to texts of tragedy and hope.

STRUCTURE OF THE BOOK

In this Introduction we have looked at the general methodology and orientation of this book. With this background in mind, we shall proceed to investigate the Psalter under the rubrics of three major trajectories. The first trajectory arises out of *individual and communal suffering* and addresses its speech to God. In the first part of the book we hear individuals and the entire community speak out of their suffering and their hopes. The movement of these first chapters schematizes the movement of the Psalter itself, namely from lament to praise. In its unceasing struggle out of lament toward trust, thanksgiving, and ultimately praise, the community and the many individuals within that community seek to wrestle with God in their suffering, their oppression, their expectation, and their liberation.

As will become clear through these chapters, the community's struggle does not take place in a political vacuum, and so the second section of the book is taken up with the *question of political structures, the politics of hope, and divine governance*. Issues of war and rule are part of the divine economy, and the demands of God impinge on the operation of the state and its several institutions. Here we see that the community's hopes and tragedies are inextricably intertwined with the political structures of the day. Only movement beyond the politics of war and triumphalism can engender the peace of God that the community so desperately needs.

The final section of the book is given over to three major strands of the biblical tradition that find expression in the Psalter, namely *the history of salvation, wisdom instruction, and prophetic admonition.* Many voices — individual and collective, traditional and radical — make their way into the kind of reflection and worship we find in the Psalter. Each voice challenges us to rethink worship's response to human suffering and social injustice.

PART I

THE COMMUNITY SINGS

1

"Out of the Depths"

Laments of the Individual

We may not think that we have done enough if we come to worship bearing only the pain of our suffering or our anger at social injustice, but even in this act of defiant worship, the psalms tell us, we have already established the foundation for a biblical spirituality. Fully a third of the Psalter is devoted to psalms of lament by the individual, telling us in no uncertain terms that authentic worship emerges when worshipers dare to express their pain and raise before God their deepest questions about the reign of injustice in the world. The singing of these psalms of lament throughout the liturgical year gives modern worshipers the opportunity to articulate their grief and come to terms with their sorrow. The psalms of lament continually call us to plumb our beleaguered condition, give voice to our radical doubts about God's action in the world, and bring to the surface our disquiet over suffering. It is true that praise, thanksgiving, and other expressions of joy stand at the heart of worship—as the rest of the Psalter makes abundantly clear—but the psalms of individual lament show us that the sufferer's call to God from "out of the depths" (Ps. 130:1) of misery and oppression is central to a vital worship. In the individual laments we find a compelling theological and human response to the reality of personal suffering and social injustice—a response that arises from inside situations of hurt and hopelessness, injustice and oppression.

TO PLEAD FOR HELP

Worship cannot remain blind to human suffering. Our liturgies cannot ignore poverty, hunger, oppression, and death, especially on the vast scale we are witnessing today. Neither should worship bury the hidden griefs and personal sorrows each worshiper carries through the portals of every house of worship. A global tragedy is also a tragedy for many individuals, and a worship that seeks justice must touch both the individual and the global—the personal and structural dimensions of suffering. Worship's task is to let us hear the cry of the poor, not in an abstract and detached way, but with all the urgency and despair that arises out of concrete situations of grief and oppression.

Worship is open to the full range of human experience and offers numerous gestures and postures that permit us to express all that lies within our hearts and souls.[1] To the person who feels strengthened by God, worship offers the raising of hands to give thanks. To those who sense the overwhelming majesty of God, worship offers the bending of knee as a sign of reverence. But what posture can worship offer the aggrieved?[2] How can the brokenhearted approach God? The psalmists answer this question with profound simplicity. No special stance can be demanded of the aggrieved; we can only hope that worship makes ample room for their *cry for help*. Thus it is that many of the individual laments open with a direct call to God to "rescue" or "save" the sufferer from a situation (Pss. 7:2; 54:3; 59:2; 70:2; 140:2). Often the psalmists will ask God to "listen" (Pss. 5:1; 55:2–3; 86:1), "hear my cry/prayer" (Pss. 17:1; 61:2; 102:2; 141:1; 143:1), and "have mercy on me" (Pss. 51:3; 56:2; 57:2). Stronger still is the plea that opens Psalm 69,

> *Help me, God,*
> *For the waters have come up to my neck!*
> *I've sunk into the miry depths,*
> *There's no place to stand.*
> *I've gone into deep water.*
> *The flood has overtaken me* (Ps. 69:2–3).

Poignant in its poetry is the opening to Psalm 42,

As the hind pants for the streams,
So does my inner self long for you, God.
My being thirsts for God, for the living God.
When will I go and see the face of God? (Ps. 42:2–3).

The cry for help is indicative of the speaker's pain, despair, grief, and longing. Bringing only this cry, and nothing more, the sufferer is free to approach God. The plea is urgent and immediate. We can sense the desperation in the speaker's moment of grief.

The psalmists are forced to acknowledge that in our pain and in so many situations of oppression, God all too often seems distant and unconcerned. When the person in need cries out, is God listening? Sensitive to this reality, several psalms open with an expression of the terrible abandonment that so often accompanies suffering. The sufferer is permitted to bring the most bitter and demanding of pleas. It is not unusual to find rather daring opening expressions such as "LORD, don't rebuke me in your anger!" (Ps. 6:2), "Don't be silent!" (Ps. 109:1), or "Why do you keep so far away?" (Ps. 10:1). The latter example is most striking, for the text's outcry is made against the wicked rich who in their denial of God abuse the orphans and poor (Ps. 10:2–18). Worship that does not give expression to this kind of pain or despair is worship that fears to touch the harsh realities of human existence and poverty:

My God, my God, why have you left me?
Why is my help so distant from my anxious pleas?
My God, I call out during the day, but you do not
  answer;
At night I find no rest (Ps. 22:2–3).

Words of anger at God are terribly uncomfortable, but the psalmists recognized that worship will remain a shallow affair if the worshiper's rage is left outside the sanctuary. This willingness to give expression to the agony of the sufferer is, in biblical terms, an act of worship. To speak from one's pain and oppression—to no longer hide one's rage over injustice—is the essential first step in approaching the God who, in our suffering, seems so aloof.

Worship that is modeled after the psalms of lament does not hesitate to face the perplexing character of human suffering, nor does it shy away from the difficult questions raised by poverty and oppression. Worship that tackles suffering and injustice will offer words and hymns that articulate this plea for help in all its rage and despair. Since this cry for help is on the lips of many individuals and even entire nations, our worship must not disregard the pervasive and global character of individual suffering. Worship rooted in a genuine concern for the disenfranchised cannot remain disconnected from the cry of the oppressed person in Southern Africa, Latin America, the Middle East, or elsewhere. Neither will authentic worship ignore the hopelessness felt by so many refugees left stranded hundreds, if not thousands, of miles away from home. Worship that wishes to articulate the cry of the oppressed and the refugee will recognize in this cry a world prayer. In an age where few theologies can be called universal, the plea for help is the one universal prayer emerging from the heart of all who suffer or who are exploited. Giving expression to this grief does not guarantee easy answers to the problem of suffering or injustice, but such a worship does open the door to a confrontation with God over the realities of human grief and political oppression.

CONDITION OF THE SPEAKER

We hear about and witness so much suffering through television, the newspapers, and the movies that we can become quite numb to the ugliness and brutality of human suffering. Yet, even in an age of numbness, we can still be thrust back into the reality of world suffering, either by pictures and stories that jar us back or, closer to home, by some tragedy that sweeps us away in the torrent of suffering. Whatever the shocking image or grievous event, we cannot long remain distant from the fact that our world battles constantly against illness or political oppression, and in many cases we are still losing that battle. These images and incidents travel with us to worship, whether we ask them to or not. They are in our minds when we are called to offer up our unspoken petitions. These situations tug at our hearts whenever the right words touch us during our worship, and we find tears welling up from inside. By dwelling on the condition of the worshiper, the psalms of lament use worship to penetrate our numbness to human suffering. These psalms recognize that the deepest form of worship roots itself in a firm confrontation with the ills and injustices that people endure daily. Worship that dares to exhibit the degree of openness toward suffering that we find in the psalms of lament is not a comfortable or pleasant sort of worship; nevertheless, this act of worship is a necessary spiritual exercise for all who hope to remain open to God in the midst of suffering.

Where we might find it uncomfortable to deal with suffering during worship, the psalmist feels free to speak in a direct way to God about illness and other forms of suffering that tear away at the worshiper's physical being. For the speaker in Psalm 6, anguish and pain consume the body:

> *Show me favor, LORD, for I am wasting away.*
> *Heal me, LORD, for my bones are terrified.*
> *My inner self is terribly frightened.*
> *And you, LORD—how long?* (Ps. 6:3–4).

The graphic character of these psalms is shown in the range of body parts that are mentioned: bones, tongue, eyes, throat, and knees all find their way into the painful poetry of the psalmist:

> *I've been poured out like water.*
> *All my bones are out of joint.*
> *My heart is like wax,*
> *Melted within me.*
> *My strength has dried up like a piece of pottery.*
> *My tongue sticks to the roof of my mouth.*
> *And you lay me down in death's dust* (Ps. 22:15–16;
>   cf. e.g., Ps. 6:7–8).

Often we find the speaker weary and faint from pain and grief, as seen, for example, in Psalm 69,

> *I am exhausted from crying out,*
> *My throat is dried out,*
> *My eyes have failed,*
> *While waiting for God* (Ps. 69:4).

Psalm 109 makes it clear that this kind of grievous suffering can result from poverty and oppression.

> *For I am oppressed and poor.*
> *My heart is pierced within me.*
> *I go like the shadow that has lengthened.*
> *I am shaken off like the locust.*
> *My knees shake from fasting.*
> *My body has shriveled up; there's no fat left.*
> *I have become their object of scorn.*
> *When they see me, they shake their heads* (Ps. 109:22–
> 25).

Whether the product of illness or poverty, human suffering in all its concreteness moves the psalmist to speak out. It is the psalmists' conviction that God must hear and see what is happening to the world that God has made. The psalmists' songs are vivid and compelling, teaching us that worship is the appropriate place for us to bring our greatest grief and deepest suffering into the presence of God.

In Psalms 31 and 69, the language of the sufferer bears a strong resemblance to the motif of the "suffering servant," better known from Second Isaiah (cf. Isa. 42:1–4; 49:1–6; 50:4–9; 52:13–53:12).[3] In Second Isaiah, God's servant's work has ended in failure and the servant has suffered terribly. Second Isaiah makes it clear that God's support is clearly with God's servant, yet the servant must endure this time of suffering and scorn before finding consolation. In Psalms 31 and 69, the speaker has also "become an object of ridicule" because of "all my enemies" (Pss. 31:12; 69:5, 9–12):

Those who see me in the streets, flee from me.
I'm put out of mind, like someone who has died.
I'm like an object that has disappeared (Ps. 31:12b–
   13).

To serve God and to know that we are not exempt from suffering can be a source of great frustration. In fact, this suffering may become all the more maddening because God fails to act. "Don't hide your face from your servant. I'm in distress. Answer me quickly" (Ps. 69:18; cf. 31:17). The Psalter's "suffering servant" laments firmly underscore the fact that, as in the Book of Job, being a "servant" of God is no passport out of a world of suffering and injustice.

The words of comfort that are found at the ends of Psalms 31 and 69 are reminiscent of the great word of consolation spoken by Second Isaiah (Pss. 31:20–25; 69:31–37; cf. Isa. 40:1–10). Yet, we will develop a superficial view of these words of comfort if we do not bear in mind that these are words spoken only *after* much grief and loss. Neither the words of Second Isaiah nor of the Psalter function as a magic elixir that smoothes over the pain to numb the sufferer. Both of these collections recognize that those who proclaim messages of hope must not create false expectations about what faith can accomplish in the midst of suffering. The words of comfort linked to the suffering–servant image remain fully aware of the hard work that remains in rebuilding the ruined land (Ps. 69:31–37; Isa. 40:3–5; 41:17–20; 44:24–28; cf. Isa. 58:13). The anguish and grief inherent in the notion of the suffering servant refuses to let us turn this image into a pleasant, redemptive vision of suffering. The image actually points out how shocking suffering is and how sharply suffering pierces the soul. Reflecting carefully on the image of the suffering servant, we are reminded that it is often quite difficult to find adequate consolation in situations of suffering. The biblical message of consolation comes to a servant who has experienced great grief and terrible despair.

Some suffering is so bitter and grievous that mere words cannot contain the sorrow or pain. In those situations, if we even dare resort to words, few symbols are weighty enough to express the sufferer's burden. In the psalms of lament, Sheol and the

Pit—symbols of the grave and the netherworld—are used to give expression to the deepest levels of mental anguish and physical exhaustion:

> *Come back, LORD! Rescue me!*
> *Help me for your mercy's sake.*
> *No one remembers you in death.*
> *Who can give thanks to you in Sheol?*
> *I am exhausted from my groaning.*
> *I drench my bed [with tears] every night.*
> *I dissolve my couch with my tears* (Ps. 6:5–7).

The suffering of Sheol and the Pit is a suffering that has left the worshiper feeling abandoned and in great despair:

> *I am bloated by troubles.*
> *My life approaches Sheol.*
> *I am reckoned with those who descend to the Pit.*
> *I am like a warrior without a rescuer,*
> *Loose among the dead,*
> *Like the slain lying in the grave,*
> *Whom you remember no longer.*
> *They are cut off from your power.*
> *You put me in the lowest Pit,*
> *In the dark places, in the depths* (Ps. 88:4–7).

Through the powerful symbols of Sheol and the Pit, the voice of worship confronts the painful possibility that God cannot or will not act, and even when God does act, these terms symbolize great suffering:

> *I thank you, O Lord my God, with my whole heart.*
> *I honor your name forever.*
> *For you showed great kindness to me,*
> *by rescuing me from Sheol's lowest depths* (Ps. 86:12–
> 13).

True expressions of worship will dare to touch these distressed sentiments. The challenge for worship, whether ancient or modern, is to find a way to move on to praise and thanksgiving without negating the grief of abandonment. To offer praise when grieving is really needed only compounds the emptiness the worshiper feels and leads to a painful separation between worship and life. The worship that offers strength is a worship that is willing to follow the worshiper down to Sheol and the Pit, to the lowest levels of abandonment.

Certainly, worship cannot be driven solely by symbols such as Sheol or the Pit, but neither should worship overlook the underlying personal pain implied by these symbols. The consolation of God only takes on flesh as the sufferer's pain and loss are truly heard. Our liturgies cannot afford to remain numb to human suffering, especially if our hope is to construct a spirituality rooted in justice. Hence, we must find a way to speak about and symbolize these realities in worship. Worship for us is no different than for the psalmist—it is the decisive moment when we demand to know if God has been numbed to the suffering and injustice that abound in our world. The daring approach of the biblical laments is to insist that God look squarely at human suffering, physical pain, humiliating oppression, and despair.

ENEMIES AND OPPRESSORS

While much of the suffering discussed in the individual laments concerns internal suffering or illness, a great number of these psalms speak about suffering created by "enemies" and "the wicked" who assault the speaker. Since we are far removed from the original context of these writings, it is now very difficult to be sure precisely who these attackers are.[4] However, the frequent references to the "enemies" and "the wicked" are significant enough for us to single out these terms as a special feature of individual laments.

The enemies encircle the speaker. Sometimes they mock and taunt, pelting the sufferer with derisive words: "They surrounded me with words of hate; they attacked me without cause" (Ps. 109:3; cf. 64:3–9; 71:10–13). The suffocating danger

the worshiper faces is graphically brought out by depicting the
enemies and the wicked rich as dogs, bulls, or lions:

> *They [the wicked rich] set an ambush in a hidden place*
>   *like the lion in his lair.*
> *They set an ambush to catch the oppressed person.*
> *They catch the oppressed by drawing them in with their*
>   *net* (Ps. 10:9).

> *Many bulls surround me.*
> *Mighty ones of Bashan encircle me.*
> *They open their mouths against me,*
> *Like a prowling, roaring lion* (Ps. 22:13–14; cf. 22:17–
>   19; 59:7–8, 15).

Sometimes the enemies are said to be seeking the life of the
sufferer: "Those who seek my life lay traps for me. Those who
look for my misfortune say destructive things; they mutter
deceptive words throughout the entire day" (Ps. 38:13). In
response to the enemies and the wicked, the sufferer calls on
God to slay and frustrate them (Pss. 69:19–27; 143:9–12).

A few of the individual laments suggest that this talk of the
enemies ought to be given a political interpretation. Psalm 55
portrays the enemies as the oppressor who ravages the people
of Israel:

> *Hear me! Answer me!*
> *I am restless about my complaint; I am disquieted,*
> *Because of the voice of my enemy,*
> *Because of the oppression of the wicked,*
> *For they throw iniquity at me,*
> *And they begrudge me in anger. . . .*
> *Confound them, Lord. Mix up their language.*
> *For I have seen violence and strife in the city.*
> *Day and night, they surround it on its walls.*
> *Iniquity and trouble are inside it.*
> *Destructive things are within.*
> *Oppression and deception never leave its town square*
>   (Ps. 55:3–4, 10–12).

In Psalm 59, the enemies are the "nations" who surround Israel: "They come each evening growling like dogs, roaming the city" (Ps. 59:7; cf. 59:2, 8–9). Psalm 102, set in the exile, depicts the enemies as those nations among whom the exiles are dispersed:

> *Throughout the day, my enemies ridicule me.*
> *Those who mock me curse using my name. . . .*
> *You will arise, [LORD], and show compassion to Zion.*
> *For it is time to show favor to Zion.*
> *The appointed time has come.*
> *For your servants like its stones.*
> *They adore its dust* (Ps. 102:9, 14–15; cf. vv. 16–23).

Psalm 120, also set in the political context of exile, is very specific when it speaks of the exile's frustration at having to live among people who only know how to make war,

> *Alas, I dwell with [the people of] Meshech,*
> *I live among the tents of [the people of] Qedar.*
> *I've had enough of living with those who hate peace.*
> *I am peaceful,*
> *But if I talk,*
> *They are for war* (Ps. 120:5–7; cf. 140:2).

While it is not always clear what the psalmist intends by the use of the words "enemy" or "wicked," the evidence cited here indicates that in a significant number of cases these terms are used to refer to (1) domestic oppressors, (2) foreign conquerors of Israel, and (3) opponents of Israel's exiles. As we shall see in the next chapter, the community laments tend to support a political interpretation for this language in the Psalter.[5]

These references to political enemies in the individual laments indicate quite clearly that worship cannot shy away from political realities. In a first-world context, all this talk about political enemies and oppression is often deemed inappropriate to worship language. Yet, when read from a third-world perspective or from the point of view of those who are exploited in the first world, these words are explosive. To those, for example, whose lives are lived out under dictators and death squads, talk of political enemies is extremely relevant subject matter for worship. Ancient Israel, overrun as it was by the superpowers of its day, was really in no different a situation than most third-world or eastern block countries in our century. Surrounded, beleaguered, and exploited, these countries have known what it means to cry out to God to end the assault by the wicked and the enemy. Worshipers in these political contexts may understandably utter before God this seemingly scandalous language about the enemy, the wicked, and the oppressor. They must not be told that worship has nothing to do with politics, when they know that it is worship's task to confront those who prey on the populace like packs of dogs (Ps. 22:17).

INNOCENT OR GUILTY?

Are we responsible for our suffering? Is suffering some kind of punishment for our evil deeds? These are age-old theological conundrums, subject to intense debate in the biblical tradition. To the Deuteronomistic Historian—that is, the writer(s) of the books of Deuteronomy through Kings—it was obvious that Israel was morally and theologically responsible for its own destruction. Similarly, the writers of Proverbs blame the poor for their suffering, treating poverty as a punishment for laziness.[6] In contrast, the Book of Job questions Israel's standard theology of rewards and punishments by posing the counter argument: What about the innocent who suffer? The Psalter, not standing in one ideological stream of tradition, is divided on the question of personal responsibility for suffering.

It is true that some of the individual laments foster in worshipers a sense of personal responsibility and guilt for their situation of suffering. These psalms directly link suffering and transgression:

> *For I am prepared to stumble.*
> *My pain is with me continually.*
> *I confess my iniquity.*
> *I am anxious over my sin* (Ps. 38:18–19; cf. 7:4–6).

The sufferer's act of worship makes the sufferer ever more conscious of personal wrongdoing: Grief over suffering is transformed into grief over sin. Certainly, the most eloquent psalm in this regard is Psalm 51, a text which calls on God to "Wash me completely from my iniquity; purify me from my sin" and the famous, "Create in me a clean heart, God; renew a steadfast spirit within me" (Ps. 51:4, 12). Psalm 51 gives heightened expression to the notion of personal responsibility for wrongdoing, articulating the worshiper's desire that God bring about a cleansing of the worshiper's guilt.

However, the individual laments also acknowledge that not all suffering is the product of one's own sin or wrongdoing. As Westermann observes, few laments can be termed "penitential psalms."[7] Of the seven texts he cites, only two, namely Psalms 38 and 51 (cited above), actually focus on the topic of sin in any full way.[8] By contrast, the speaker in Psalm 26, confident of personal faithfulness, challenges God to inspect all that lies within:

> *Judge me, LORD, for I have acted with integrity.*
> *I have trusted in the LORD. I have not slipped.*
> *Inspect me, LORD. Test me.*
> *Test my conscience and my mind* (Ps. 26:1–2).

The vast majority of the individual laments simply detail situations of distress and make little or no mention of personal guilt. Psalm 86 comes from the mouth of a worshiper who is "oppressed and poor" and who speaks only of the "time of my trouble" and of a "group of violent people" who "seek my life" (Ps. 86:1, 7, 14). Such a lament, spoken by an innocent individual, carries a Job-like quality, especially in its protest against a God who, in the midst of suffering, appears to be the enemy. The psalmist can say, for example, "You are my God, my stronghold. Why have you rejected me? Why must I walk about gloomily under an enemy's oppression?" (Ps. 43:2; cf. Job 7:17–21; 13:23–24; 30:19–21). The psalmist recognizes quite clearly that so much of human experience is out of our control. The theology of rewards and punishments—one of Israel's standard theologies—is flatly contradicted by the reality of the suffering of the innocent. Knowing that most suffering cannot be explained as a punishment for personal misdeeds, the psalmists boldly address words of protest to God, lifting a critical voice against undeserved suffering and victimization.

Do we consider such challenges to God to be words of worship? If we do not, perhaps this is because deep down we still think that most, if not all suffering, is the deserved result of personal wrongdoing. Worship based on the lament moves us beyond guilt feelings to confront a situation that is really out of our hands. Worship may empower us to fight an illness or protest an injustice, but worship should never make us feel responsible for our suffering if, in fact, we are not to blame for that suffering. In these situations, the Psalter recognizes that the sufferer must be permitted to speak the unspeakable before God. Who has not felt cheated by God when they are overwhelmed by disease, by the pains of old age, by the sorrows of death or the miseries of poverty? Many of the individual laments give expression to these feelings, acknowledging that such sentiments are an appropriate part of worshipful prayer before God. Worship must become the place where all who suffer for no reason or who suffer unjustly can find a hearing for their personal anguish and their rage against God.

DOUBTS AND AFFIRMATIONS

Out of the depths of concrete misery, torment, torture, exploitation, and exile, the worshiper is permitted to address some hard questions to God. In the individual laments, the questions directed at God can be rather pointed, such as, "Has God forgotten how to show pity?" (Ps. 77:10a), or "If you keep track of people's sins, Lord, who will survive?" (Ps. 130:3). Questions like these speak to the harsh reality of human suffering in the face of divine indifference. Now that the sufferer has been allowed to articulate feelings of grief, the weary condition of the body, the situation of danger from without, he or she is able to articulate a cry to God from the depths of suffering with a clarity not possible before the act of worship began. The laments bring about a free expression of grief, thereby opening the way to a deeper struggle with God.

Hand in hand with the worshiper's doubts come affirmations concerning God that are sources of encouragement and hope for the worshiper. Throughout the individual laments, the sufferer seeks to affirm God's ability to help those in need. God has been and continues to be a refuge for the sufferer: "For you have been my refuge. A tower of strength in the face of the enemy" (Ps. 61:4; cf. Pss. 25:20; 31:2). Sometimes the affirmation is bald and simple, as in "[God] leads the humble with justice and teaches the humble [God's] way" (Ps. 25:9). God's knowledge of the sufferer since birth and even prior to birth also forms the basis for hope:

> *I have leaned on you from the womb.*
> *You are the one who drew me forth from my mother's*
> *loins.*
> *I always offer my praise to you* (Ps. 71:6; cf. 139:11–
> 18).

At times the affirmation of the laments is rooted in God's faithfulness in the past. In one text the psalmist invokes scenes from Israel's primordial history, recalling God's "miracles in the past," when God parted the exodus waters and led the people "like a flock" (Ps. 77:12, 21). The past is never used as an escape in the laments. In this text, on the contrary, the past is invoked to induce a sense of possibility for the present.

Worship attuned to suffering and social justice merges doubt and affirmation. Through the confrontation between doubt and affirmation the psalmist gains enough strength to remain in the presence of God. The most creative worship—the most powerful affirmations of God—emerge as we speak to human frailty, suffering, and pain. The liturgical environment is the place to bring our deepest griefs, our greatest fears, and our ever-recurring unbelief. It is the main task of the laments to articulate this sense of "dislocation," to use Brueggemann's phrase.[9] We short-circuit worship if we deny the dilemmas of doubt raised by the reality of personal suffering and social injustice. Yet, in the articulation of grief and doubt, worship becomes the occasion for an ever-tentative exploration of God's kindness, faithfulness, and presence.

WORSHIP AS A RESPONSE TO SUFFERING

The psalms of individual lament are driven by the belief that God can be worshiped without negating the reality of human suffering. Yet, as Westermann observes,

> There is not a single Psalm of lament that stops with lamentation. Lamentation has no meaning in and of itself. . . . What the lament is concerned with is not a description of one's own sufferings or with self-pity, but with the removal of the suffering itself.[10]

The end the psalmists have in mind is the return to the posture of worship—to the altar of God and the lyre of praise:

> *Send out your light and your truth;*
> *They will guide me.*
> *They will bring me to your holy mountain,*
> *To your dwelling-place.*
> *Then, I will go to the altar of God—*
> *To God, my exultant joy.*
> *Then, I will give thanks to you with the lyre, O God, my*
>   *God* (Ps. 43:3–4; cf. 51:16–19; 54:7–8).

Some laments conclude by envisioning a situation where people will be restored to recount God's fame and deeds:

> *When the LORD has rebuilt Zion,*
> *When God has appeared in glory,*
> *When God has taken note of the prayer of the destitute,*
> *And has not despised their prayer,*
> *This will be written down for the coming generation,*
> *And the nation that is created will praise the LORD*
>   (Ps. 102:17–19; cf. 35:27–28; 57:8–12).

Presumably, the sufferer will be able to return to tell of God's faithfulness and assistance in the midst of suffering and oppression:

> *Let me exult and rejoice in your kindness,*
> *For you have seen my oppression,*
> *You know my troubles* (Ps. 31:8).

> *I will give great thanks to the LORD with my mouth,*
> *I will praise God in the midst of the crowd,*
> *Because God stands at the right hand of the poor,*
> *To save them from those who would judge their lives*
>   (Ps. 109:30–31).

At the very least, the sufferer will return to the place of worship with the sense that he or she is free to be present with every pain, loss, doubt, hope, and dream (cf. Pss. 56:11–14; 71:14–24).

Psalm 42 suggests that our very opportunity to worship is one possible response to suffering. The sufferer pointedly remembers having participated in worship and wonders why he or she is disquieted now:

> *My being thirsts for God, for the living God.*
> *When will I go and see the face of God?*
> *My tears have been my food day and night,*
> *As they say to me throughout the day,*
> *"Where is your God?"*
> *May I remember and pour out these things inside me:*
> *That I went with the throng,*
> *And I walked with them to the house of God,*
> *With a joyous voice and with thanksgiving,*
> *With a crowd keeping the holiday.*
> *Why am I so low?*
> *Why do I groan within?*
> *Hope in God, for I will again give thanks for God's help*
>   (Ps. 42:3–6).

This psalm is filled with the despair of the sufferer. Yet, the sufferer discovers that worship can fashion a response to suffering. While we cannot always remove pain and misery, nor answer the deepest questions about suffering, we can worship. Worship gives us a way to look at the world. Worship gives us a place to bring our disquiet over suffering. However, worship, we are told, is more than pouring out our grief. It is also the reservoir from which we can draw our greatest strength to cope and keep going.

The individual laments raise difficult questions about worship in a world of suffering and injustice. We must continue to assess how we bring matters of suffering and justice into the worship environment. We need to ask if our worship serves as a genuine source of consolation to those who suffer. Do the oppressed find in our worship a credible protest against the injustices rampant in our world? The individual laments call for a worship that strives to touch those who suffer, without negating their suffering or making them feel further abandoned. Worship should seek to create a space for grief, an opportunity for protest, an occasion to wrestle with God. If our worship environment achieves this blending of grief, protest, and wrestling, we will have captured the dynamic spiritual sensibilities that underlie the individual laments.

2

"By the Rivers of Babylon ... We Wept"

Community Laments

Reflection on suffering and worship presents us with a paradox: We often suffer and seek God as individuals, but we can only worship as a gathered community. The sixteen community psalms of lament broaden the vision of the previous chapter by giving collective worship a way to articulate the fear, grief, and anger of an oppressed and defeated nation. The psalmists' faith incorporates communal woes as a necessary dimension of worship: the pain of war, the despair of exile, and outrage at the continued exploitation of the nation. The psalmists recognized that communal tragedy is more than an amalgam of individual tragedies. Hence the need for a poetry that arises out of the community's experience of war, dislocation, refugee flight, exile, oppression, and despair. These are the occasions and the contexts of the communal laments.

To what extent are the individual and communal laments related? There are some who would argue that the individual psalms of lament studied in the previous chapter actually have a strong communal dimension. In a number of cases one could argue that the "I" of the individual laments is figurative for the entire community.[1] This, if true, would deepen and extend the present chapter. However, it does appear that most of the individual laments do indeed intend to articulate the suffering of individuals, and so the question of the "I" must remain open for these psalms. Furthermore, the emphatic "we" and the dominant "us" of the community psalms of lament invite us to reflect on worship's response to the communal dimension of suffering. The community psalms of lament press us to consider how worship can, and indeed must, speak to a society and a globe that is beset by suffering. For modern worship the issues posed by the community laments are politically challenging: Does our worship shy away from global suffering? Is our articulation of grief in the global village conscious of the individuals who are suffering, or have we let our worship become distant to collective pain? The community psalms of lament give the worshiping community a compelling vocabulary for confronting a God who oversees social dislocation and tragedy.

A COMMUNITY EXPRESSES ITS GRIEF

How does the community approach God when its members feel abandoned by God? This is a question that has gnawed away at me for a number of years. A black pastor from Namibia once formulated it for me this way: "What do I tell my parishioners who, in their oppression, ask me why God has abandoned us?" Lacking the international attention of a South Africa, the people of Namibia had every reason to feel doubly abandoned by God. The communal laments do not offer an easy road out of this sense of abandonment, but they do offer the language that a community can use to begin speaking to God from out of the midst of communal distress. How does the community penetrate the veil of divine silence? Here it is instructive to look at the variety of ways in which the communal laments open.

Simple Pleas

As with the individual laments, many of the community laments open with very simple pleas to God. Phrases such as, "Help, LORD!" (Ps. 12:2), "Listen, Shepherd of Israel" (Ps. 80:2), and "God, do not be silent!" (Ps. 83:2) are words that are not far from the lips of any community that suffers. Sometimes the opening pleas are even more desperate, such as, "God of retribution, appear!" (Ps. 94:1).

Questions of God

Throughout the community laments, disturbing questions are raised about God's actions toward Israel. In one case, such a question opens the lament: "Why, God, do you forever reject? Why are you so angered with the flock in your pasture?" (Ps. 74:1). The poet wrestles with the contradictions of a theology which believes in a God who rewards and punishes but must contend with a world that knows war, destruction, and injustice. The realities of that world press so hard that God seems to be an angry enemy — a view that is startlingly close to the Book of Job (cf. Job 7:17–21; 13:23–24; 23:10–15; 30:19–21).

Statements Concerning Exile or War

Several of the texts begin by rooting themselves in situations of profound social disruption. Psalm 137 opens with the plaintive, "Along Babylon's rivers, there we sat and cried, remembering Zion" (Ps. 137:1). Still more vivid is the statement in Psalm 79:1 which recounts the moment of the Babylonian invasion that led to the exile: "God, the nations have entered your inheritance! They have defiled your holy temple. They have turned Jerusalem into ruins." These laments exhibit a theological perspective that is born out of the profoundly concrete experience of war and the aftermath of exile (cf. Ps. 129:1).

Statements Concerning the People's Relationship with God

Although many of the community laments reflect the disarray and despair of war, in several texts, this conflictual atmosphere serves to focus the community's ongoing dialogue with God. This relationship is thought of in generational terms: "God, we have heard with our own ears, our ancestors have told us, you acted in their day, in former times" (Ps. 44:2). Yet, the community laments are hardly content with nostalgia; rather, they explore

the contradictions between such an affirming history and a dis-
rupted present in which the only sensible theological response
seems to be, "God, you have thrown us off and torn us down"
(Ps. 60:3a; cf. 74:1). However, the dissonance between the
received tradition and the radically probing questions raised by
the experience of invasion and war also led the psalmists to
affirm, "Lord, you have been our refuge generation after generation" (Ps. 90:1b). The community laments open the doors to
a radical reassessment of the people's relationship with God.

An Individual Speaks up for the Community

One psalm opens as a liturgical moment in which an individual approaches God on behalf of the community: "I look up
toward you—to the one enthroned in heaven" (Ps. 123:1). Elsewhere, the notion of a singular voice is adapted to give expression to the unified character of the community's suffering: "Let
Israel say, 'They have abused me since my childhood' " (Ps.
129:1). Several texts speak to collective suffering as an experience that binds the people together as one person (cf. 44:5, 16;
60:11; 74:12; 83:14).[2]

Accusation against the Enemy and the Wicked

Two community laments open by directly addressing the issue
of the enemy and wicked who exploit and assail the people (Pss.
58:2, 129:1). These diatribes against the enemy become disturbing acts of worship. We might also note here Psalm 83, which,
though it does not open with a note about the enemy or wicked,
is almost entirely taken up with a political alliance that, under
Assyrian leadership, threatens to bring the nation's destruction.
The concrete reality of the political moment—the experience of
violence and exploitation—guides the language of prayer and
worship.

Note of Expectation

There are several texts that begin in a more affirmative tone.
We can hear the deep conviction in the poet who says, "LORD,

you have favored your land, having restored Jacob's captives" (Ps. 85:2) and "My mind is assured, God, I will sing" (Ps. 108:2a; cf. 123:1; 126:1). These more positive opening pleas indicate that the worshiping community did at times muster a sense of God's presence in the midst of tragedy. And yet, these texts do not skirt around their context of adversity (cf. 85:6–9; 108:12–14).

Despite the rare positive opening plea, the rather more numerous negative opening statements remind us that in situations of communal suffering, the community's sense of despair or rejection must stand at the heart of the community's theological reflection and worship. Both approaches, whether positive or negative, lead to powerful religious acts if they correctly gauge the community's status and needs in its moment of tragedy.

THE POLITICS OF SUFFERING

No doubt we could imagine a variety of catastrophes and evils that would provoke a community to respond in lamentation. However, the Psalter chooses to focus on three well-defined and highly charged political roots of national suffering, namely: the plundering and oppression of Israelite society; Israel's military defeats; and the starkest sign of communal humiliation, the destruction of Jerusalem and Solomon's temple by the Babylonian military machine in 587 B.C. Since several of the communal laments find their roots in this destructive invasion, let us enter Israel's politics of suffering through this event that looms so large in the biblical imagination.

A Community Devastated

The destruction of Jerusalem and its temple in 587 B.C. is the defining issue for the community's lament in Psalms 74, 79, and 137 (we will discuss Psalm 137 below). To the community, the destruction of Jerusalem is a sign that the community has been rejected by God (74:1). This sense of abandonment is more than simply an exile's wistful musings for the days of old. The descriptions of destruction are too vivid for us to think that the speaker

is far removed from the events. The psalmist speaks out of
the whirlwind of war, developing a prayer for a community that
is desperately reaching for God after suffering the carnage
wreaked by foreign invasion:

> *Bestir yourself because of the perpetual ruins,*
> *Because of all the harm the enemy has caused in the*
>   *sanctuary. . . .*
> *They have set your sanctuary on fire.*
> *They have profaned the place where your name dwells.*
> *They said to themselves, "Let us destroy them alto-*
>   *gether."*
> *They have burnt all God's shrines that are in the land*
>   (Ps. 74:3, 7–8).

Psalm 79 likewise depicts the destruction of the temple (Ps.
79:1), offering a vivid and wrenching description of the horrors
of that hour:

> *They have made the corpses of your servants to be food*
>   *for the birds,*
> *They have made the flesh of your holy ones to be food*
>   *for wild animals.*
> *All around Jerusalem, they shed their blood as if it were*
>   *water,*
> *With no one to bury them.*
> *We have become an object of scorn to our neighbors,*
> *An object of ridicule and derision to those around us*
>   (Ps. 79:2–4).

For both Psalms 74 and 79 the recounting of this disaster gives
birth to still further pleas and questions, "How long, God, will
the foe reproach, will the enemy revile your name?" (74:10) and
"For how long, LORD, will you remain angry?" (79:5). The community laments depict the devastation in haunting images and
with deep emotion. We are in no doubt that the destruction left
the community angry, desolate, defeated, ashamed, and venge-
ful.

A Community Defeated

Several of the communal laments focus on military conflicts and defeats (Pss. 44, 60, 83, 108). These texts are probably to be connected with the Babylonian invasion, although we cannot be absolutely certain of this. Unlike the individual laments where the identification of the enemy is less certain, in these texts, the enemy is a coalition of foreign powers that intends to destroy Israel:

> *Your enemies are in an uproar,*
> *Those who hate you are walking proudly.*
> *They conspire secretly against your people.*
> *They counsel together against those you treasure.*
> *They have said, "Let's cut them off as a nation.*
> *The name of Israel will not be mentioned ever again"*
> (Ps. 83:3–5).

Psalm 83, in which the enemy element dominates, specifically names many of the nations that surrounded Israel as members of this advancing coalition: Edom and the Ishmaelites, Moab and the Hegrites, Gebal, Ammon, Amalek, Philistia, Tyre, and Assyria (Ps. 83:7–9).[3] Psalm 60 draws on the image of an earthquake to depict the arrival of an invading army (Ps. 60:3–5). In this defeat, the psalmist sees the failure of God to "march forth with our armies" (Ps. 60:12; cf. 108:12–14). Psalm 44 likens the devastation and dispersal brought by the enemy to being devoured like sheep (Ps. 44:12). The disaster of deadly warfare is at the heart of these communal laments, making ever more striking the phrase, "we are considered sheep to be slaughtered" (Ps. 44:23). When the community suffered terrible devastation because of foreign intervention, it became the task of worship to speak to God out of the horrors of war. There is a strong lesson for us here. Living as we do in an era of war, it is a crime that so little of our hymnody attempts to come to grips with the real tragedy engendered by the conflicts that riddle our world community. When one part of the world community is racked by the agony of war, how can we not feel this suffering and sing of its pain?

A Community Plundered

To the topics of the destruction of Jerusalem and military defeat, we must also add a third politically laden category central to the community laments, namely exploitation and plundering. How is the community that has felt "assailed" and "plowed" since its youth (Ps. 129:1–3) supposed to speak to God except from within its experience of political oppression? How is the "plundered vine" (Ps. 80:9–16) supposed to worship without informing God about the bitter realities of exploitation? The community laments make room for the worshiping community to say to God: "You fed them [the people of Israel] the bread of tears. You had them drink tears in great measure. You set us at strife with our neighbors and they ridicule us" (Ps. 80:6–7). Worship must not remain blind to the interior realities of oppression; the community must be willing to name its distressed condition. Only this sort of communal lamentation will be able to see past the arrogant speech making of those who hold power (Ps. 12:3). Beyond the lies, the community discovers the God who says, "Because of the violence against the oppressed and the groaning of the poor, I will now take action" (Ps. 12:6).

Foreign invasion, military defeats, and oppression: This is the "theological" stuff that gives shape to most of the community laments.[4] These psalms acknowledge that worship cannot operate above or apart from the grievous realities of international politics. Worship must articulate and confront the sorrow that empire building spreads. In a world rife with social injustice, we must ask ourselves if we have written hymns that give expression to the awfulness of that injustice? Such hymns cannot be detached, but, like the community laments, should articulate the pain of people who are forced to suffer so much. We do not usually think of worship as a time to groan with the world community. Yet, the community laments teach us that worship is the decisive occasion for us to use a language of world suffering — a language that knows war, exile, defeat, and violent abuse.

THE COMMUNITY SPEAKS TO THE GOD OF SILENCE

Does the community's lament ever breach the wall of silence that suffering can build between God and God's people? Three of the community laments are conceived of as discussions between the community and God (Pss. 44, 79, 90; cf. Ps. 85). One of the notable features of each of these dialogues is that they do not immediately begin with the plea for help. Psalm 44 opens with the psalmist addressing God, reminding God that the community knows that God used military might in the past to establish Israel (Ps. 44:1–4). Psalm 79 opens with a disturbingly concrete description of the conquering army entering God's domain, turning Jerusalem into ruins, and leaving corpses in their wake (Ps. 79:1–4). Psalm 90 begins with a reflection on the eternal character of the God who has been "a dwelling place in every generation" (Ps. 90:1–4). Each of these psalms seeks to place the community's pain into a larger divine context.

The plea for help is set several verses into the psalm in order to jar the worshiper into seeing the community's suffering against the backdrop of sacred history and divine power. Thoughts of past victory sharpen Psalm 44:10: "Yet you have rejected and disgraced us." Pictures of the temple's destruction, with its ruins, dead bodies, and blood shed "like water," puts a keen edge on the anger in Psalm 79:5: "How long, LORD, will you be angry forever, will your anger blaze like fire." Psalm 90's opening reflection on God's eternal perspective heightens the urgent plea that emerges in Psalm 90:13: "Turn, O LORD! How long?"

Following these pleas, Psalms 44 and 79 offer some pointed words intended to jar God. In Psalm 44, for several verses after the plea, the psalmist depicts God as the one responsible for the enemy's plundering of Israel (Ps. 44:10–17). The psalm then affirms that though God may have abandoned the community in its moment of distress, "We have not forgotten you, or been false to your covenant" (Ps. 44:18). In trying to make sense of the dissonance between the community's current crisis and the community's story that in the past God has acted, the psalmist looks inside the community to find and affirm both its faith in God and its sense that God is to blame for this disaster. In Psalm 79, the words after the plea call on God to avenge the blood spilt during the invasion of Jerusalem and the destruction of the temple: "Pour out your wrath on the nations that do not know you, upon the kingdoms that do not invoke your name" (Ps. 79:6; see 79:5–11). Communal outrage in time of war is a religious act, even a duty—however foreign that outrage has become to us who rest ensconced in more settled forms of worship and politics. By expressing this anger, the oppressed community begins to affirm its own faithfulness amid the rage, thereby probing the character and faithfulness of God.

The realities of war and destruction make it difficult if not impossible for worship to conclude on a pleasant or hopeful note. Nearing the end of Psalm 44, the poet painfully exclaims, "Why do you hide your face, forgetting our misery and oppression?" (v. 25). Similarly, Psalm 79 rather strongly asserts, "Let the groan of the prisoner reach you; in accord with your great strength, set free those who are to die. Pay back our neighbors sevenfold for the abuse they have shown you, Lord" (Ps. 79:11–12). The brutality of the world does not permit us to assume that worship will always be easy or soothing. In fact, if Psalms 44 and 79 are a guide, there are times when worship might end with us lying prostrate on the ground, calling on God to "Arise and help us, redeem us in accord with your faithfulness!" (Ps. 44:26–27). At times it is appropriate to ask, as in Psalm 90, "Give us joy for as long as you have made us suffer, for the years we have seen misfortune" (v. 15). This is a note of hope bound up with the realism only a survivor of suffering knows.

Worship will undoubtedly reopen old wounds of death, loss, and hopelessness, for worship is the place where the community acknowledges its despair, gives vent to its anger, and mourns its losses. These are the things a community will offer in its dialogue with God. There is, of course, a practical lesson in all of this for modern worship. A community should not bare its suffering only to receive a trite song in response. Shallow music cannot reach into the depths of a community's pain. In the midst of suffering, a community needs to find tough language that will go so far as to dare God to speak to the community's suffering. In so doing, worship creates a bridge to the silent God.

THE COMMUNITY LOOKS WITHIN

The attempt to articulate communal suffering leads to a more self-reflective mode in Psalms 126 and 137. This self-reflection takes two forms in these psalms, offering alternative ways for communities to face their grief. Psalm 137 looks back to the *not-so-distant and ever-so-painful past*. Psalm 126 looks forward to the *ever-so-dreamlike but laughter-filled future*. Through these psalms, the community asks what sorrows have we known together (Ps. 137) and what joys will we share together (Ps. 126). Both approaches — looking to the past or to the future — produce a self-reflection that allows the community to seek God in the present.

Reflecting on a painful past without covering up sorrow can help to focus and articulate present grief. Psalm 137 most poignantly recalls Babylonian captivity: "By the rivers of Babylon, there we sat and we wept as we remembered Zion" (v. 1). Jerusalem remains a bittersweet memory. The exile's anger is sharpened by the experience of that memory. The anger that emerges gives us one of the most troublesome passages in the Psalter:

> *Remember, LORD, against the Edomites,*
> *The day of Jerusalem's fall,*
> *On which they said,*
> *"Strip! Strip!*
> *Down to the foundations!"*
> *Babylon, the one to be destroyed,*
> *Happy is the one who repays you,*
> *Who rewards you in kind for what you have done.*
> *Happy is the one who takes and dashes your babies*
> *Against the rocks!* (Ps. 137:7–9).

Even the anger of the refugee or the exile can become an act of prayerful worship. These are, of course, words of desperation, but who has not at one time or another called on God to really mete out justice against governments, companies, and corrupt leaders who steal land, murder the innocent, and make so many live lives of virtual slavery? This is a natural reaction, and Psalm 137 teaches us that these are not words, feelings, and realities that we have to hide from God.

The more hopeful Psalm 126 gives us a communal self-reflection on the future. This is not a future vision that represents an escape from the present. We know this because the psalm's talk about the future permits the worshiper to gain perspective on the present: "Those who sow in tears will harvest in joy" (Ps. 126:5). Yes, the present is bitter, but the psalmist seeks to infuse the present with a sense that God can and will provide joy. One of the tasks of worship is to assist the community in reflecting on its suffering. This reflection must not cover over past grief or feelings of anger, but can also envision a future in which the community rejoices. All reflection, whether on the past or the future, should seek to help the community gain perspective on its present suffering. The act of worship needs to make room for the frustration felt by exiles and for all who "sow in tears" (Ps. 126:5). Yet, for the sake of the suffering community, the act of worship must also seek to make room for dreams, visions, and unexpected joy. This offers a great challenge to the sensitive liturgist, for in trying to make people dream again, the liturgist is not there to take people on flights of fancy which will only further depress the sufferer when the act of worship is ended. In the laments, bitterness often tempers the search for a land where "kindness and truth meet, and justice and peace kiss" (Ps. 85:11; cf. 85:6–10). The liturgical task is, rather, to bring to the suffering community the possibility that a joy will arise that can fully embrace the sorrow the community has borne.

CONCLUSION: THE POLITICS OF WORSHIP

The political question dominates the community lament genre. The community laments focus on the dire consequences of empire building. War, colonialism, refugee flight, and international exploitation are all occasions for communal grieving. The community laments ask us to develop a worship that lays bare the grief behind the politics of suffering. The challenge to the modern worship setting is enormous. Where civil religion will regularly want to affirm that "God is on our side," the community laments compel us to look at the politics of suffering in our world community and in whichever land we call home. Where are the places that our nation is really in agony? Have these voices made their way into our worship? This is the challenge that the community laments pose for worship.

Of course, some of the realities and feelings the liturgy is called upon to express through these psalms are disturbing, but this is simply a reflection of the disturbing reality of mass human suffering presupposed by our psalmists' verses. National injustice, foreign invasion, suffering in exile—these experiences tore at ancient Israel's soul. Whereas politicians, kings, generals, and bureaucrats like to portray their conquests as swift and ever so glorious, the community psalms of lament show us that beneath royal decrees and martial glories lie fields strewn with dead bodies, severed families, and fallen city walls. It is, therefore, the task of worship to articulate the grief not only of suffering individuals but also of distraught communities.

The psalms of lament of the community create a space for the community as a whole to gather and reflect on its stricken condition. These psalms do not try to give final answers. In fact, the psalmists' call to destroy the wicked and the enemy certainly introduces a disturbing and discordant note into worship. Such desperate words are not easy to pray, but for a suffering community these are the very words the worshiping assembly needs to address to a God who seems altogether detached and aloof. Who could fail to hear the desperation in these words?:

> *Why should the nations say, "Where is their God?"*
> *Before our eyes, let the nations know that you avenge*
>   *the spilled blood of your servants* (Ps. 79:10).

I would say that if the psalmists' call to destroy the enemy makes us uncomfortable, we should ask ourselves if this is not a sign that we are among the power holders who are threatened by such a call. However uncomfortable the outcry makes us feel, we must bear in mind that for far too many in our troubled world, this embittered longing for God to act decisively against the triumphant oppressors is not a theological embarrassment but a dire necessity. If we find the call inappropriate to the worship setting, we should at least try to understand why those who live amid oppression and war are forced to make such a desperate plea, even as an act of worship.

For the most part, the community laments are capable of only bringing to the surface the pain of war and the frustrations of exile. There is little hope in these songs. No political solutions are offered. We must recognize that there are periods in history and places on this planet where there is little reason to hope because the political climate is so oppressive; in these situations, the tone of worship cannot restrict itself to simple praise and thanksgiving. Worship will always try to move toward praise, but in situations of communal grief, the act of worship must dare to speak to the politics of suffering.

3

"My Soul Thirsts for You"

Psalms of Trust

When Mahatma Gandhi, the well-known proponent of non-violence, came to write his autobiography, he spoke of his life story as, "my numerous experiments with truth."[1] In a parallel way, the Psalms of Trust (or Confidence) discussed in this chapter represent the results of Israel's life-restoring *experiment with trust* — tentative, yet concrete, steps toward a hope not yet fulfilled. To learn how to trust God in the difficult and bitter circumstances discussed in the previous chapters is nothing short of a dangerous experiment with truth and action. It is the risky venture of every generation of believers. Like the ancient Israelites, we seek to trust God in the midst of suffering in order to find the *strength* not to be overwhelmed by our grief. Like our spiritual ancestors, we seek to trust God in order to find, if not answers, then at least some *comfort* and reason for enduring our suffering. Again, like them, we seek to trust God in order to find the *courage* to stand up against those who crush us. In every generation, as reflected in the Psalms of Trust, all these — strength, comfort, courage — have been considered valid reasons to seek God.

Yet, the Psalms of Trust wish to go even deeper, to let prayer and worship begin to express a sense of our relatedness to God even in the midst of suffering. The Psalms of Trust are designed not only to strengthen, comfort, and encourage the worshiping community, but, more importantly, to awaken in the worshiper a sense of the spiritual quest—a quest that is like thirsting for water in a "dry and weary land" (Ps. 63:2). The Psalms of Trust or Confidence represent eleven such humanizing experiments. Two of these psalms are community Psalms of Trust (Ps. 115, 125); the rest are individual Psalms of Trust. The Psalms of Trust represent the first substantive movement away from alienation and abandonment toward hope and a renewal of life. We have here a poetry that gives worshipers a way to reach to God without either drowning in suffering or fancifully imagining that all is well.[2]

AN ACTIVE SEARCH FOR GOD

The paradox of suffering is that the very circumstances that can breed anger and distrust of God can also be the circumstances in which the most profound quest for God can begin. The modest proportion of the Psalter that is devoted to Psalms of Trust reminds us that any act of trust in God is far more tentative than the acts of lament which express the worshiper's grief and frustration. Indeed, it would seem that taking the step of trust requires first experiencing in full the expressions of anger and torment appropriate to the psalms of lament. The person or community that can lament experiences both a profound sense of God's absence and a fleeting sense of God's presence. The Psalms of Trust seek to capitalize on the latter without neglecting the former to remind us that worship is more than lament, it is an active search for God.

The active search for God is born out of the realization that no matter how tormented and pained we are as individuals or communities, in our relation to God we must say with the psalmist, "my inner being cleaves to You; your right hand supports me" (Ps. 63:9). The Psalms of Trust draw us to *discover an attachment to God* that is as basic as the suffering and injustice we experience. This bond is so deep that it forces us, even in the most difficult circumstances, to seek out the presence of God. This linkage with God is expressed most poignantly in Psalm 63:

> *God, you are my God.*
> *I seek you.*
> *My throat thirsts for you,*
> *My body aches for you,*
> *In a dry and weary land without water* (Ps. 63:2).

There can be no doubt that these words come out of a desperate search for God. There is no glossing over the harshness of human suffering. Psalm 63 shows us that the search for God in the midst of suffering must face squarely the worshiper's pain. There is not even the slightest hint that we find God by hiding from our suffering or our soul searching. Instead, there is the hope that in the "dry and weary land" we will find the water that can sustain us in our grief. This psalm acknowledges that trust in God is not an easy sensibility to cultivate, but cultivate it we must.

Where can we go to find God? Where is the heart of our spiritual landscape? For the psalmist, this painful search for God *leads one back to the temple* — back to the concrete center of worship:

> *One thing I ask of the LORD,*
> *I seek it:*
> *That I may live in the house of the LORD all the days*
>   *of my life* (Ps. 27:4)

> *I have looked for you in the sanctuary,*
> *In order to see your power and your glory* (Ps. 63:3).

> *Surely goodness and steadfast love shall pursue me all*
>   *the days of my life,*
> *and I will live in the LORD's house for the longest time*
>   (Ps. 23:6).

The psalmist deliberately sets out to find the power of God in the holy places. Through laments and songs of trust, the sanctuary becomes a locus where all of life can be brought and offered to God. It is the place where we can speak of war and injustice, and that in the midst of suffering we can demand of

God, "Teach me your way, LORD, and lead me on a level path because of my enemies" (Ps. 27:11; cf. 27:2–3, 12). This is no ethereal, detached request. The psalmist's prayer in the temple is an active call to trust in God in the midst of suffering and oppression.

Scripture tempers the worshiper's desperate search for God by *a call to wait for God*. This is the note on which Psalm 62 begins: "Only for God does my being wait in stillness" (v. 2). This patience is not something easily had. One cannot force the issue of patience. Such patience only comes as a discovery—a discovery in the midst of violence (Ps. 62:4–5, 11). It is a discovery that arises only from sensing God as "my rock and my help, my haven; I shall not be shaken" (Ps. 62:7; cf. 62:3). It is a discovery that comes from knowing that,

> *Humanity is nothing at all.*
> *People are a lie.*
> *Put on the scales,*
> *They weigh less than nothing.*
> *Do not trust in oppression.*
> *Do not put false hopes in robbery.*
> *Even if wealth increases, don't pay much attention to it*
>   (Ps. 62:10–11).

The psalmist has wrestled with human violence. The psalmist knows that much of what we say will endure really does not. Through these realizations, the psalmist is able to discover the substantive presence of God. It is this God that the psalmist is willing to wait for—a God who is "rock" and "haven," a "deliverance" and "refuge."

An even more beautiful and meditative sense of *waiting* for God is found in Psalm 131. The psalmist has arrived at the place of contentment and likens this to the intimacy of mother and child: "Surely I have stilled and quieted my inner being. Like a weaned child with its mother, like a weaned child is my inner being" (Ps. 131:2). These simple verses have inspired the modern adaptation of Christopher Walker, "Like a Child Rests."[3] The meditative strains of Walker's song ably capture the posture of waiting cultivated by Psalm 131.

Yet not all waiting in the Psalms of Trust is meditative and reflective. We have to keep in mind that the counterpart to "patient" waiting is a rather "impatient" waiting. Certainly anger and rage are more prominent in the laments, but such a stance is by no means foreign to the Psalms of Trust. Psalm 63 offers these very strong words,

> *May those who seek to destroy my life*
> *Descend to the lower depths of the earth!*
> *May they be given over to the sword!*
> *May they become the prey of the jackals!* (vv. 10–11).

We find similar words in Psalm 125 for those who are corrupt: "May the LORD lead them away with the evildoers" (v. 5). Certainly, these words express the raw emotions we saw more fully expressed in the psalms of lament. The angry words of Psalms 63 and 125 should tell us that not all Psalms of Trust are gentle and reflective. There is no dramatic chasm standing between the Psalms of Lament and the Psalms of Trust. Trust that is born of lament may indeed become reflective and meditative, but the waiting that trust fosters can be either patient or raging.

How is it, then, that the Psalms of Trust are able to move beyond the psalms of lament? One thing that a psalm of trust will not do is dwell on the contradiction between human suffering and God's power, as the psalms of lament do. Where the laments are at times paralyzed by God's failure to act in a time of very real individual or communal suffering, the Psalms of Trust attempt to renew the search for God in the midst of suffering. The Psalms of Trust urge us to see that it is the burden of worship to search for God in the midst of our sorrow—in the midst of war, violence, and oppression (cf. Ps. 63:10–11; also Ps. 27). The Psalms of Trust may not dwell on the particulars of human suffering, as do the laments, but the Psalms of Trust do root themselves vividly enough in concrete suffering for us to know that the search for trust goes on in the midst of death and suffering. The Psalms of Trust show us that one of the major tasks of worship is to awaken in the parched and beleaguered community a sense of the presence of God.

Of course, far too often situations of suffering cast their

shadow over all that the sufferer does and lives for. Years can be spent recovering from the devastating experiences touched on in the laments. Serious illness, economic strangulation by oppressive rulers and landowners, or foreign domination all leave their mark on those who suffer. The Psalms of Trust derive their strength from the fact that they find a way to take up the more active search for God without losing hold of the deep pain known in the laments. Terrible tragedy and God's power are allowed to commingle, neither negating the other. In the conjunction of tragedy and the divine presence, trust is born.

THE GOD OF THE QUEST

Who is this God of the quest? Who is this Eternal One that we thirst for? The God we meet in the Psalms of Trust is certainly not a God with many answers. These psalms do not seek to give simple explanations or reasons for suffering; instead, the Psalms of Trust ask us to let God be God. In order for the worshiper to awaken, the Psalms of Trust ask the worshiper to dwell on the character of the nameless God to whom we cry out. Whereas the psalms of lament derived their strength by forcing open the contradiction between human suffering and divine *silence*, the Psalms of Trust juxtapose human suffering with divine *presence* and out of this conjunction awaken in the worshiper the desire to trust in the One who, although silent, is nevertheless present.

What images and words does the psalmist use to depict this divine presence? Undoubtedly the most frequent and profound image is that of God as "refuge" and "haven." The psalmist is able to say to God, "Protect me, O God, for I take refuge in you" (Ps. 16:1; cf. 62:3, 9). The psalmist senses the divine presence in places where insecurity might dominate (cf. Ps. 16:8, 9–10). When physically threatened, this awareness of God as refuge gives the worshiper courage to face the foe and not flee like a bird to the mountains (Ps. 11:1). Perhaps the most powerful expression of God as refuge appears in Psalm 91:

> *I say of the LORD, my refuge and my fortress,*
> *My God in whom I trust,*

That God will rescue you from the snare of the fowler,
From the ruinous plague.
God will cover you with God's pinions,
And you will find refuge under God's wings.
God's trustworthiness is an encircling shield.
Do not fear the terror of the night,
Or the arrow that flies during the day.
Do not fear the plague that moves in the darkness,
Or the disease that destroys at noon.
A thousand fall at your side,
Ten thousand fall at your right hand,
But it will not approach you (Ps. 91:2–7).

Note that the psalmist is *not* saying that trust in God will allow one to easily escape terrible situations. What the psalmist is trying to do is to enable the worshiper to remember God's active presence even when dangers threaten. To say that God is our refuge is to say more than God is our way of escape. Rather, to say that God is our refuge means that in God we find the strength to stand up for what is right and just in situations of unrelieved violence and injustice. The psalmist raises the hope in the worshiper that someone, perhaps even the entire community, will live to see God's judgment against the wicked.

The other images of divine presence that pervade the Psalms of Trust, namely "help" and "shield" (Ps. 115:9–11), "rock" and "deliverance" (Ps. 62:7–8), and "guard" (Ps. 121:5), likewise bring out the nurturing, watchful, and guiding character of God. Perhaps the most famous image of guidance is that of God as shepherd, developed in Psalm 23. God is the one who "leads me to the water of the resting places" and "guides me in the right paths" (Ps. 23:2, 3). Yet, these pleasant pastoral images should not cause us to overlook the tensions that are present in the psalm—the context of insecurity that forces open the question of needing to trust God—namely, the "valley of deep darkness" and the "presence of my enemies" (Ps. 23:4–5). The protection of God is sought against the backdrop of the concrete realities more fully described in the psalms of lament. In the encounter between tragedy and trust, the psalmist is able to find a God who "renews my life" (Ps. 23:3).

In the image of shepherd, and in the other images discussed above, the psalmists cultivate the view that God is life-giving, but the psalms do not develop this vision in a detached or abstract manner. Rather, both the Psalms of Lament and the Psalms of Trust show us that we will only gain an awareness of God's presence to the extent that we let our worship resolutely seek God, not in spite of, but in light of human suffering. Worship can assist us in penetrating the haze of divine silence to gain a deeper sense of God's presence. Our images of God, like those employed by the psalmists, should strive to evoke an awareness of the divine presence in the midst of a hurting community. Certainly, we cannot guarantee that every act of worship will achieve this level of consciousness, but any worship that seeks to circumvent the expression of lament and sorrow will never foster an abiding sense of the divine presence.

While there is much in these Psalms of Trust that is indicative of our search for God, one of these psalms turns this notion around and intriguingly suggests that the God of the quest is One who searches for us. It is in the character of God to seek out the person that is just and to "despise the wicked and those who love violence" (Ps. 11:5). It may not be in the character of God to immediately destroy oppressors or heal our wasted bodies, but it is in the character of God to search our hearts and weigh the justice of our deeds. This psalm raises our level of awareness about the search for a God to trust. Trust in God comes to fruition not only as we seek God but also in our discovery of the God who searches for us. We do not worship the Unmoved Mover of Aristotelian philosophy; ours is an active God who is caught up in the process of creation and change, life and death, birth and rebirth.

A QUESTION OF ALLEGIANCE

Unfortunately, the spiritual quest has numerous detours. For the ancient writers, the major problem was that the people deliberately failed to trust God, opting instead to worship other gods. We know this as the problem of idolatry. The issue surfaces in both an individual song of trust (Psalm 16) and a communal song of trust (Psalm 115), indicating that idolatry poses dangers not only for the individual but also for the entire community. In Psalm 16, it is the individual who must choose not to participate in sacrifices to another god (Ps. 16:2–4). In Psalm 115, the whole community is challenged to accept what is really the teaching of the entire Hebrew Bible, namely that idols are merely the work of human hands and that humans do not answer to lifeless statues (Ps. 115:4–8).

If we are to fully appreciate the question of idolatry, we must bear in mind that this is more than a matter of an artistic debate over the use of statues in worship. Destroying all the statues does not necessarily cure the interior malady that causes us to deny the centrality of God in our lives. In fact, the problem of idolatry is in many ways a question of misplaced allegiance and of deficient spiritual understanding.

Yet the problem of idolatry goes even deeper than this, for isn't idolatry really a matter of not letting God be God? We prefer to fashion a God that we can pin down and manage. We often act as if our God is a god who will fix everything and attend to our every whim and desire. Like Job, we are unable to confront the terrible splendor of the God who can harness the power of the entire universe and fashion the wild and untamed creatures of our world (Job 39–41). A statue is very tame. As the psalmist says, "They have mouths, but they do not speak. They have eyes, but they do not see" (Ps. 115:5). The ancients knew how to take care of their statues: They fed them, carried them in processions, and put them to rest at night. They knew how to take care of their gods. They knew how to domesticate divinity. The psalmist's response to idolatry raises a new question: What if ours is a wild and untamed God? It is a frightening thing indeed to think that God cannot be limited to only what we will let God be, and yet this can be the point of departure toward a revitalized understanding of God's relation to a suffering world. Therefore, the taunt found in the laments, "Where, now, is their God?" becomes in Psalm 115 a point of insight and affirmation concerning this unbridled divinity: "Why do the nations say: 'Where, now, is their God?' Our God is in heaven and whatever God wishes to do God does" (Ps. 115:2–3). God is free and unrivaled.[4]

Of course, to worship an unnervingly elusive and untamed God raises some disturbing questions in a world filled with suffering and injustice. Like the psalmists' taunters, there are times when we must wonder where God is in the midst of suffering. Is the God we see in the breath of a baby's sighing also active when unjust governments fall? Does God move among the poor and suffering and know their pain? Living as we do in a century of mass murder, perhaps one way to speak of God's presence is to say that God is being murdered too. In one of the most theologically challenging passages of his book *Night*, Elie Wiesel can only locate God in the face of the young boy hung by SS guards and "struggling between life and death." Wiesel writes,

> Behind me, I heard the same man asking:
> "Where is God now?"
> And I heard a voice within me answer him:
> "Where is He? Here He is—He is hanging here on
>   this gallows."[5]

Christians struggling with the illogic of Jesus' death find God executed and hanging from a cross—an event of disturbing theological implications. Jesus, like Gandhi and Martin Luther King, Jr., was obliterated by the logic of idolatry: How many innocents have been trampled by leaders who have turned national security and the state into a god?[6] How many reformers have been caught between what people expect God to be and what God looks like to the prophet?

The forceful challenge of the reformer to break the conventional codes about God has led to many a prophet's death precisely because, as a society, we know that a change in thought about God means a change in the power structures, politics, and economics of society. For those wedded to the ways of an oppressive socioeconomic order, such a change must be countered and stifled by every available means. By contrast, those who are working for change may not always have an exact blueprint for the society they would like to build, but they know that the search for the untamed and unbridled God can never be without consequence for the worshiping community's understanding of social justice. For those who seek such a God, this insight is freeing: If God is not content to sit at the top of whatever social pyramid we have created, then we are able to call on God to help us build a more just world and God will be with us, even in the most frustrating and dangerous moments in this world's rebirth. Idols were useful to the ancient kings and rulers because they could use them to symbolize the royal family's intimate connection to the society's gods. The gods gave legitimacy to the status quo. The biblical challenge to idolatry counters royal pretensions: What if the idols turn out to be powerless and untrustworthy? What if we say, with the psalmist, "The heavens are the LORD's, but [the LORD] has given the earth to humankind" (Ps. 115:16)? If we seek to worship the unchained God in a world that is content to enslave its Creator, we know that it will be very difficult to work to unchain all who are enslaved by society. Yet we also know that the untamed God would have us seek a world beyond enslavement. This knowledge can serve as an anchor in our search for God in a world stained by evil and violence.

"NO HARM" AND THE DANGER OF UNREALITY

All hymnody faces the grave danger that it will promise things that are not true and that it will raise hopes and expectations not easily fulfilled. Two Psalms of Trust appear to promise the worshiper far more than God can deliver in this world, and we must pause to consider this problem more closely, for if we offer our songs as opiates there is a danger that our worship will be clouded by an air of unreality. The hopes that we raise will be dashed at the first sight of danger or difficulties. So much of modern worship is caught in this mode that we know that every generation is given to escape and fantasy when it comes to God-talk in worship.

Psalm 91 lists a number of things that God will do and not do for the one who "dwells in the shelter of the Most High" (Ps. 91:1). How encouraging it is to affirm that God's protection means not falling into the "snare of the fowler," being killed by the "ruinous plague," or suffering from injury or disease (Ps. 91:3, 10). How comforting it is to be told that "God will command the divine messengers to keep watch over you wherever you go. . . . You will tread on the lion-cub and the asp; you will trample on the young lion and the serpent" (Ps. 91:11, 13). Likewise, Psalm 121 makes similar affirmations when it claims that "God will not let your foot move; the one who guards you does not sleep. . . . During the day the sun will not strike you, nor the moon at night. The LORD will protect you from all harm; God will guard your life" (Ps. 121:3, 6–7).

If we had only these psalms to go on, we would think that ancient Israelite religion was given over to astonishing flights of fancy. We might think that the psalmists' view had no attachment to lived reality, where things are not quite that simple. From what we know of Israel's tragic history, we might even think that such poetry was written as an escape mechanism designed to temporarily free the worshiper from earthly toil, tears, and troubles. This would be a plausible conclusion if we only possessed these two psalms. Yet the bulk of the material we have studied—the numerous laments and the other Psalms of Trust—are far too concrete for us to treat these two psalms superficially. Certainly any talk of "no harm" must be subsumed to the harsh realities confronted in the other psalms, and such language must not dominate a characterization of the Psalms of Trust. In modern worship, it would be misleading to lift out only these psalms and not invoke the bitter cries and longings of the other Psalms of Trust.

Given the ambiguities and dangers inherent in using these psalms in isolation, the modern use of these psalms will very much depend on a careful attention to the context of worship in which they are to be used. There are times where the use of Psalms 91 and 121 would raise false hopes. It is the task of the liturgist and musician to know when music adds to suffering instead of relieving it. Perhaps this is why so few Psalms of Trust make untoward claims. Biblical religion was far too rooted in the politics of suffering to become an opiate to cover over personal or communal pain. Our modern worship must display the same sensibility when trying to create trust for God in situations filled with pain and hopelessness.

WORSHIP THAT AWAKENS US

The Psalms of Trust work to awaken in the worshiper a sense of the presence of God. Can this really be done apart from giving expression to all the other emotions that are bound up with the pain of human suffering? For the psalmist, this can never be. The Psalms of Trust are too closely tied with the psalms of lament. The Psalms of Trust show us that in order for the individual or community to move beyond the anger, frustration, and even numbness of human suffering, the worshiping community must dare to unlock not only the emotions of lamentation but also the dangerous sense that God is indeed present. The Psalms of Trust remind us that lamentation, however necessary, is never enough.[7] The worshiping assembly must risk speaking about the God who is present in the midst of human suffering.

The psalmist seeks to articulate the trust that can be discovered in the contradiction between human suffering and God's power. If our worship can help reawaken a sense of God's presence in all who suffer, that worship will have offered solid grounding to the type of thanksgiving and praise the community can offer. This thanks and praise will not be hopelessly out of touch with real human pain, nor will it be terribly sentimental, but it will arise out of those places where individuals and communities sing of tragedy and trust as inseparable theological companions.

But there is a danger here: Worship must not promise too much. Music that offers comfort must not be like a drug that imposes a new form of emotional numbness. We know that suffering can numb the emotions, but we also know that lament can be one way to open the emotions to again feel alive. Yet, if after lamenting, we begin to sing songs that are so unrealistically positive about life that they make us numb again to the suffering we have experienced, have such songs really helped us in our quest to find God? Depending on the words or on the worship context, the more positive song of trust can choke the very emotions that the lament has released. We must consider when and in what contexts a song of trust will awaken the worshiper and not stifle the real rage that the sufferer feels and needs to express to God.

4

"You Turned My Lament into Dancing"

Psalms of Thanksgiving

How can we possibly give thanks in a world dominated by war and disease, drought and famine, refugee flight and death squads? Where are the acts of God that bring relief to our agony? There is no doubt that we place a great burden on worship when we ask our liturgies to open us to God in a suffering world. Yet we cannot hide our struggles from the worshiping community. The previous chapter showed us that one of the fundamental tasks of worship is to help us find a way to trust God in the midst of our world's pain. The present chapter will go even further, to argue that worship must enable us to see where God is at work in the world, affirming the acts of God through thanks to God.[1]

In a world of suffering, confrontation with evil demands not only that we denounce what is wrong but also that we announce what is right. To see the good in this world and to give thanks for it is a radical act. To point out where God is at work is to point out where injustice fails and to see where the world's transformation is taking place. Our struggle with evil demands that we search for and proclaim the acts of God that counter suffering. The Psalms of Thanksgiving, both individual and communal, give thanks for those moments when suffering and death do not triumph, and allow us to see in those moments the hand of God. We must, through our worship, bring to light what is hopeful. In the eternal battle between good and evil, there are many defeats.[2] Through laments and songs of trust, we mourn these defeats and work to recover from the losses. By contrast, the Psalms of Thanksgiving give the worshiping community a way to offer thanks to God when healing defeats suffering, forgiveness blots out sin, and humane deeds triumph over political expediencies. The ability to give thanks is a radically humanizing endeavor, by which we refuse to let the triumphs of evil destroy our capacity to see God at work in our torn world.

WHAT DOES GOD DO THAT DESERVES THANKS?

Of paramount importance to the Psalms of Thanksgiving is the affirmation that *God hears our prayer.* For us it is often difficult to believe that God listens to us, yet the Psalms of Thanksgiving are designed to remind us that God hears us even in the midst of our sorrow: "I sought the LORD, and God answered me; God rescued me from all that terrified me" (Ps. 34:5; cf. 138:3). The psalmist asks us to look at our lives to bring to mind the times when it has been clear to us that God was listening and offered comfort. Recalling the moments in which we have found strength gives depth to our rejoicing:

> *I waited in hope for the LORD;*
> *God inclined to me,*
> *and listened to my cry.*
> *God raised me out of the tumultuous pit,*
> *out of the miry clay.*
> *God set my feet on a rock,*
> *and gave foundation to my steps* (Ps. 40:2–4;
>   cf. 116:1–8).

This passage gives expression to those times when God breaks through the chaos of our lives to set us firmly on the ground. The story of individual triumph can become an occasion for the entire community to rejoice. The community as a whole can then say, "I thank you, for you have answered me, and you have become my deliverance. The stone that the builders rejected has become the chief cornerstone" (Ps. 118:21–22; cf. Ps. 66:16–20). Whenever individuals or communities find relief from suffering, this is an occasion to give thanks to God.

God not only hears us, but *God forgives our sin*: "Iniquitous things weigh heavily on me, but it is you who forgives our transgressions" (Ps. 65:4). The words "iniquity" and "transgression" do not dominate most people's vocabulary, but it is useful to remember that the various Hebrew words for sin denote a break in our relationship with God and other persons. Forgiveness, therefore, is needed to put our lives and our communities back together. To what extent, then, can we identify with the psalmist's anguish over sin?:

> *When I kept silent, my bones wasted away,*
> *Through my groaning the entire day.*
> *Your hand bore heavily on me day and night.*
> *My vigor was wasted by the droughts of summer.*
> *I told you of my sin;*
> *I did not cover up my iniquity.*
> *I said: "I will confess my transgressions to the LORD,"*
> *And you forgave the guilt of my sin* (Ps. 32:3–5; cf.
> 41:5).

Setting aside pietistic or sentimental notions of sin, who can deny that the ills of racism, sexism, and ethnic warfare are symptomatic of unjustly structured relationships that mark every individual, family, and community? The anguish of the psalmist is an appropriate response to the sins that mar our world. Inequitable power relationships, whether in the home, the Church, or the world, are sinful and call for remorse.

However, we must be on our guard here, for *remorse by itself can be an introverting and destructive force*. Remorse alone is not sufficient to produce change in either self or society. As the psalmist realizes, penitence needs to be balanced by forgiveness. This forgiveness is not some passive quality that forgets evil and permits people to continue to ruin themselves or retain a destructive hold over others. Forgiveness in the biblical conception is an active, transformative agent, namely the power of God that works to overcome fractured relationships. This more dynamic view permits us to rise out of remorse to seek substantive changes in ourselves and in our world, and to see in those changes the reality of divine forgiveness.

One dimension of renewal that is specific to the Psalms of Thanksgiving of the individual is that of *healing*. The act of healing from physical illness calls for thanksgiving. In Psalm 41, the speaker recalls the time in the past when the enemies gathered around the speaker, "All who hate me whisper together against me, plotting some terrible disaster for me: 'There's something evil entrenched in him, so that he lies down. He'll never get up again!' " (Ps. 41:8–9). Yet the speaker rejoices in the fact that in crying out, "LORD, have mercy on me, heal me, for I have sinned against you," God sustained the speaker (Ps. 41:5; cf. vv. 4, 11). Elsewhere in the Psalms of Thanksgiving, the psalmist simply affirms that God brought healing, but does not detail the circumstances (Ps. 30:3, 8–13). In the case of physical recovery, we need to see the power of God to give life, and in those circumstances, we are right to rejoice.

Of course, every illness cannot be overcome. In an era of terminal cancers and AIDS, we know only too well that neither God nor science can offer all the cures we would desire. Medical tragedy abounds, along with medical miracles. In these situations we find God in the act of human comfort. No human should suffer and die alone, nameless and faceless. Sometimes the community is faced with the task of being with people in their death. Can worship play a role in bringing some measure of relief to the dying? Are we prepared to let those in desperate straits design liturgies that actually speak to their pain, fear, and moments of despair? How are these individuals being empowered to take their rightful place in the worshiping community? Those with AIDS, in particular, need to know that they are not going to be cast aside by the worshiping community. The Church must dare to be an advocate in this regard, since there is a tremendous act of healing that it can perform by bringing strength, friendship, forgiveness, and relief to the dying and their loved ones. Where healing cannot mean physical restoration, healing can still mean not abandoning people in their hour of anguish, thereby allowing them to continue to experience and express their giftedness within the community.

The community Psalms of Thanksgiving place a special emphasis on God's *provision of food for the world*. There is no greater affirmation in these psalms of God's global concern than that found in Psalm 65:

> *Those who live at the ends of the earth are awestruck*
>   *by your signs.*
> *You make the places of sunrise and sunset rejoice.*
> *You have taken note of the world,*
> *Irrigating it,*
> *And enriching it greatly.*
> *The river of God is filled with water.*
> *You ready our grain, for this is how you prepare it:*
> *Drenching its furrows,*
> *Pressing down its ridges,*
> *You soften it with showers.*
> *You bless its growth.*
> *You crown the year with your goodness.*
> *Your paths are richly filled.*
> *The desert pastures are full,*
> *And the hills are girded with joy.*
> *The pastures are clothed with flocks,*
> *And the valleys are covered with grain.*
> *They shout for joy.*
> *Indeed, they sing* (Ps. 65:9–14).

God is to be thanked not only for listening, forgiving, and healing us, but in our worship we must thank God for the food that is graciously spread across this planet. We ought to sing with the psalmist, "The earth has yielded its produce; may God, our God, bless us" (Ps. 67:7).

However, we should not glibly rejoice over God's provision of plenty, when around the world our brothers and sisters are dying from starvation and when land is being expropriated from farmers. Organizations such as the Institute for Food and Development Policy in San Francisco have challenged us to see that world hunger is caused by unjust political and economic power arrangements and not by a lack of food.[3] The sin here is clear. We cannot rejoice over "God's provision" if our plenty actually comes to us as the result of world economic exploitation and hoarding. The need for forgiveness and restructuring is imperative. What will galvanize us to work for political change, so that we can again rejoice with the psalmist that God does indeed provide abundance for this planet?[4] Every time food manages to reach those who really need it, we have a reason to rejoice. Every time arable land is restored to the disenfranchised for cultivation, God may legitimately be praised. *The food question challenges our thanksgiving songs to their very core.* A positive response to this challenge is to develop liturgies that enable us to envision a world economy wherein the fruits of the planet find just distribution. We need not wait for the politicians to stumble onto this vision; such a global understanding ought to emerge directly out of worship and prayer.

The Psalms of Thanksgiving affirm that God hears and forgives, God heals and gives nourishment. The Psalter's concern for healing challenges us on the *individual level*, asking us to rejoice when individuals find care, comfort, and healing. The food question moves us into the *global realm*. Both levels are essential for developing a healthy worship environment, for we live in a world that is desperate for words of thanksgiving that address individual needs and tackle global concerns. When worship can do this, the body of gathered worshipers will be transformed into a humane and freeing community.

THE GOD WHO JUDGES THE NATIONS

The Psalms of Thanksgiving confront us with a worship that is wide-ranging and relevant to the lives of individuals and indeed to entire communities. However, the global vision of these psalms goes even deeper, to raise questions about God's oversight of the world and God's response to the poor. What does it mean to say that God is the judge of the world? What does it mean to say that God hears the cry of the poor? These are the deeper issues raised by the Psalms of Thanksgiving.

For the psalmists, worship is the place where we are to affirm that God is the supreme judge of the nations, who defeats the people's enemies. God's rule over the world is declared in Psalm 9:

> *The LORD endures forever;*
> *God has set up a throne for judgment.*
> *God will judge the world justly,*
> *And will render judgment over the peoples equitably.*
> *The LORD will be a refuge for the one who is crushed,*
> *A refuge in times of distress* (Ps. 9:8–10).

God's just rule over the world is also highlighted in Psalm 67, where the psalmist states:

> *May the peoples give you thanks, God.*
> *May the peoples give you thanks, all of them.*
> *May the nations be glad and rejoice,*
> *For you judge the peoples with equity,*
> *And you guide the nations of the earth* (Ps. 67:4–5).

The God that we rejoice in is the God who seeks to bring about justice among and within the nations.

Of course, this poses a difficult question for worship. How can we laud the God of justice, when there is so much injustice to overcome? Worship's twofold task is to open the world to the God *who rules over the nations* and *who wills the defeat of the forces of injustice* arrayed against God's people. Psalm 9 is most forceful in its thanksgiving when it speaks of God's ability to overcome unjust nations:

> *You rebuked the nations.*
> *You destroyed the wicked.*
> *You wiped out their name forever and ever.*
> *Enemy! The wastelands have forever met their end.*
> *The cities you uprooted, their memory has been oblit-*
> *erated. . . .*
> *The LORD has made [the LORD's] self known.*
> *God has executed judgment.*
> *The wicked have become ensnared in God's handiwork.*

> *The wicked have gone down to Sheol,*
> *All the nations that forget God.*
> *For the poor will not be forgotten forever,*
> *Nor will the hope of the oppressed be absent forever.*
> *Arise, LORD, let no person exert force.*
> *May the nations be judged in your presence* (Ps. 9:6–7,
>   17–20).

This psalm forcefully expresses the view that when unjust governments topple and the needy are not ignored, this is an occasion for joy.

Once again we face the question of the "enemies" found also
throughout the Psalms of Thanksgiving. God is repeatedly
thanked for defeating the harassing foes of the people:

> *I extol you, LORD, for you have raised me up,*
> *Not permitting my enemies to rejoice over me* (Ps. 30:2).

> *Although I walk in the midst of distress,*
> *You give me life.*
> *You extend your hand against the wrath of my enemies.*
> *Your right hand rescues me* (Ps. 138:7; cf. 9:7; 34:20–
>   22; 92:10).

The psalmist sees God at work in the defeat of the enemy and
rejoices in this deed. For the psalmist, the collapse of the enemy
is a sign that God is the just judge of the world. To be sure, the
modern Church has not been terribly comfortable with this talk
of the "wicked" and the "enemy" and has therefore decided to
axe such seemingly noisome verses from the weekly lectionary.
However, the topic of God's judgment of the wicked and the
enemy is central to the politics of the Psalms of Thanksgiving,
and to omit such verses sharply curtails the affirmation that God
is the judge of the nations. To fully appreciate this reaction to
the "enemy," we must remember that ancient Israel was a tiny
nation subject to the whims of the superpowers of its day, the
"nations that surround me" (Ps. 118:10)—Egypt, Assyria, Babylon, Persia, Greece, and Rome. The wars that took place
between the great powers along the eastern Mediterranean

coast were initiated to obtain tribute, to control trade routes, and to establish spheres of military influence. The tiny cities that dotted this region were scenes of brutal warfare, as Egyptian and Assyrian reliefs and pictures attest with horrifying clarity.[5] The vassals did not weep too bitterly over the collapse of the ancient powers. In fact, their defeat would certainly have been a time of relief and celebration, as the prophetic text of Nahum makes clear.

The biblical joy at the defeat of these enemies is undoubtedly akin to the exuberance felt in our own century in those countries that have experienced the collapse of colonial rule. Like their modern counterparts, the ancient Israelites did not ask for either foreign domination or exile, but they saw in their national survival and in the collapse of their enemies an act of God worthy of thanksgiving. This might serve as a guide to worship in our own day, for when colonialism, oppression, slavery, and unemployment are defeated, should not the worshiping community give thanks? The spiritual strength of this movement of history is echoed in these words of Martin Luther King, Jr.:

> The developed industrial nations of the world cannot remain secure islands of prosperity in a seething sea of poverty. The storm is rising against the privileged minority of the earth, from which there is no shelter in isolation and armament. The storm will not abate until a just distribution of the fruits of the earth enables man everywhere to live in dignity and human decency.[6]

Worship constructed in light of the psalms empowers us to sing of these victories as acts of God (cf. Ps. 118:10–15). Of course, worship will temper our joy by reminding us that we cannot expect justice to always triumph in Hollywood-like fashion. Any such expectations are tempered by our reading of the Psalms of Lament and Psalms of Trust. Yet, songs of the collapse of tyrannical nations are part and parcel of our inherited political vocabulary of worship, and when read and adapted appropriately, this aspect of the Psalms of Thanksgiving can solidify our conviction that God is indeed the just judge of the nations.

In God's capacity as the judge of the world, the Psalms of

Thanksgiving portray God as the one who listens to the plea of the lowly and oppressed. Psalm 9, which presents God as the judge of the world, directly links God's global rule (cf. 9:8–10 quoted above) to God's care of the poor: "God, who avenges murder, has remembered them, God has not forgotten the outcry of the oppressed" (Ps. 9:13). When the community sees that God indeed hears the cry of the poor, the community can rejoice in the justice of God. However, to affirm that God is the judge who hears the cry of the poor ought not to be done lightly, for such an affirmation is actually a statement that is revolutionary in most political contexts. How powerful it is to confess that God treats the desperate situation of the poor with the utmost seriousness. Yet is it not true that most of us would rather not be bothered with having to listen to those who are poor? Sadly, we have to admit that many of us do not really care to investigate the roots of the poverty that engulfs our planet. Sometimes we hesitate because we are simply afraid of having to become involved. At other times, we fear finding out that we are actually to be numbered among the oppressors and not the oppressed.

We must be on guard here, not letting our reluctance paralyze us. The singing of the Psalms of Thanksgiving should become an opportunity for us to commit ourselves to credibility in our worship and in our deeds. The worshiping assembly needs, through its thanksgiving, to begin affirming that God is the judge who hears the cry of the poor. However, this affirmation will only be credible to the extent that it is linked to concrete efforts to do something about the political and economic injustices of the world. The world aches to draw closer to the God who does not let the cry of the poor go unheeded. The worshiping community is challenged to answer that cry both in song and in deed.

"A NEW SONG"

What is the language of this "new song" (Ps. 40:4) of justice that we need to sing? How does the song of thanksgiving bring a deeper sense of God's presence into the community's acts of worship? The Psalms of Thanksgiving often draw on the simplest of phrases to carry the profound weight of the psalmist's sense of relief and joy. The Psalms of Thanksgiving are littered with statements such as, "I give thanks to the LORD with all my heart" (Ps. 9:2) and "I extol you, O LORD" (Ps. 30:2). As Westermann observes, through the song of thanksgiving (what he terms "declarative praise"), the psalmists give expression to "the joy of the one whom God has drawn up out of the dark depths, the joy of the one who has been freed from the 'bands of death,' the joy of the one in whose mouth God has placed a new song of praise to our God, of him whose sorrow God has turned to joy."[7] The language is not complex, but appropriate to the moment for the worshiper. These are simple expressions of thanks and praise.

Of course, there are numerous problems with praise language. Such language will be hollow if lamentation is what is actually needed. We must know when words of thanks are appropriate and not a cover for our inability to deal with grief and suffering. Furthermore, praise language can seem detached from the realities of human grief and suffering. We should keep in mind that the praise language of the biblical Psalms of Thanksgiving *is never isolated* from language that touches on forgiveness, justice, enemies, or the plight of the poor. The Psalms of Thanksgiving employ a praise language that is concretely rooted in the experience of human suffering. This is praise that is tied to life lived out in a world of pain, affliction, and social injustice. For modern worship, the lesson is clear: Songs filled with praise language will fail to touch those who come to worship to the extent that such music is unable to speak to the hurts that worshipers bring with them. When it comes time to give thanks, songs not anchored in real human pain or hope will only weakly convey the joy that the worshiper desires to express to God. For our music to be profound about joy, such music must also grapple with our sorrows.

Paradoxically, the new song of thanksgiving *deepens the worshiper's sense of the importance of ancient ritual*. In several of the Psalms of Thanksgiving, thankfulness imparts to the worshiper a more profound respect for the house of prayer and ritual, the temple and its sacrifices. Psalm 65 sets this posture out clearly for us:

> *Happy is the person whom you choose to bring near to*
>   *dwell in your courts.*
> *We will be satisfied with the goodness of your house,*
> *The holiness of your temple* (Ps. 65:5; cf. 66:13–15;
>   118:26–29; 138:2).

The temple represents what is central to ancient Israelite
religion. It is the place of worship. It is the house of God.
Whether one is present at the temple, can only visit it during
the holidays, or even if one is living in exile, the temple is a
communal center of devotion, prayer, and imagination. Through
pilgrimage the temple connects all of God's people. Through its
rituals, all God's people can approach God.

Yet the new song of thanksgiving adds something more, for
it transforms the sacred halls of the temple's past into a place
where God's continuing presence can be felt by all who are
present. It is this profound sense of common worship that ele-
vates the Psalms of Thanksgiving above mere individualism.
Thus, although most of the Psalms of Thanksgiving are psalms
of the individual, a clear sense of the larger worship environment
and community permeates the texts.[8] Often there are calls for
the faithful to give thanks to God, so that the individual's release
can become an occasion for communal rejoicing (Ps. 30:5; 32:6,
11). One text states rather emphatically, "I have not hidden your
kindness and your truth from the great assembly" (Ps. 40:11).
The Psalms of Thanksgiving encourage the individual worshiper
to share specific misfortunes and joys with the larger worshiping
community. Likewise, these psalms permit the larger community
to wrestle with the sorrows of the individual and to give thanks
for the worshiper's triumphs. The new song of thanksgiving may
arise out of an event that transforms the life of the individual,
but in worship that same song works to bring individuals
together into a community of worship. The new song of thanksgiving is a song for the entire worshiping community.

Our contemporary worship music and environment must also
bring out our connectedness to other believers and to the ritual
traditions that have shaped the worshiping community for centuries.[9] Of course, the possibilities in the modern worshiping
setting are numerous and seemingly endless. We are moving into
a time where the percussion and rhythms of third-world believ-

ers will be used right alongside revitalized Gregorian modes. Stained glass with modern saints and martyrs unite our architectural traditions to the issues that galvanize the modern Church. The Psalms of Thanksgiving help us to see that the new song can work together with the oldest of worship forms and institutions, transforming worship in the received tradition into something more than an act of nostalgia.[10]

This enhanced appreciation for ritual that is nourished by the Psalms of Thanksgiving appears to be undermined in Psalm 40 when the poet states, "You did not care for a sacrifice or a grain-offering. You have opened my ears. You have not asked for a burnt-offering or a sin-offering" (Ps. 40:7). Such statements in the Hebrew Bible are not meant to negate ritual; rather, they seek to make the prophetic call for a worship that is more than mere surface ritual or that hypocritically uses ritual as a substitute for changed attitudes and actions.[11] To draw close to God, the worshiper must discover what it means to say, "I like to do what you wish, my God. Your teaching rests deep inside me" (Ps. 40:9). Only then do ritual and worship take on substance. Ritual is a vehicle for God's grace. By itself, apart from a compassionate God and an open worshiper, ritual action is worthless. In the Hebrew Bible, music, prayer, sacrifices, and offerings are the means, the temple or some other sacred place is the location, but without worshipers who are open to God's love and justice, the worship falters.

The Psalms of Thanksgiving present us with another reality, that of the community that has found a way to give thanks to the God of justice, the ruler of the world, the scatterer of the enemies, the one who protects the lowly. The new song is one in which God lives in the midst of our ritual, where God meets the people in the singing of songs and prayers that dare to touch the concrete sufferings and joys of those who come to worship. The experience is so decisive that the psalmist is able to exclaim: "God put a new song into my mouth — a song of praise for our God" (Ps. 40:4a).

"WHO GRANTED US LIFE"

The biblical songs of thanksgiving are not only developed in response to immediate events. Two of these psalms take the

longer, historical view to recognize that Israel must rejoice and
gives thanks to God for its existence as a people. Psalm 66 looks
to the time of the Exodus from Egypt, and Psalm 107 speaks
directly out of the adversities of exile—two of the most profoundly formative experiences in the history of ancient Israel.
These psalms make us conscious of the need to offer thanksgiving on a global scale and a historical level. Such psalms begin
to anticipate our next chapter on the hymns of praise, especially
those that laud God as the creator of the world and all living
things.

The psalmist thanks God that Israel survived the tumultuous
events of the Exodus and some later, unspecified military confrontation to achieve prosperity (Ps. 66:12). This thanksgiving
recognizes that the very survival of the people is an act of God,
that God is to be remembered as "the one who has given us
life" (Ps. 66:9). Psalm 66 invokes the Exodus to elaborate on
the power of God. The deeds of God are recounted in order to
cause "all the earth" to "sing the glory of God's name" (Ps.
66:1–2). The psalmist sees in the events of the Exodus the mirac-
ulous birth of the community (Ps. 66:5–9; cf. 65:8). These were
the deeds that gave the community life. The Exodus becomes
the defining point for the later military disaster, for in these
events the psalmist can see that the people have been refined,
having gone "through fire and water" (Ps. 66:12). The fact of
survival is reason enough for the psalmist to give thanks to God
and to offer a variety of offerings and sacrifices (Ps. 66:13–15).
For the psalmist, each situation of communal survival is an Exodus event, an act of God.

Psalm 107 finds the life-granting act of God in the return of
the exiles (Ps. 107:3).[12] This ballad-like psalm divides into four
major sections, each of which depicts a grouping of exiles who
survive great suffering. There were those who "lost their way in
the desert" (Ps. 107:4). Others "dwelt in deepest darkness" (Ps.
107:10). Some "were fools who were made to suffer for their
rebellion and their iniquities" (Ps. 107:17), while still others in
ships "went down to the depths" of the sea (Ps. 107:26). In every
case, the psalmist affirms, "Out of their distress they cried to
the LORD, and God rescued them from their troubles" (Ps.
107:6, 13, 19, 28). For the psalmist, to survive is an occasion for

rejoicing. In each case the psalmist says to the survivors: "Let them give thanks to the LORD for [the LORD's] steadfast love, God's wondrous deeds for humankind" (Ps. 107:8, 15, 21, 31).

When an oppressed people find their way out of the political "desert" (Ps. 107:4, 6), when they break free of the "iron bars" of oppression (Ps. 107:10, 16), when they are spared the "gates of death" and can eat again (Ps. 107:18–20), when God reduces their "storm to a whisper" (Ps. 107:29)—these are occasions for the community to rejoice in God. Each section of the psalm plumbs the depths of dislocation and oppression. Emerging out of specific political realities and a specific moment of Israel's survival, this psalm provides concrete images that can be attached to many other situations of political oppression and liberation. The psalmist, for example, moves on to argue that the wickedness of a land's inhabitants leads to the land's physical deterioration, but that God can take the wilderness and revitalize it for those who have been "hungry" (Ps. 107:35–41). By expanding on the image of the release from exile, the scriptures remind us that every event of political liberation is at heart a theological event, an act of God, in response to which the community is to "exalt God in the assembly of the people" (Ps. 107:32). This psalm enables us to see that God's concern for the oppressed is not limited to one distant moment in ancient Israel's past, but is an enduring facet of God's "steadfast love" (Ps. 107:43).

The Psalms of Thanksgiving empower us to continue the search for a worship that will deepen our experience of the God of history, the God of those who are in misery and sorrow—a God who speaks to injustice, poverty, and suffering on a community and global scale. If our liturgies have offered real comfort to the beleaguered, shown gentleness to the distressed, opened a space of joy in the midst of suffering, then we will have moved beyond worship as a spectator sport toward a worship that has each worshiper actively engaging the life-and-death struggles that give depth and hue to our entire planet. The new song we seek must come from each and every mouth, from each and every heart, from each and every nation. This is a daunting task—one that requires skill, care, patience, hard work, and risk. Individuals and nations will give thanks when they have a reason to give thanks. Our worshiping communities will give thanks in a world of violence and oppression only when the reasons for rejoicing have come to light. The Psalms of Thanksgiving can sharpen our sensibilities about joy in worship, calling us to respond in words of thanksgiving when we discover that God has truly "turned my lament into dancing" (Ps. 30:12). When this renewal occurs, whether to one person or to an entire oppressed people, our worship must stand ready to translate that sentiment into a song of thanksgiving.

5

"You Renew the Face of the Earth"

Hymns of Praise

Although photographs of the earth from space have become commonplace, I still find myself reacting with amazement at pictures of that clouded, blue-green orb we call home. There in all its grandeur and fragility is our tiny lifeboat, floating in a sea of stars, lost in a galaxy amid ten thousand other galaxies. I know that my personal problems are real, but they seem to pale in significance when seeing the world as a whole. I know that ethnic and national conflicts are the result of genuine concerns, yet they often seem petty or arrogant when looking at this borderless globe. Then, when I think that our rivers, seas, and even oceans are filling with garbage, I wonder if these photos from space have really helped us to develop a deeper appreciation for this delicate planet and its many inhabitants.

Outer space provides us with a potent vantage point from which we can think about ourselves, our world, and God. In a strikingly similar fashion, the Psalter's Hymns of Praise take the perspective of eternity to jar the worshiper into rethinking all that is earthly. Like the astronauts' photographs of the earth, the eternal perspective of the Hymns of Praise compels us to redefine all that it means to be human. In worship we are to see with new eyes and hear with new ears. The eternal perspective

of the Hymns of Praise in the Psalter brings a reexamination of
military power, poverty, idolatry, and earth's resources. Worship
asks us to take God's vantage point and look again at all that
we do and all that we hold to be so terribly important.

Beyond the human dimension, the Hymns of Praise show us
that worship is a time to encounter the glory and majesty of
God. In worship we are to revel in the compassion and love of
God for us. This does not mean that in worship we seek to
escape from earth to hide with God in eternity. On the contrary,
worship is a very human act whereby we bring heaven and earth
closer to each other, allowing us to glimpse the creative spirit
that shapes our planet. This meeting with God calls us to care
for our world and stand by the side of the poor. In this worship
encounter, we sense the presence of the compassionate God of
eternity who tends the earth and watches over its inhabitants.

LIVING BETWEEN DUST AND DIVINITY

The Hymns of Praise teach us that the deepest form of divine
praise actually sharpens our understanding of what it means to
be human. It is in our daring to come to terms with both the
earthly and the eternal within ourselves that we discern who we
are as God's creation. Thus, even though the Hymns of Praise
look toward God, they are no less concerned with the human
than the laments, the songs of trust, or the Psalms of Thanksgiving. The Hymns of Praise differ only in those aspects of our
humanness that they wish to draw out for further inspection and
redefinition. These psalms urge us to reflect on our humanity
against the backdrop of the eternal. Wishing neither to humiliate
us nor to exalt us, the Hymns of Praise are designed, in part, to
help the worshiper gain some perspective on power and poverty,
history and idolatry.

The spiritual search reveals that we live somewhere between
dust and divinity. This central paradox of human existence is
expressed most eloquently in Psalm 8:

> *When I look at your sky,*
> *The work of your fingers,*

The moon and the stars that you have established,
What is humankind, that you keep us in mind?
What are mortals, that you take note of us?
You have made us a little less than gods.
You have crowned us with glory and honor.
You let us rule over what you have made.
You put everything under our feet (Ps. 8:4–7).

Our praise of God ought to cause us to ask this question over and over: "What is humankind?" In trying to answer that question in worship, we will be confronted with both our immense capacity for creativity and our terrible ability to destroy. We will grapple with our longing for eternity and the reality of our finitude. Worship asks us to come to terms with birth and death. To gaze at the eternal and to know that "we are dust" (Ps. 103:14) is not to denigrate what is human; rather, for the psalmist, knowledge of our finitude is the ground for appreciating God's love for us. Even out of eternity, God wishes to touch us in our frailty:

For as high as the sky is over the earth,
So deep is God's love for those who fear God.
As far as the east is from the west,
So far does God remove our sins from us.
Just as a father shows compassion to his children,
So does the LORD show compassion to those who revere
    God (Ps. 103:11–13).

At the juncture between the eternal and the finite emerges God's enduring compassion for the fading grass that is humanity:

Humankind
Their days are like grass,
Like wild flowers, they bloom.
But then a wind passes by and they are gone,
Their place does not recognize them any longer.
But the kindness of the LORD is from everlasting to
    everlasting to those who revere God.
God's righteousness extends to the grandchildren,

> *To those who adhere to God's covenant,*
> *To those who remember to carry out God's decrees*
>   (Ps. 103:15–18).

Conscious of its fragility, the worshiping community can still experience the eternal love of God. Yet by cultivating an awareness of our ties to the divine — that is, by seeking to live out the teachings of God — the worshiping community can begin to discern God's "rule over all" (Ps. 103:19). It is the task of praise to probe both our divinity and our dust to gain a deeper knowledge of the human–divine relationship.

ETERNITY AND EARTHLY WAR MAKING

Of what practical value is this reflection on the eternal and the finite? What will we gain in acknowledging, with the psalmist, our createdness? In Psalm 33, for example, the vantage point of the eternal offers a more critical perspective concerning humanity's military arrogance. Looking down from heaven (Ps. 33:13–14) — i.e., taking the divine perspective — the psalmist finds that,

> *The king is not saved by a large army.*
> *The warrior is not liberated by great might.*
> *The horse is a deception in rescue,*
> *Even by its great strength it cannot flee* (Ps. 33:16–17;
>   cf. 147:10).

By invoking the perspective of eternity and creation, the poet is led to question the enduring value and effectiveness of military might. Worship from the eternal vantage point will highlight those forces that really bring about lasting change in human affairs, guarding us against any illusions about military quick fixes. Our worship should remind us that, depending on the course history has chosen, all the weapons in the world will not necessarily insure victory. The divine perspective will even cause us to ask if we can dare use the word "victory" when so much death and destruction is involved in our conquests.

Certainly, one danger in adopting a "divine perspective" is that we will march forth with a sword in one hand and the Bible in the other, convinced that God is on our side. This is much the image that we are given in Psalm 149:

> *Let the pious exult in glory.*
> *Let them shout for joy in their beds.*
> *Let the praises for God be in their throats,*
> *And the two-edged sword be in their hands,*
> *To bring vengeance against the nations,*
> *And rebukings on the peoples,*
> *To bind their kings with chains,*
> *And their nobles with iron fetters,*
> *To carry out the written judgment against them.*
> *This is an honor to all who are pious.*
> *Hallelujah* (Ps. 149:5–9).

It has ever been the danger of religion and ideology to impose "the truth" by threat or coercion. We must recognize that the Bible itself is laden with a politics that at times can breed a conquest mentality. South African and Palestinian liberation writers have drawn our attention to this dilemma.[1] In a way, Psalm 149 readily lends itself to a model of theology that calls for revolutionary social change, as do the Book of Joshua and the tales of the Maccabees. Given the "third-world" character of ancient Israelite religion, where tiny Israel was constantly beleaguered by far greater military competitors, we should not dismiss this psalm's militant words too quickly. The Hebrew Bible does not entirely eschew the use of force to throw off oppressive regimes or exploitative foreign powers. This is a difficult strand of the biblical tradition that we must recognize and attempt to deal with. However, rather than attempt to harmonize the militant and pacifist texts of the Psalter, it seems more intellectually honest and theologically beneficial simply to acknowledge that there are diverse views toward military force in the psalms. This means that neither the pacifist nor the militarist will be entirely comfortable with the psalms, but this is as it should be, since we could never automatically expect that an eternal perspective would dictate simple, clear answers for every possible use of military force. Yet, I think that it is also fair to say that few wars have ever had clear divine authorization, and the record shows that unfortunately most military action finds its roots in human greed for wealth or in a lust for power. The eternal perspective enables us to see our war making as a wretched and largely futile enterprise, which produces little positive social change.

ETERNITY AND POVERTY

Praise not only helps us gain perspective on military power, but praise also enables us to rethink our approach to the question of poverty. The act of praise is an occasion to exalt God as the one who comes to the aid of the poor. Psalm 113 invokes the perspective of eternity to have us look at the world of the poor from God's vantage point. Although enthroned on high, God's compassion goes out to the poor and to the childless woman (Ps. 113:5–9). God does not remain detached from the poor, and neither can the worshiper who utters these words:

> *God lifts the poor out of the dust.*
> *God raises the poor out of the garbage pile,*
> *To have them sit with the nobles,*
> *With the nobles of God's people* (Ps. 113:7–8).

The eternal cuts through all our blinders to focus our attention on the plight of those who suffer. Praise requires a politics of poverty—not a politics that sees spiritual value in poverty, but one that treats poverty and suffering as scandalous conditions requiring liberation. Similarly, Psalm 146 identifies the creator God as the one "who brings justice to the oppressed and gives bread to the hungry" (Ps. 146:7), as opposed to the "nobles" who apparently do not do these things (Ps. 146:3; cf. 107:40–41; 113:7–8; 118:8–9). The writer refines the notion of divine justice by speaking of God as the one who sets prisoners free and restores sight to the blind (Ps. 146:7–8). God watches over the "strangers, orphan, and widow" (Ps. 146:9).[2]

These psalms intimately link talk of the creator God with

practical concern for justice. There is no separation of politics from praise. In fact, these psalms suggest that the eternal perspective ought to cause us constantly to reevaluate our politics. If our worship is not drawing us to sympathize with the plight of the poor and, indeed, all who suffer, can we really say that our worship is imbued with a divine perspective? The Hymns of Praise show us that our theology of God and creation must also be a justice theology. In order to develop such a theology, we need liturgies that link creation and justice, God and hunger. As the eternal perspective confronts us with the issues of poverty and justice, we will be in a better position to define what it truly means to fight to retain a shred of human dignity in the midst of scandalous poverty. Our reflection on the eternal may convince us that we are indeed dust, but we will also develop the strong conviction that no one should be forced to live as dust only. God wishes to lift the poor out of the dust, and that is our task, too. By imitating God, the worshiping community will cultivate a liturgical life that respects the humanity of those who are poor and all who suffer. In siding with those who suffer, our worship will cut through limp praise language to galvanize the worshiping community to act on the urgent and pressing justice issues of our day.

If God raises the poor out of the dust, then God is an actor in history. This, at least, is the conviction of Psalm 135, where God is praised as the creator God. In the first place, God is praised as the creator of the natural order—heaven and earth, the seas, clouds, lightning, and wind (Ps. 135:5–7). In the following section, the psalmist proceeds to connect God's creative power to the formative events in Israel's history, namely the exodus from the land of Egypt and the conquest of Canaan. God is the creator of Israel,

> *Who struck the firstborn of Egypt—*
> *Both people and animals.*
> *God sent signs and wonders into Egypt—*
> *To Pharaoh and all his officials.*
> *Who struck many nations,*
> *And slew mighty kings:*
> *Sihon, the king of the Amorites,*

Og, the king of Bashan,
And all the kingdoms of Canaan (Ps. 135:8–11).

God, as the actor in history, gave the lands of the defeated kings to the Israelites as their "heritage" (Ps. 135:12). For the psalmist, the existence of the natural order and of Israel are the primary indications that God is at work as a creative power. The reality of God's creative work sets into sharp relief the impotence of the idols fashioned and worshiped by the nations (Ps. 135:15–18). Our encounter with this God will cause us to reconsider all that we are as creators in history. Praise of God throws up a mirror in front of all our actions in history, in war, and toward those in need. Each time we praise God, we are consequently urged to reconsider what it means to create and recreate the world. Are we using our power to build a better and more just world? Will our actions bring relief to those who suffer and who are oppressed? Or will we remain impotent like stone and wooden idols, choosing not to look too closely at God for fear that we will have to refashion ourselves and our society?

RECREATING THE WORLD

One of the major purposes of the Hymns of Praise is to permit the worshiper to speak of God as the Creator and to extol the beauty of creation as a product of God's handiwork. The world of the psalmist is a magnificent place. Psalm 19 gives us the famous phrase, "The skies tell of the glory of God, and the vault speaks of God's handiwork" (Ps. 19:2). The poetry of the psalms revels in the splendor of the sun, "which is like a bridegroom coming out of his room, rejoicing like a hero to run the track" (Ps. 19:6). For the psalmists, the whole of creation is a repository of praise to God's creative power. Psalm 148 looks to both the heavenly and earthly realms as vehicles of praise. In the first part of the psalm, the divine messengers and the celestial bodies are called on to give praise to God: "Let them praise the name of the LORD, for it was God who gave the order and they were created" (Ps. 148:5). Likewise, in the second half of the psalm, the earth's creatures and landscape are called on to give praise to God: "Let them praise the name of the LORD, for God's name alone is exalted. God's splendor covers the earth and the sky" (Ps. 148:13). These psalms present the worshiper with a positive vision of creation as the wellspring of joy and beauty. Nature sings with joy to God.

Of course, the latter part of the twentieth century has not always presented us with pictures of creation as a beautiful place. War and pollution have scarred the earth. Certainly, the Gulf War's image of hundreds of Kuwaiti oil wells burning out of control will long endure as a visual indictment of our war making. This event is but one of many that warn us that we have arrived at the point where we can ruin vast reaches of our planet. Closer to home, who does not shudder to think about what chemical evils might lurk in our backyards? Is the toxic waste dump truly leak-proof? Is our water drinkable? Can I breathe the air today? Questions such as these tell us that the issue of our relationship to creation is an urgent one.

There are many locales of stunning beauty left on the planet for poets to laud, but there is no hiding the fact that we must redefine our relationship with nature. On the practical level, we need to creatively restructure our management of the earth's resources and of our waste. Yet the problem is deeper than simply asking how we can make better use of the planet and its wealth, for this rather detached approach keeps nature at an arm's length from us—frozen, unfeeling, manipulable, exploitable. Our reflection on the pollution problem will take on a radically different character if we regard nature, as the psalmists do, as an active, responsive partner in an intimate relationship with the human community and God. Gerhard von Rad ably captures the biblical view when he writes,

> Israel was not familiar with the concept of nature, nor did she speak about the world as a cosmos, i.e., about an ordered structure that is self-contained and subject to definite laws. To her the world was primarily much more an event than a being, and certainly much more a personal experience than a neutral subject for investigation. . . . For Israel the world was, to formulate it somewhat epigram-

matically, an unceasing, supporting, ordering activity of
God.[3]

By treating nature as a subject and not simply an object, we
will start asking more probing questions about our use and abuse
of creation. Matthew Fox reminds us, "Experiencing our world
in a deeper way heralds a new relationship to it — especially for
those cultures that have preferred exploitation to wonder."[4] If
nature is lover and friend, mother and life-giver, we cannot
remain distant and detached from activity that endangers the
health and well-being of the planet.

Admittedly this redefinition of our relation to creation asks
most of us to make a radical about-face in our attitudes. To say
that we are willing to let nature shape us instead of us always
trying to make creation do our bidding is not an approach that
we moderns will readily adopt. Part of the problem is that Eur-
opeans and their North American descendants have long
become accustomed to being, quite literally, the shakers and
movers of the planet. In the western world we cultivate a mentality of domination and control over resources, people, and
commerce. Those who share this mentality can readily identify
with the psalmist who says,

> *You let us rule over what you have made.*
> *You put everything under our feet.*
> *Sheep and oxen, all of them,*
> *Even the wild animals,*
> *The birds of the sky and the fish of the sea,*
> *Whatever traverses the paths of the seas* (Ps. 8:7–9).

Certainly, there is something quite positive about taking
charge of our own affairs as individuals and our own destiny as
a people. To seek to dominate and control can mean that we
will wipe out diseases or produce richer crop yields. Such are
the benefits of taking charge of and wrestling with creation.
However, we are learning all too vividly that domination has its
arrogant side. Sadly, there is a global unwillingness to do much
about the crushing problems created by our abuse of the earth
and its resources. Yet, if we were open to developing a more

intimate relationship with creation, we would find ourselves free from the tyranny that comes with always insisting that we alone must set the growth and development agenda for the planet. If nature were given more of a say in our decision-making process, we might then begin to discover ways to care for the world God has made. Certainly, this is not to say that we should stop creating and refashioning our environments — it is a human necessity that we remake our world — but today we need to learn to measure our labor according to the needs of nature and to work with nature in revitalizing the planet. Domination of creation must be entwined with a willingness to listen to creation.

There is no more beautiful expression of a biblical love for creation in the Hymns of Praise than that found in Psalm 104. The psalm can be divided up into five main sections. In the first part of the psalm, the psalmist begins by reflecting on the greatness of God witnessed in the larger elements of creation, the sky, water, and clouds (Ps. 104:1–3). Against this backdrop God "established the earth on its foundations; it will never be moved" (Ps. 104:5). The psalmist goes on to speak of the creation of mountains and valleys by the "rebuke" and "thunder" of God (Ps. 104:7).

In the second part of the psalm, God is said to have brought forth wild beasts and birds (Ps. 104:10–12). The grasses grow for cattle (Ps. 104:14). On the basis of Genesis 1, which is so similar to this psalm, we undoubtedly expect the creation of humans at this point; instead, the psalmist presents us with a litany of those items that bring life and good cheer to the human palate, namely wine, oil, and bread (Ps. 104:14–15). Trees, mountains, and crags fill out the landscape (Ps. 104:16–18). The third section of the psalm (Ps. 104:19–23) recounts the function of the moon and sun. Poetically, night becomes a time for the forest animals to roam and for the lion to roar in search of prey, whereas day is the time for human labor.

The ordering and phrasing of Psalm 104 is probably more familiar to us from the creation story as told in Genesis 1. In fact, Psalm 104 underscores the inclination to read Genesis 1 as a *poem* that extols the beauty of creation. More than this, however, the fourth section of this psalm (Ps. 104:24–30) offers us a deeper way to read Genesis 1. These and other creation texts found in the Bible are not simply about creation in isolation but about creation as the product of the "wisdom" of God (Ps. 104:24). For the psalmists, the world of nature not only sings to God but also opens us to the God who is our provider and caretaker, the one who gives life and takes it away:

> *You hide your face, and they are terrified.*
> *You take away their breath and they die,*
> *To dust they return.*
> *You send forth your breath, and they are created,*
> *And you renew the face of the earth* (Ps. 104:29–30).

We have much to learn from God's relationship to God's creation. The key to God's creative acts is the renewal of the world.

The fifth section of the poem (Ps. 104:31–35) leaves the speaker in a posture of worship, singing of the greatness of God. In the end, the worshiper takes up the chorus of praise that begins in creation but which now carries on in the voices of the worshiping community. Reflection on nature has a twofold purpose in the psalms: to evoke a greater awareness of the glory of God and to loosen our tongues to sing with joy to God.

If our sensitivity to the degradation of creation has been heightened, then the psalmist's vision of creation will give us occasion to pause. The Hymns of Praise show us that sky and sea, mountains and valleys, beasts and birds are all to be freed to offer praise to God. Creation was never meant to be enslaved as a humanly fashioned eyesore. Once shackled, creation cannot sing with joy to God, neither can the spoiling of nature inspire us to sing of God's greatness. Our task as worshipers of God is to let creation continue to sing, but this means that worship must be combined with an active concern to renew creation. For Matthew Fox, this pursuit of renewal engenders a hope-filled future for the planet and its children:

When creation spirituality offers effective resistance to those who would despoil the earth by enlisting adults in an effort to defend mother earth, the young are given hope. For it is they and their descendants who will suffer most if the earth they inherit is desecrated.[5]

If we tend the world with care, the sanctuary of creation will continue to give witness to God's abiding love and creative power. However, if we refuse to respect nature's wonders, stifling its song of praise, we will find that even heaven's tears will not be able to wash away the stain of our violation of this planet.

THE GOD OF ETERNITY

The Hymns of Praise work to expand our comprehension not only of ourselves and of creation, but ultimately of the God of eternity. It may seem presumptuous that we should even try to give voice to what is really inexpressible. How can our words and metaphors, our images and signs, really communicate what it means to be God? The probing of ourselves and of creation that we find in the Hymns of Praise is critical to our emergent spirituality, but these psalms go further, to suggest that worship can indeed foster a sense of God's grandeur and God's compassion. The Hymns of Praise are not philosophic tracts designed to pin down in precise terms the nature and substance of the divine. This is neither possible nor desirable for the worshiper. However, the Hymns of Praise do open us to the God who lives in an enduring relationship with humanity and creation. We may not penetrate the dark veil that ultimately separates us from the divine, but in worship we can begin to speak of the God who exhibits great love and compassion toward the world and toward us.

The God who creates the world is a God enshrouded in mystery. The very name of God, YHWH, is unpronounceable, and as Exodus tells us, reveals only of God, "I am who I am" (Exod. 3:14).[6] The name of God, therefore, becomes an object of wonder and awe in the Hymns of Praise:

> *God has offered redemption for God's people.*
> *God has commanded God's covenant forever.*
> *Holy and awe-inspiring is God's name* (Ps. 111:9).

God is the God of the ineffable name and the God of great glory:

Let the name of the LORD be blessed,
From now unto eternity.
From the place of the sun's rise to its setting,
The name of the LORD is to be praised.
The LORD is high above all the nations.
Above the sky is God's glory (Ps. 113:2–4).

The name of God not only expresses God's otherness and mystery, but also God's efficacy and power:

LORD, your name is eternal.
LORD, memory of you lasts from generation to genera-
tion.
For the LORD renders judgment on behalf of God's peo-
ple,
And God will be comforted about those who are God's
servants (Ps. 135:13–14; cf. 33:20–21).

It is this name that renews worship as we are freed to let God be God (cf. Pss. 33:10–11; 145:1–4). Worship is to cultivate a sense of amazement toward this God. In the community's reflection and song, there must be room for the God who transcends all our mundane images and symbols, who cannot be contained by our groping vocabularies and our feeble metaphors.

However, even though God is mystery, praise enables us to discover that God reaches out compassionately to humanity.[7] God is the gentle parent (Ps. 103:13), the God who heals and forgives (Pss. 103:4–5; 146:8; 147:3), the God of steadfast love (Pss. 100:5; 103:8–11; 117:2). Concretely, God is the one who gives food to those who hunger (Pss. 33:19; 111:5; 145:15; 146:7; 147:9, 14). Praise helps us to envision a God of love who reaches out to a world in need. This talk of a concrete compassion is reinforced by the psalmists' vision of God as the God of the poor and the lowly (Pss. 113:5–7; 146:7; 149:4), the just judge (Ps. 103:6), and the one who defeats the wicked and the enemy (Pss. 8:3; 104:35; 145:20). For ancient Israel, this conviction about God's compassion was grounded in God's covenant with Israel:

> *God has made a memorial for God's awe-inspiring deeds.*
> *The LORD is gracious and compassionate.*
> *God has given food to those who revere God.*
> *God remembers forever God's covenant* (Ps. 111:4–5, cf. 111:9).

It is this covenant that separates Israel out from other nations, for Israel alone was fashioned by the teachings that God brought to God's people (Ps. 147:19–20). It was Israel's confession that God liberated the slaves in Egypt in order to create a people empowered to bring God's compassion to the poor and the oppressed (e.g., Exodus 21–23; Leviticus 19, 25; Deuteronomy 24).

Divine name, glory, steadfast love, compassion, just judge, giver of food, covenant—all these are images of the eternal God in relationship to God's people. Through praise, the worshiping community inaugurates the venture to find the eternal God who is creating and recreating the world. Praise not only cultivates a sense of mystery and wonder toward God, but also fosters a desire to extend the love and compassion of God to all who are in need. Once again, praise of God brings us back to ourselves and our world. Yet our turning to God also permits us to discover that creative love which desires to transform the whole world. It is a love that is found wherever food is shared, exiles and slaves are freed, and justice breaks out. In our Hymns of Praise, we may not entirely penetrate the veil of eternity, but we can at least glimpse the enduring love that binds God to God's creation.[8]

AN ORGANIC VISION OF GOD

The three dimensions that we have isolated here in the Hymns of Praise—human, creation, and eternal—are not entirely separable. The nature of philosophic and theological knowing is such that any effort to fathom one dimension leads to a probing of the others. If we want to know what it means to be truly human, we must grapple with matters concerning God and our createdness. If we wish to delve into creation, we find that we are touching the wonders of the Creator and encountering ourselves as actors in creation. Finally, when we try to understand who God is, we invariably reflect on God's relation to the created world and to ourselves as creatures in that world. The human, creation, and the eternal are interlocking elements in a divine maze that confronts us in every quest for justice and truth. These three dimensions are the backbones of the biblical Hymns of Praise.

6

"They Who Do Justice"

Liturgical Psalms

By this point in our study, it should be apparent that no act of worship can proceed without a concern for the condition of those who suffer or who are oppressed. Whether we are speaking of psalms of lamentation, trust, thanksgiving, or praise, each level of worship remains open to the God of justice. Several psalms, termed liturgical or processional psalms, more overtly presuppose the worship setting, with its vibrant liturgical movement and resounding music.[1] While other psalms were undoubtedly part of the liturgical life of ancient Israel, the Liturgical Psalms make it plain that the justice question was at the heart of Israel's worship. The issue of justice is not an add-on to worship; it is not something we get to after our entrances, after our prayers, after our offerings, and after our dismissals. For those who set up a dividing wall between faith and politics, God can never emerge as the biblical God who—in the midst of worship—challenges all our faiths and all our politics.

WORSHIPERS WHO SEEK JUSTICE

The Liturgical Psalms cultivate worshipers who seek justice in the community. Two of these psalms—15 and 24—raise the question of who shall worship and live in the presence of God,

91

answering the question by grounding worship in ethics.[2]

To the psalmist in Psalm 24, the fundamental question is, "Who shall ascend the mountain of the LORD? Who shall stand in God's holy place" (Ps. 24:3). The decisive answer is, "The one with clean hands and a pure heart, the one who has not vainly invoked 'God's life' [i.e., make a false oath using God's life or name] or sworn deceitfully" (Ps. 24:4; cf. Exod. 20:7). Truth in actions, intent, and speech are to characterize those who wish to live in God's holy place.

Similarly, for the psalmist in Psalm 15, the question is, "LORD, who will dwell in your tent? Who will live on your holy mountain?" (Ps. 15:1). Here the answer is more extended than that of Psalm 24 and details several facets of justice. The one who may ascend, according to the psalmist, is, "the one who lives blamelessly and does what is right and thinks about the truth" (Ps. 15:2). As in Psalm 24, worship is to shape one's character and one's conduct toward others. Psalm 15 is quite specific in naming several areas of conduct. The true worshiper does not slander or malign others (Ps. 15:3). When it comes to economics and law, worshipers who seek to enact God's ways "do not give out their money at interest, neither do they take bribes against those who are innocent" (Ps. 15:5). For the psalmist, the question of participation in worship *automatically* raises the issue of justice. There is not the slightest hint that economics, law, and politics are to remain outside the sanctuary and off the lips of the worshipers. On the contrary, worship is to empower the community through a renewed vision of justice that transforms both personal conduct and community relationships.

Acts of justice constitute the worshiping community's entrance rite to God's holy mountain. By intimately linking worship and ethics, the Liturgical Psalms challenge the kind of piety, prevalent even in our own day, that lifts up the name of God but avoids tangling with questions of suffering and injustice. These psalms remind us that we are *not* forced to choose between an internal spirituality and external acts of liberation. The two go hand in hand. A justice spirituality will emerge within each of us as we work to bring comfort to those who suffer and liberation to those who are oppressed. To nurture this spirituality, our collective worship must be responsive to both the interior and external dimensions of a justice spirituality. We need liturgies that raise questions about the many economic and legal injustices in our world, but we also need a worship that fosters personal commitment to the work of justice. By rooting our worship in individual and communal acts of justice, a deeper concern for justice will emerge in the heart of each worshiper.

GOD-TALK AND JUSTICE

The issue of inclusive language has jumped to the forefront in recent years, reminding us that while it is indeed true that worship is deeper than words, worship involves terribly difficult but absolutely necessary choices about the words we will use when speaking about God in our worship. The need for inclusive language becomes more urgent as we tangle with liturgies and scripture readings that seem hopelessly infused with male-dominated language.[3]

It is, however, the Church's affirmation that the Bible as the Word of God is directed to all women and men, consequently the Church has chosen to revise the lectionary readings of the mass to reflect its belief in the inclusive character of the Bible's enduring message. In the words of the U.S. Bishops,

> The word of God proclaimed to all nations is by nature inclusive, that is, addressed to all peoples, men and women. Consequently, every effort should be made to render the language of biblical translations as inclusively as a faithful translation of the text permits, especially when this concerns the people of God, Israel and the Christian community.
>
> When a biblical translation is meant for liturgical proclamation, it must also take into account those principles which apply to the public communication of the biblical meaning. Inclusive language is one of those principles, since the text is proclaimed in the Christian assembly to women and men who possess equal baptismal dignity and

reflects the universal scope of the church's call to evangelize.[4]

Unfortunately, while the Church has taken positive steps in relation to language about the community, the debate over the language used when speaking about God in worship has been far more divisive. All too often, the discussion revolves around whether or not we should continue to refer to God as father.

To settle on a few images for God, however central they are to the tradition, seems to me to miss the point about our use of language in worship. Our view of God, and hence our vision for justice, will remain quite narrow if we fail to take advantage of the full range of images the Bible utilizes when speaking of God. On the one hand, worship language should be plain and intelligible, but worship language should also be rich and evocative, pointing us to the mysteries of God and to deeper levels in the spiritual quest. God is certainly the compassionate father (Pss. 68:6; 103:13), and all parents can cherish this image of God, but God is also the nurturing, protective mother and midwife (Pss. 131:2; 22:9–10; cf. Isa 46:3–4, 66:12–13; Hos. 13:8). However, we are not limited to only talk of the divine mother/father. The Psalter is rich in images and metaphors: God is rock and refuge (Ps. 18:3). Comfort is found beneath God's wings (Pss. 17:8, 57:2, 63:8, 91:4). God's right hand exercises power (Pss. 17:7, 20:6, 44:3, 138:7). God is portion and cup (Pss. 16:5, 119:57). God is help and deliverer (Ps. 70:6), compassion and kindness (Pss. 103:8, 145:8), creative spirit (Ps. 104:30) and wondrous glory (the Hebrew *kabôd*, "glory," occurs numerous times in the psalms). The Psalter's language for God is as rich and as varied as Israel's experience of God. To be more creative in our God language, our worship needs to be tapping these and the many other biblical, traditional, third-world, and feminist images that open the community to the multifaceted nature of God's being.[5]

THE GOD OF JUSTICE: PSALM 68

Concern for social justice brings a new set of issues to the language debate. To draw us closer to the God of justice, we need to recover the rich language of justice that appears in the Psalter and elsewhere in scripture. Psalm 68, for example, portrays God as "a father to orphans, a champion to widows" (Ps. 68:6). This phrase reminds worshipers not only about God's compassion but also about the plight of those who suffer. It is this God that the people experience as worshipers enter the sanctuary with their instruments of praise (cf. Ps. 68:25–27). This psalm offers strong evidence of the Psalter's ability to fashion a rich language in order to depict God's concern for justice:

> *Sing to God, sing to God's name.*
> *Extol the one who rides on the clouds.*
> *The LORD is God's name.*
> *Exult in God's presence!*
> *God in God's sacred residence is a father to orphans*
>   *and a champion to widows.*
> *God settles the homeless in houses.*
> *God brings prisoners into prosperity,*
> *Even the rebellious who lived in a parched land. . . .*
> *God, you prepare your good things for the oppressed*
>   (Ps. 68:5–7, 11b).

The image of God as the cloud-rider — an image ancient even to the biblical poets — is refashioned to stress that God does not remain aloof from the needs of the disenfranchised among God's people.[6] Taking this psalm as a guide, we too should feel free to merge our traditional language of God with modern images of homelessness, refugee flight, famine, and unemployment. The words we use in worship must open us to the God of justice and awaken us to the world's desperate need for hope and genuine social change.

Psalm 68 envisions God as the universal power broker. The psalmist does not shun political language and images when speaking of God. God scatters the kings who are at war with one another (Ps. 68:12–15). God commands thousands of chariots and takes captives (Ps. 68:18–19). "Deliverance," in this psalmist's vocabulary, is a concrete political deliverance that involves the smashing of the enemies' heads and the presentation of tribute from the defeated kings (Ps. 68:20–22, 30–32).

Even the procession into the temple appears to consist of representatives from the ruling tribes (Ps. 68:28). Whether it is wishful thinking or not, the psalmist envisions all the kingdoms of the earth singing to God (Ps. 68:33–36). The language that we might relegate to the realm of abstract theology, namely words referring to God's strength, majesty, thunder, and might, are all politically charged terms for the psalmist. The psalmist intends to sound a political word in saying of God:

> *From your holy places, God, you are awe-inspiring.*
> *The God of Israel gives strength and power to the people*
>   (Ps. 68:36).

Here is an image of God that challenges the standard view that kings are the source of their own power. God alone is the one about whom the psalmist can say, "God has scattered those who take delight in war" (Ps. 68:31).

This talk of God as king and warrior opens us to a potentially troubling aspect of the Psalter's politics. The language is rooted in ancient monarchic politics.[7] As such, we must not blithely import the psalms into our worship without carefully examining the extent to which the Psalter fosters a royal politics, in particular a politics of domination couched in the form of benevolent paternalism. Caution is advisable here, because monarchic politics is perfectly capable of speaking about social justice while leaving unjust institutions and structures firmly in place. In the next three chapters, we will investigate the critical question of the Psalter's monarchic imprint. Only through this analysis will we see how and to what degree the psalms subvert hierarchical politics in favor of the justice of God.

WORSHIP ROOTED IN JUSTICE

The Liturgical Psalms call us to creatively evoke a concern for justice in the heart of the worshiper. Such a concern will guide the ways that we construct our hymns, our homilies, our petitions, and our lectionary readings. Justice is not only a goal; it is an expression of our being—one that shapes all that we say and do in our worship. For worship to invigorate us to work for justice, it must charge our imaginations to see God as the God of the poor, the homeless, the lost, the hurting. Our striving for justice needs to be nourished by a liturgical movement that is grounded in a keen vision of God as "a father to orphans, a champion to widows" (Ps. 68:6). Words of justice must echo not only in our halls, but also reverberate in our hearts. Entrance rites and prayers, offerings and eucharist, homilies and dismiss-als—every segment of our collective and inclusive worship should nurture and strengthen us to struggle against what is unjust and to work to ease the pain and sadness of those who are crushed by this world.

PART II

THE ROYAL SPHERE

7

"A Scepter of Equity"

Psalms of the Earthly King

For the ancient Israelites, the sanctuary was the place where the king came to hear the demands of justice and wrestle with the realities of broken covenants and military defeats. Questions of royal power form an important matrix in the Psalter—a trajectory that we shall follow for the next three chapters. In the Psalms of the Earthly King, the so-called royal psalms, we hear the fruits of Israel's ongoing conversation between the temple and the palace.

To be sure, there is a martial atmosphere that pervades many of the royal psalms, and, to the extent that these psalms present a picture of the king as God's chosen conqueror, we may react negatively to worship's embrace of the monarchy's seemingly insatiable quest for land and wealth. Our discomfort with this abuse of worship undoubtedly explains why the Church has chosen not to highlight this block of the Psalter during its Sunday worship and why traditional Judaism has elected to read these texts in a messianic, future-oriented fashion. Both groups recognize the dangers inherent in manipulating worship to say that God is on "our" side, supporting imperial whims. However, contrary to the messianic approach, we shall see that these psalms are most definitely about earthly rulers. Our hermeneutic needs to retain something of the Psalter's concrete political orientation, for in their here-and-now focus, the royal psalms afford the worshiping community the opportunity to speak to and about human political power and authority. This is a critical dimension of ancient Israelite worship. The royal psalms nurture a worship that boldly sets the demands of justice before those who hold the reins of power. Certainly, this issue remains alive for us today.[1]

THE MONARCH AS CONQUEROR

What kind of a monarch do the royal psalms envision? What does this king do for the people? On one level, the royal psalms are very clear: The biblical king is a conquering king. Like King David of old, the psalms speak of a king who extends the nation's political dominion:

> *Ask me, and I will make the nations your inheritance.*
> *Your property will be the ends of the earth.*
> *You will break them with an iron rod.*
> *You will smash them like a potter's vessel* (Ps. 2:8–9).

Victorious in battle, the king can confess: "You have set me at the head of nations; peoples I knew not must serve me" (Ps. 18:44b). In support of the king, it is the community that prays, "Let all kings bow to him, and all nations serve him" (Ps. 72:11; cf. vv. 8–10). The biblical king makes war and expands the royal domain, marching forth with the firm conviction that God engineers the size and holdings of a king's territory. One psalm even speaks of God as the one who readies the king for battle, "Blessed is the LORD, my rock/ the one who trains my hands for battle,/ my fingers for war" (144:1).

While we may justifiably shy away from this thinking, preferring instead to believe that socioeconomic and political forces shape a ruler's destiny, we must acknowledge the pervasiveness of the biblical belief that God plays chess with the world's rulers. The prophetic literature goes even further, to argue that God works in and through all the kings of the earth (e.g., Isa. 13–26, 44:28, 45:1; Jer. 46–51; Ezek. 25–32; Amos 1:1–2:16; Hab. 1–2). Tempered by modern political science, we will undoubtedly extend a Job-like skepticism to the psalmists' view that world politics could be run so deftly by a behind-the-scenes divine hand. Yet, when interpreting the royal psalms, we must recognize in these texts a royal ideology that is steeped in the common ancient Near Eastern view that the gods carry out their purposes through the earthly king.[2]

This focus on the king as conqueror constitutes one possible approach to these texts. However, there is another way to look at poetry concerning a king at war. A more sympathetic reading of the royal psalms would call to mind the community laments — texts which portrayed ancient Israel as a nation threatened by invasion from without. Knowing the harsh world of the laments, we must ask if, in fact, the royal psalms are really about a heroic battler, as the conqueror approach would lead us to believe, or are we to see in the royal psalms a beleaguered king who is representative of an entire people faced with destruction? There is no martial heroism in Psalm 2, where seemingly triumphal royal language is juxtaposed with the dark reality of a nation under siege:

> *Why are the nations restless?*
> *Why do the peoples mumble emptily?*
> *The kings of the earth position themselves.*
> *The rulers consult one another,*
> *Against the LORD and [the LORD's] anointed [ruler]*
>   (Ps. 2:1–2).

Such a text forcefully reminds us that the Psalter's hopes for a royal conqueror were kindled on the ashes of so many Israelite national defeats. Indeed, if there is one political fact that has marked the eastern edge of the Mediterranean since antiquity, it is that of foreign domination and the threat of such domination. The Egyptians, Assyrians, Babylonians, Persians, Greeks, Seleucids, Romans, Arabs, Turks, and even the British, all sought to conquer and control the resources and peoples of the Levant. To simply list the players is enough to indicate the scope and persistence of external danger faced by this region from its earliest days.

Concern about war and the enemy provides the context for

six of the royal psalms (Pss. 2; 18; 20; 72; 89; 144).[3] When read against this backdrop, the language of the king, even the language of victory, takes on a more strained, desperate quality. The king's prayers for divine support are indicative of potentially destructive battles Israel faced against vastly superior foreign forces:

> *"Praised is the LORD," I call out.*
> *I am saved from my enemies. . . .*
> *In my distress, I called to the LORD.*
> *I cried out to my God.*
> *In God's temple, God heard my voice.*
> *My cry came before God, to God's ears. . . .*
> *God sent forth [messengers] from the heights and took*
> *   me.*
> *God drew me out of the deep water.*
> *God freed me from my powerful enemies,*
> *From my opponents when they became too strong for*
> *   me.*
> *They arrayed themselves against me on the day disaster*
> *   fell upon me.*
> *But the LORD served as my support.*
> *God brought me out into open territory,*
> *God took me out, for God favors me (Ps. 18:4, 7, 17–*
> *   20; cf. 144:7–11).*

The king's distress embodies the fears and heartache of a populace that has experienced firsthand the grim realities of battle. There is no Homeric glorying in war here. From the mouth of Israel's king comes the remembrance of protection on the day of battle, with death too proximate and national disaster hauntingly imminent. Certainly, in the Levantine playground of the superpowers, any local victory would seem to the people to be a gift from God, an escape that offered a temporary respite from the burdensome rule of the foreign powers.

In these two very different approaches to the royal psalms—the one more heroic, the other more troubled—we can see texts marked by the double-edged nature of monarchic politics. At times, the Psalter's talk of victory is undoubtedly reflective of nothing more than sheer conquest of territory and peoples. Ancient kings were frequently inclined to be misled by such delusions of power. Yet the Books of Kings, wherein conflict — both internal and external — reigns throughout, inform us that a series of such rulers erringly sowed the bitter seeds of Israel's and Judah's destruction. The lesson of the Books of Kings is clear: Victory as conquest — i.e., the quest for purely political solutions to human conflicts — only brings further affliction and oppression. At other times, however, "victory" for the Psalter must certainly have meant relief from foreign domination. As such, Israel's praise of the king resembles the hope and joy of many third-world countries today which seek and sometimes find relief from the burdens created by modern empire building. In these cases the royal psalms embody the political hopes of an entire people.

THE MONARCHY AND JUSTICE

Apparently conscious of the oppressive nature of territorial expansion, the psalmist calls for conquests that leave justice in their wake:

> *All kings will bow to him [i.e., Israel's king].*
> *All nations will serve him.*
> *For he will rescue the poor person who cries out,*
> *The one who suffers and has no help.*
> *He will have mercy on the bedraggled beggar.*
> *He will save the lives of the poor.*
> *He will intervene to free them from oppression and vio-*
>   *lence,*
> *For their lifeblood is valued in God's sight* (Ps. 72:11–
>   14).

A worship steeped in justice seeks rulers who are not simply bent on conquest. Limited as the royal psalms are to a hierarchical worldview, they nevertheless look to those in power to use their positions to seek economic justice. It is the prayer of the worshiping community that the king's just judgment will effect justice for the lowly:

> *God, pass on to the king your legal judgments.*
> *Give the king's son your justice.*
> *May he judge your people justly,*
>   *your poor rightly.*
> *Let the mountains bring well-being to your people.*
> *[Let] the hills [bring peace] through justice.*
> *May he defend the poor of the community.*
> *May he help those who are poor.*
> *May he crush the oppressor* (Ps. 72:1–4).

Psalm 72 gives disquieting expression to the ills of society and openly calls on the king to address the situation of the poor. Worship's inescapable political character is found in this need to remind the king of the proper use of political power. In the Church year, this psalm is read on Epiphany, appropriately juxtaposing the reign of Christ with biblical ideals for earthly rulers. Politicians and rulers in all times and places are to be reminded by the religious community that the poor are *not* to be neglected in the formation of national legislation. The king's ability to effectively address the situation of the poor constitutes the cornerstone of a just social policy.

The varied strains of Psalm 72 blend the warrior image of a King David with the wisdom-seeking image of King Solomon. In this respect, we will not have a full appreciation of this psalm unless we pause to consider the broader import of the Davidic and Solomonic images. David is remembered in the Books of Samuel as the conqueror unequaled among Israel's kings, unlike in the Books of Chronicles, where he is remembered for establishing and supporting the ritual guilds.[4] It is David, not Solomon, who, as king over all Israel, conquers Jerusalem and various territories in Transjordan and Syria, thereby establishing Israel as a major political actor in the region (2 Sam. 8:1–15; 10:6–19). Solomon, by contrast, is remembered for fortifying the national defenses and building the temple—that is to say, for his "wisdom" (1 Kgs. 5:21–32 [in English versions 5:1–18]; 10:1–29). What did Solomon desire? In his prayer to God, Solomon asks for "a receptive mind with which to judge your people and by which to perceive the difference between good and evil" (1 Kgs. 3:9). Whereupon, God is said to have granted Solomon not only a "wise and discerning mind," but also a great deal of wealth and a long life (1 Kgs. 3:12–14). This section from 1 Kings reveals a key insight into ancient Israelite political thought that is shared by the Psalter, namely that questions of power and authority are *not just Davidic territorial matters but also Solomonic questions of wisdom* (cf. 1 Kgs. 5:9–21 [in English versions 4:29–5:7]). By emphasizing these qualities of both David and Solomon, the compilers of the Deuteronomistic History (i.e., Deuteronomy–Kings), like the writer of Psalm 72, highlight the twin virtues that must undergird Israel's monarchy: military prowess and public policy wisdom.

With wisdom as a guiding political virtue, we may ask, what makes for wise rule? Psalm 101 — a psalm that has been treated by scholars as a royal confession of conduct before God — indicates that such a ruler is led by a heart that is nurtured on "merciful judgment," "integrity," "eyes" not set on any "base thing," and the avoidance of "crooked dealings" (Ps. 101:1–3).[5] In the royal "house," the just ruler desires to be surrounded by upright advisors:

> *I look to the trustworthy ones in the land,*
> *That they may live with me.*
> *Those who act with integrity shall assist me.*
> *No deceiver shall live in my house* (Ps. 101:6–7a).

Extending wise rule to the "city," the king polices the streets and rids the land of evildoers (Ps. 101:5, 8). According to the psalmist, then, the ethical ruler cultivates an interior integrity that extends to the royal cabinet and is, in turn, expected of the populace at large.

Taking Psalms 72 and 101 together, we can see that worship has a dual role to play in relation to those in power. On the one hand, Psalm 72 *gives voice to the people's expectations* of their king. Through this psalm, worship goes to the heart of the nation's politics to challenge its measurement of justice and its norms for assisting those in need. In the sanctuary, the psalmist declares, it is appropriate for the people to speak to the powers about poverty. Yet it is not enough for the religious community to simply proclaim a message of justice. Psalm 101 penetrates more deeply, showing us that *unless those in power learn to sing songs of justice and mercy*, the community's call will fall on deaf ears and be rendered ineffective. The worshiping community must hold open the opportunity for those in power to stand in the sanctuary of God, cultivating hearts of integrity, seeking advisors with vision, and instituting policies that respond to the needs and distress of the poor. The danger here is, of course, that kings and rulers will coopt the worshiping community by having power holders appear beside prelates, creating a semblance of a concern for justice but giving no substance to that appearance. While the danger is great, the need for good governance is so acute that the worshiping community must seek in its worship to counsel political leaders in the ways of integrity, ethics, and justice.

THE MONARCHY AND PROSPERITY

For the psalmists, the king's upright conduct is but one dimension of the royal office that commands attention. The poet's imagination is also enlivened by the prosperity of the king, as shown in this royal wedding song, written for the king and his bride. To the king, the poet says:

> *My mind is stirred by a good word.*
> *So I say,*
> *My work is for the king.*
> *My tongue is the readied pen of a scribe.*
> *You are more handsome than anyone.*
> *Favor is poured on your lips.*
> *Therefore, God has blessed you forever. . . .*
> *You are adorned in myrrh, aloes, and cassia.*
> *From palaces of ivory, stringed music gladdens you.*
> *The daughters of kings are among your favorites.*
> *Standing at your right hand is the favored woman cov-*
> *   ered with the gold of Ophir* (Ps. 45:2–3, 9–10).

Elsewhere, in Psalm 72, the king is credited with being the source of prosperity for the whole of society:

> *May he [the king] come down like rain on the cut grass,*
> *Like abundant rain on the earth.*
> *The just will flourish in his days,*
> *And well-being will abound until the moon ceases.*
>
> *May [God] make them [the poor] live and give them*
> *   gold from Sheba. [Alternate reading: Let him (the*
> *   king) live and let him receive gold from Sheba.]*
>
> *Let there be abundant grain in the land, on the moun-*
> *   tain tops.*
> *May his fruit abound like that of Lebanon.*
> *May they blossom from the city like the grasses of the*
> *   earth* (Ps. 72:6–7, 15a, 16).

In speaking of wealth and abundance, the psalmists are actually invoking one of the themes connected to the topic of royal wisdom: The royal psalms not only seek a king endowed with wisdom and understanding but also wealth and life:

> *Lord, the king rejoices in your strength.*
> *How greatly the king exults in your victory!*
> *You have given him what he desires.*
> *You have not withheld what his lips requested.*
> *Instead, you have led him into the best blessings.*
> *You have put a fine gold crown on his head.*
> *He asked for life from you and you gave him it —*
> *Long days, eternity.*
> *His glory is great through your victory.*
> *Splendor and majesty you have granted him.*
> *For you have made him blessed forever.*
> *You have gladdened him with the joy of your presence*
> *   (Ps. 21:2–7; cf. 20:5–6).*

Unfortunately, this poetic reveling in royal splendor serves to obscure an oppressive economic and political reality that is exposed only by the prophets. The fragments of masterfully carved ivory found at Israel's capital, Samaria, for example, ought to remind us not only of Ahab's "house of ivory" (1 Kgs. 22:39), but also of the criticisms of Amos, who castigates the rulers for living in such luxury, "resting on their ivory beds" (Amos 6:4).

For the royal psalms, the link between monarchy and prosperity produces a social vision that bestows justice from the top down. What are we to make of the embrace of royal power found in these psalms? What does it mean theologically to say that the king is the source of society's prosperity? For A. R. Johnson, this prosperity is rooted in the just conduct of the king—a topic discussed in the preceding section of this chapter:

> It is the king's function to ensure the "righteousness" or right relationship within the borders of his territory which will ensure the economic well-being of his people and at the same time will safeguard them from foreign interference. There can be no prosperity and no assurance of continuity for the nation without righteousness; and there can be no righteousness without the fidelity to Yahweh and His laws to which the tribal brotherhood of Israel was pledged under the terms of the Sinaitic covenant. In the ultimate, therefore, the righteousness of the nation is dependent upon the righteousness of the king.[6]

However, the covenant is also a theological factor grounding prosperity. It would seem that the psalmists' assessment of the king is guided by the Deuteronomistic conception of the king as God's anointed or specially designated ruler. Israel's positive dynastic theology is given its most elaborate definition in 2 Samuel, where the writer has God say of David's son, "I will become his father, and he will become my son" (2 Sam. 7:14). As with the Deuteronomistic History, the royal psalms cultivate an intimate relationship between the king and God, a relationship that is spoken in terms of father-son language. Consistent with the phraseology of 1 Samuel, God reaffirms, in Psalm 2, the king's installation on Zion's throne. The king announces the decree of the LORD: "You are my son, I have begotten you this day" (Ps.

2:7).[7] Such language places the king on a level above normal human beings. This language seeks to undergird the throne with divine power and support. In biblical terms, God's support means that the dynasty or the throne is a permanent and eternal institution (2 Sam. 7:11–16; cf. Ps. 45:7, from which the chapter title is taken).[8]

The everlasting character of the dynasty is traced back to the promise of God to David, but the psalmists also acknowledge the conditional character of the throne:

> *The* LORD *swore to David truthfully,*
> *And will not cancel it:*
> *"One of your very own offspring I will place on the*
>   *throne.*
> If your sons will adhere to my covenant,
> *And to my testimony that I will teach them,*
> *Then their sons shall also sit on your throne, forever"*
>   (Ps. 132:11–12; cf. 1 Kgs. 3:14, emphasis added).

This shift in consciousness toward a more conditional royal promise is indicative of Israel's collective wisdom regarding its royal theology, after centuries of life under a number of disreputable rulers.[9] The psalmist hints at a type of royal *reassessment* that is expressed much more fully, for example, in the books of Jeremiah and Ezekiel. Jeremiah made it clear that divine commitments to the king and to the temple were not irrevocable (Jer. 7:1–20; 21:1–22:30). In Ezekiel, the oppressive shepherds/ rulers of Israel are to be judged and eventually replaced by a regathered people and the elevation of a just shepherd/ruler, namely the new Davidic king (Ezek. 34:1–31). In Brueggemann's words, "The justice refused before 587 is now to be a social reality."[10] A conditional promise means that the simple fact of the institution of kingship's *existence* does not by itself guarantee social stability, prosperity, or divine support.

The prophetic critique of royal ideology sends the discussion in a new direction. Is there any counterpart to this critique in the royal psalms that would lend weight to the notion that worship should be more thoughtful about royal wealth and durability? The royal psalm that goes the furthest in this direction is

Psalm 89—a psalm which opens up a very different evaluation of the connection between the monarchy and prosperity. In the final verses of this text, the ancient theology of God's support for the king collides directly with the harsh reality of the king suffering a stunning military defeat:

> *You have cast off and rejected.*
> *You have shown anger with your anointed.*
> *You have spurned the covenant with your servant.*
> *You have profaned his crown down to the ground.*
> *You have wrecked all his defensive walls.*
> *You have made his strongholds into ruins* (Ps. 89:39–
>   41).

The careful way this psalm builds, perhaps unexpectedly, to this conclusion is instructive. The psalm opens with an eloquent statement of the standard royal theology, where God's steadfast love is revealed in the promise of permanent kingship given to David (Ps. 89:2–4). The next section of the psalm confirms the vision of the monarch as conqueror, recalling that God's creative power and justice stood behind the warrior David, that is, the dynasty (Ps. 89:6–27).[11] The psalmist speaks of God's intimate relationship with the king, using "father" language (Ps. 89:27). Several verses take up and affirm the theme of the permanence of the throne (Ps. 89:30–37). However, by incorporating a fairly negative statement regarding the conditional character of this royal covenant, the psalmist indicates there is a need for the worshiping community to use its liturgical celebration as a time to wrestle with the contradiction between its official theology and the historic reality of military defeat:

> *I will make his offspring eternal.*
> *His throne will last as long as the heavens endure.*
> *If his sons abandon my instruction,*
> *And do not follow my judgments,*
> *If they profane my rules,*
> *And do not adhere to my commandments,*
> *I will use a rod to exact a punishment for their trans-*
>   *gressions,*

> *And [I will send] plagues for their wrongdoing*
> (Ps. 89:30–33).

These contradictions lead directly to the final verses of the psalm, where the rejection of the king is made apparent. Unfortunately, the Church's lectionary omits these final verses, thereby presenting only the positive aspects of the divine-royal covenant. Yet the full psalm indicates that times of war and national disaster are the moments when worship must be willing to reexamine faulty and incomplete political theologies. A lectionary that presents a simple, positive reading of this psalm overlooks the larger political context, namely the historic reality of the demise of Israel's monarchy. Without the final verses of Psalm 89, we lose a valuable opportunity to critically assess questions of political power, divine mandate, and hierarchy.

While the royal psalms by no means develop a full-scale critique of the kingship, it is clear that they vary in their overall estimate of God's support for particular kings. Such support is never guaranteed. At the very least, worship should remind us of this fact. Psalm 89 is a model for a hymnody that would dare to scrutinize official theologies when they clash with the lived history of a people. This psalm warns us against using worship to lend unqualified theological support to a nation's rulers. The community must not foster the illusion that kingship or any other political structure will be an endless source of prosperity. Indeed, if Psalm 89 is any guide, worship must help us cope with and expose the unstable nature of our political and economic institutions.

THE COMMUNITY AND THE KING

While our discussion of the royal psalms to this point has had the monarch as its main focus, implicit throughout our discussion is the fact that the worshiping community has a vital relationship with the king. The worshiping community nurtures the values and questions that are central to the quest for a just social order and makes these issues known to those in power through the medium of prayer and liturgy. Let us consider the community's role in more detail.

Given the military orientation of a number of these psalms, it is not surprising to find that the people sing of the king's victories and pray for future victory (Ps. 21:2–6, 14). In one psalm, the people volunteer to fight for the king (Ps. 110:3).[12] Elsewhere, the people pray to God for support of the king (Pss. 20:2–6, 7–10; 72:15).

Despite these rather straightforward statements of commitment to military success, the worshiping community actually has a complex and not altogether uncritical relationship to the royal theology. While the worshiping community may foster and reenact key elements of the Davidic royal covenant, it also serves as a conscience to remind the ruler and the people of the roots of the royal promise. In Psalm 132, which might very well be termed a royal liturgical psalm, the psalmist speaks of the advancing of the ark of the covenant to its place of rest (Ps. 132:8).[13] Its arrival is the occasion to ask God to reaffirm the covenant with the dynasty, calling on God not to reject the current ruler:

> *For the sake of David your servant,*
> *Do not turn away from the face of your anointed [ruler].*
> *The LORD swore to David.*
> *It is firm.*
> *God will not turn from it:*
> *"From your offspring I will make your throne.*
> *If your children adhere to my covenant*
> *And my testimony which I have taught to them,*
> *Then their children will also sit on your throne forever.*
> *For the LORD has chosen Zion.*
> *God desires it as a place to live"* (Ps. 132:10–13).

This ceremonial invocation of the conditional nature of the royal promise bears a strong resemblance to the more critical theological dynamic that infuses Psalm 89.[14] These psalms serve to remind us that the worshiping community must constantly assess contemporary reality in light of the received religious tradition and reevaluate the tradition in light of lived national experience. Herein lies the key to a powerful interaction of worship and politics: If worship remains dynamic in relation to both tradition and experience, it will successfully grapple with the changing face of politics. If, on the other hand, worship seeks to cling in a sterile way to tradition, it will fail to provide satisfying answers to the questions raised by the nation's history of defeat, dynastic transition, faltering prosperity, and social injustice.

While it is true that not all of the royal psalms take a more critical stance, there are enough passages in the royal psalms to convince us that the path to justice is not paved by flowery speeches about royal power and wealth. Talk of eternal dynasties will not bring needed social changes. Of course, for us today, the psalmist's critical assessment of political power remains a vital tool for constructing liturgies that address a world in need of justice. Our liturgies should remind us that political, economic, and military questions pose new agendas for worship. Even the royal psalms have to confess that weapons alone do not make a cause just or successful:

> *Now I know that the LORD helps the LORD's anointed.*
> *God answers from God's sacred abode,*
> *Through the mighty acts of God's right hand that rescues.*
> *Some [mention] chariotry and others horses,*
> *But we mention the name of the LORD our God* (Ps. 20:7–8).

The more fully we press this expectation for social justice, the more deeply critical worship will become of existing social injustices. At times, the community of worship will raise questions about our loyalties and commitments in a world scarred by imperial conflict, civil war, and economic enslavement. In these times, the worshiping community must call on those in power to seek a more just and constructive social order. It is the worshiping community's duty not to leave it solely to the power holders to frame the parameters of the justice question.

8

"Who Puts an End to Wars"

Hymns of Zion

To this day the city of Jerusalem remains a sacred city and because of this, even in its strife, this meeting place of Judaism, Christianity, and Islam continues to cry out to us in expectation of peace and justice for the world.[1] Likewise, many centuries ago, Zion — the city of God, Jerusalem — did not escape the psalmists' theological imagination:

> *God's foundation is in the sacred mountains.*
> *The LORD loves the gates of Zion*
> *more than all Jacob's dwelling places.*
> *Honorable things are uttered about you,*
> *city of God* (Ps. 87:1b–3).

Once an ancient Jebusite city and later the royal capital of King David, this city became a locus of reflection on justice, warfare, and peace in psalms commonly referred to as Hymns of Zion. In the Psalter's imagery regarding Zion, we have a powerful religious symbol — one that has emerged from the bitter struggles of a nation that hoped for a world in which wars would end. As symbol, Zion has spoken to successive generations (see Ps. 48:14). Yet, in elevating the symbol, we must not lose sight of the concrete dimension of the Zion hymns as *a response to war*. Fortress walls and guard towers may not be the stuff of modern warfare; nevertheless, in their physicality, the Hymns of Zion can continue to guide us to reflect critically and specifically on issues of military security and warfare today.

THE CITY OF GOD

Jerusalem. This illustrious city was the location not only of the royal palace of Judah (2 Sam. 5:5–11) but also the site of the Solomonic and postexilic temples (1 Kgs. 7:1–51; Haggai 1:2–11). As such, Jerusalem was the hub of ancient Israel's political and religious life. The Hymns of Zion are framed around the notion that Zion is the abode of God. However, contrary to what we might have expected from the royal psalms, the psalmists do not use the image of Zion to legitimize royal politics or the dynastic covenant.[2] The poets use Zion to raise far different issues. They want to know what it means to say that God dwells in Zion. Specifically, for our purposes, they want to know what it means to say that God dwells in a world of violence, armies, and war.

In speaking of Zion as the "city of God," the psalmist seeks to affirm boldly and directly that God dwells in Zion.[3] This presence makes God a "refuge" and "haven" for the people (Pss. 46:2, 8, 12; 48:4; cf. 84:2–6).[4] The words *haven* and *refuge* are powerful, but leave us asking what it meant for the psalmist to speak of God in this way. The Hymns of Zion emphasize that God's presence provides a physical protection and military security.[5] In a world shredded by war and violence, the city of God becomes the symbol and the reality of the possibility of peace:

> *God is in its [Zion's] citadels,*
> *God is known as a high place [of safety]* (Ps. 48:4).

Likewise, for the writer in Psalm 46, God is a "refuge" (Ps. 46:2) in a world of political turmoil and military confrontation:

> *Therefore, we will not fear when the earth changes,*
> *Or when the mountains slide into the sea,*

Or when the water roars and foams,
Or when the mountains quake at its [the sea's] swelling.

God is in its [the city's] midst.
It shall not totter.
God will give aid when morning comes.
Nations are in turmoil.
Kingdoms reel.
God speaks.
The land melts (Ps. 46:3–4, 6–7).

To say that God is "refuge and strength" (Ps. 46:2) is not merely a matter of detached interior contemplation for the psalmist. To say that "A river—its branches gladden the city of God" (Ps. 46:5a), is not to invoke a pleasant pastoral image but to say that God's protective presence brings about Israel's military security in the face of surrounding hostile powers:

The LORD of hosts/armies is with us.
The God of Jacob is our high place [of safety].
Look now at the LORD's works—
The one who has done astonishing things in the world,
The one who ends wars throughout the world.
God breaks the bow and cuts the spear.
God torches the wagons (Ps. 46:8–10).

The psalmist affirms the dynamic presence of a God who dwells in and brings concrete peace to Zion. With God in residence, Zion becomes the city of God.

DEFINING SECURITY

The belief that the gods dwelt in their temples in the midst of the people, providing security, is not unique to ancient Israel but pervades the societies of the ancient Near East.[6] Indeed, the phrasing of Psalm 48, with its reference to "Zaphon," carries on traditions of the divine abode paralleled elsewhere in the Ugaritic mythological texts:

> *Beautiful in its elevation,*
> *The joy of the entire world —*
> *Mount Zion —*
> *The remote Zaphon (ṣapon).*
> *The city of the great king* (Ps. 48:3).

In the Ugaritic texts, the god Baal is termed *bᶜl ṣpn*, "Baal of Zaphon," i.e., Mt. Cassius.[7] Behind the biblical and ancient Near Eastern mythic understanding of the divine presence on the sacred mountain stood two major social institutions: the palace and the temple.[8] The theological/mythological belief in the presence of the god in the temple and city, common to these cultures, generated a complex series of relationships between the palace and the temple. For example, the close proximity of the palace and temple, together with their profitable interaction and cooperation, was considered a source of societal stability and prosperity. In this regard, the temple frequently functioned as a passive ally of the state, simply invoking the gods to lend support to the king. At other times, documents from Mesopotamia inform us, temples could — through divination and prophetic speakers — demand the attention of the local rulers.[9]

We have already seen in the royal psalms the extent to which worship embraced and to some extent critiqued royal ideology in the "Psalms of the Earthly King." Yet the Hymns of Zion offer an even more vital, critically reflective social role for the temple. When the poet calls worshipers to look at the walls of Zion, the psalmist is saying, quite frankly, Look at our weapons system:

> *Go around Zion,*
> *Circle it.*
> *Count its towers.*
> *Note carefully its ramparts.*
> *Go through its citadels,*
> *So that you may tell a later generation* (Ps. 48:13–14).

The psalmist is not speaking of some ethereal Zion but directs the worshiper's attention to the city's defensive apparatus and *asks worshipers to critically reflect on the realities of security*. The walls, towers, and citadels that provided God's people a haven also panicked enemy armies:

> *The kings assembled themselves.*
> *They crossed together.*
> *What they saw astonished them.*
> *They were terrified and left quickly* (Ps. 48:5–6).

The peace of God experienced by the psalmist is not an interiorized peace, but safety in time of war. Worship, for the psalmist, becomes an occasion for the community to reflect on the realities of defense against war. In worship, the psalmist chooses to linger over the structures that appear to buy peace. Not surprisingly, the psalmist prays that such a haven be preserved by God "forever" (Ps. 48:9). Yet, in this very appeal to the divine we have the recognition that citadels and walls by themselves are not enough. *Without God there can be no lasting peace and stability.*[10] Therefore, to preserve this peace and security requires determined effort, open persistence, and prayerful observance on the part of the community. Worship in the city of God is a necessary act if the community hopes to find some measure of safety in a threatening political environment.

BRINGING AN END TO WAR

The Hymns of Zion not only make us conscious of peace and security issues, but they also *raise fundamental questions about war*. In what is perhaps the most provocative of the Hymns of Zion, the psalmist proclaims that it is from Zion, God's "lair" (Ps. 76:3), that God "breaks the flaming [arrows of the] bow, the shield, the sword, and war" (Ps. 76:4).[11] God "cuts down the princes' spirit and terrifies the earth's kings" (Ps. 76:13). For the psalmists, to speak of Zion is to speak about a God who acts to end war:

> *The one who has done astonishing things in the world,*
> *The one who ends wars throughout the world.*
> *God breaks the bow and cuts the spear.*

> *God torches the wagons.*
> *Cease [war making]!*
> *Know that I am God!*
> *I will be exalted among the nations.*
> *I will be exalted throughout the earth* (Ps. 46:10–11).[12]

The word translated "the one who ends [wars]" is built from the root *šbt*, meaning "to rest." Reflecting on the psalmist's choice of words, we can say that the very God who rested and ceased after the act of creation (Gen. 2:2) is the God who will employ that same creative power to make the nations rest and cease from their warring. God acts because, as Ollenburger observes, "War and its equipment are recognized as threats . . . not only against the created order established by Yahweh, but against his stature as 'God, exalted among the nations' " (Ps. 46.11b)."[13]

Since the psalmists conceive of God as the one who puts an end to fighting, it is probably not surprising that the Hymns of Zion do not speak about earthly kings who succeed at battle. There are no calls to go forth and destroy the enemy. The Hymns of Zion are certainly conscious of the city's walls, but these psalms do not embrace the royal ambitions that lurk behind those walls.[14] Instead, the psalmist uses the image of Zion to sustain a vision of a God who "executes judgment to aid all the earth's poor" (Ps. 76:10). War is an obstacle to a full realization of both God's peace and God's justice for the poor.[15] The image of Zion fosters a yearning for a security that is not based on war, conquest, or destruction. It is not a peace that is secured solely by kings or walls. The presence of God in the city roots this peace—a peace that is intentional—a peace that brings an end to war.

The Hymns of Zion point to another way to achieve communal peace and global security. City walls are useful to secure and preserve a type of peace, but not a peace that goes beyond those walls to transform the world. Perhaps the most politically compelling notion to emerge from these psalms is the idea that *critical reflection on Zion's walls ought to lead to the construction of a world beyond war*. The peace of God cannot remain locked behind fortress walls; it is a peace that engages the armies and kings of the earth. There is a profound hope in this understanding of Zion's peace. In gazing at these impressive city walls we are not to become transfixed; rather, we must sense God's presence in the city and begin to perceive the power of a divine peace that can go forth from the city to challenge the armies of the earth. Zion is to be a birthplace for peace.

Some scholars speak of God's protection of Zion in terms of the doctrine of the inviolability or invincibility of Zion.[16] On this understanding, the psalmists are said to believe that God's presence in Zion guaranteed Jerusalem's safety against enemy attack. This is a rather static interpretation of the texts. Needless to say, the Zion image is far more dynamic: God's presence in Zion launches a new era in which warfare comes to an end. The Hymns of Zion are not solely concerned with Jerusalem's ability to survive attack, as suggested by the inviolability doctrine; rather, they are looking beyond, to see how the divine presence within the city can creatively transform the warring world beyond the walls of the city. From Zion, this reality of peace is to spread and change the world as we know it.

This more dramatic interpretation of the Hymns of Zion finds a striking counterpart in the Zion vision of the prophets Isaiah and Micah—prophets who both held out the hope that,

> *In a later era,*
> *The mountain of the LORD's temple will be established*
>   *at the top of the mountains,*
>   *and be carried above the hills.*
> *All the nations will shine because of it.*
> *Many peoples will come and say,*
> *"Let us go up to the LORD's mountain,*
> *To the temple of Jacob's God,*
> *So that God might instruct us in God's ways,*
> *And so that we might walk in God's paths."*
> *For instruction will go forth from Zion,*
> *The word of the LORD [will go forth] from Jerusalem.*
> *God will judge between nations.*
> *God will arbitrate for many communities [Micah reads:*
>   *for nations vast and distant].*
> *They will beat their swords into plow tips,*

And their spears into pruning hooks.
One nation will not bear the sword against another
nation.
They will not train for war ever again (Isa. 2:2–4; Mic.
4:1–3).

For the psalmists and these prophets, Zion is an image of the power of God's transformative peace in the face of war. The weaker doctrine of inviolability might leave one thinking that peace stops at Zion's walls. The sentiment that rings so clearly in the Hymns of Zion and in Isaiah and Micah is that Zion is the starting point of a new way of living and worshiping in a world filled with war. The image of Zion broadens the definition of security to encompass not only city walls and towers, but also divine presence, the breaking of the bow, and hope for an end to war.

ZION AND MODERN WARFARE

If Zion is the entry into this new era, how does this reality impinge on our thinking about modern warfare? The major Christian contributions to this discussion have followed two major lines: nonviolent resistance and just-war analysis. Both schools of thought have sought to root themselves strongly in scripture and theological tradition.[17] However, whether one embraces strategies of nonviolence or the just-war theory, both approaches have encountered significant challenges in the political and national realities of the last several decades.[18] The Hymns of Zion can create a space for this discussion in the context of faithful worship, but it remains our task to extend the discussion of war into the modern worship setting.[19] When global violence, deprivation of human rights, and unjust rule persist, what issues do we need to raise in our worship?

In the North American context—insulated as it is from open military conflict—it has become far too easy for many people of faith to think only in terms of nonviolent struggle as the solution to war and violence. However, in the third world, as revolutionary movements have been forced to mobilize against intransigent regimes, the absolute purity of some theories of nonviolent resistance is called into question.[20] In far too many situations in Latin America, Asia, Africa, and the Middle East, horrible evils have been perpetrated by police states whose brutal power has gone unchecked. Can outsiders really expect the populace at large to respond only with picket signs and strikes? Worship must help us wrestle with the complexities of a response to tyranny. We ought not to pray glibly for peace without first considering the cost of peace in terms of lives and property. We must also ask if counterviolence is always ruled out when one's village or family hangs in the balance and it is certain that the regime intends only harm. In these cases it appears that concerted action, including military confrontation, seems to be the only way to dislodge such regimes. There is a great need for the proponents of nonviolent resistance to reexamine the question of national or communal defense.[21] Such concrete global realities raise very real challenges that must not be lightly dismissed.

These questions will spur us to further analysis, action, and prayer: Are there times when nationalist movements need to wrest forcefully human rights or democratic reforms from intransigent rulers? In the event of civil strife, is international military intervention a legitimate recourse for quelling belligerent parties and for bringing an end to senseless killing? If nonviolence is the final response, are we ready to deal with the risk and cost in terms of human lives? The Hymns of Zion should provide the worshiping community the opportunity to reframe the psalmists' concerns and vision in the modern worship context.

The Hymns of Zion can also provide us a valuable opportunity to assess critically the just-war tradition. In our analysis of war, we must bear in mind that difficulties in the nonviolent stance do not automatically translate into an affirmation of warfare. In fact, just-war theory, when used appropriately, is not intended to "justify" war. Indeed, this tradition has tried to narrow and define those conditions under which wars may be considered just or right. Questions central to just-war analysis include: Is there a credible authority that is empowered to carry out the war? Is the cause just, as opposed to being a war for glory or profit? Is there a right intention in fighting the war — is it being fought to promote good rather than to bring harm? Is there a basic desire for peace on the part of the defender? Is there some semblance of proportion between the effects of the war and the level of injustice against which the war is being waged? Have all alternatives to war been exhausted in the pursuit of a solution to the injustice or act of aggression?[22]

The questions raised by just-war theory are thoughtful and compelling, yet, for all these attempts to clarify the matter of the just war, there are those who will ask if warfare in the modern world can ever really be just. The document "Modern War and Christian Conscience," written in light of the 1991 Gulf war, makes the case that modern technological "total warfare" can never be just, for by its nature modern warfare is so thoroughly brutal and destructive that its immorality is plain.[23] The document points to the Gulf war's high casualties, sweeping destruction, *and our silence in investigating the effects of this tragedy* as support for its devastating critique of just-war analysis. This critique strongly suggests that modern warfare can never bring about a peace built on justice. Such a profound and provocative document undoubtedly has many implications for worship, but to my mind the most significant is that worship must grapple with the human toll of modern warfare. We must look beyond the technological sophistication of our missiles and bombers—our "walls"—to discern the divine presence in Zion that would break every weapon on earth.

ZION—AT THE HEART OF WORSHIP

The language of "ramparts" and "citadels" makes its way into another of the Hymns of Zion, Psalm 122. Here, however, the topic is not war, but peace. The psalmist exhorts the community, "Ask for [pray for] the well-being [peace] of Jerusalem; may those who love you find tranquility" (Ps. 122:6). The topic is peace, but our previous discussions remind us that the reality of war cannot lie far away from this prayer:

May there be well-being [peace] inside your ramparts,
Tranquility inside your citadels.

> *For the sake of my kin and companions,*
> *Let me say, "Well-being [peace] be within you"*
>   (Ps. 122:7–8).

Again the city's "ramparts" and "citadels," even its "gates" (Ps. 122:2), inspire a reflection on Zion's peace. What was once the site of the "thrones of the house of David" (Ps. 122:5) is, for the pilgrim to Jerusalem, a place to find inspiration for and rededication to the cause of peace. The psalmist's prayer is concerned and active, acknowledging that worship must dedicate time to prayer for peace.

The well-being of Jerusalem creates a location for reflecting on the peace of God:

> *We have meditated on your kindness, God,*
>   *within your temple.*
> *As with your name, God,*
>   *likewise praise of you*
>   *[reaches] to the ends of the earth.*
> *Your right hand is filled with justice.*
> *May Mount Zion rejoice!*
> *May Judah's daughters [cities and towns] exult,*
>   *because of your judgments!* (Ps. 48:10–12).

From that location, the worshiper discerns that humanity's highest calling is not to the glories of the battlefield but the chambers of prayer and praise:

> *How delightful are your dwellings, LORD of Hosts.*
> *I long deeply for, I need, the courts of the LORD.*
> *My mind and body sing joyously to the living God.*
>
> *Happy are they who live in your house.*
> *They praise you always.*
> *Happy are those who find their strength in you.*
> *[Your] paths are on their minds* (Ps. 84:2–3, 5–6).

In the cause of peace, new allies are formed: All who worship God in Jerusalem become residents of that city:

> *Concerning Zion it is said:*
> *"Each and every person was born there."*
> *It is God Most High that readies it.*
> *The LORD pens it in the national registry:*
> *"This one was born there"* (Ps. 87:5–6).

Worship in Zion has the power to transform the distant pilgrim into a person reborn within the gates of Zion, the city of God. Against the backdrop of the psalmist's vision of Zion's peace, the psalmists' message is clear: Only the pilgrim who is deeply rooted in Zion can carry Zion's peace to the world. Inside Zion's walls, the worshiper tastes the new era of Isaiah and Micah. Upon departure from the walls, the worshiper walks away with a powerful vision of the God who puts an end to war. It then falls to the worshiper to nurture Zion's peace in the towns and villages of the land, well beyond the safety of Jerusalem's mighty towers and walls.

ZION: MORE THAN SYMBOL

We have discovered in this chapter an image of Zion that is alive to the issues of politics and war, peace and justice. Worship discovers, in the image of Zion, not some limp spiritual metaphor, but a symbol that gives a theological focus to our efforts to end war. It is an image that encourages us to transform our war-ravaged world into a place of healing and community building. To bring these sensibilities into modern worship, we need to redefine words such as *haven* and *refuge* in terms of a constructive theological response to a world at war. Through the Hymns of Zion, sacred liturgy actively directs worshipers to search for God both within the city and outside the city walls in a world at war—to discover the God who is "a help amid distress" (Ps. 46:2)—not simply a help in relation to some narrowly construed spiritual problem, but a much-needed help in a world all too often fatigued by war. By locating God both at rest in the city and in conflict with external armies, the Hymns of Zion empower worshipers to experience the divine presence as a reservoir of communal peace. In taking this more directive stance, the temple enhances its relationship to the palace and to the society at large. The Hymns of Zion help the community to discover that it is the God in the city, not the king in the palace, who brings well-being and peace to the world outside Zion's walls. Worship that is active will openly raise questions about the community's understanding of security, peace, justice, and solidarity. Far beyond simply performing a social maintenance function, the worship found in the Hymns of Zion probes the foundations of the city and the world.

9

"The LORD Sits Enthroned"

Psalms of God as King

As a constant reminder of the reign of God, Jewish prayer regularly intones the phrase, "Blessed are you, O LORD our God, king of the universe." The Christian worshiper similarly prays, "Our Father in heaven . . . May your kingdom come, may your will be done on earth as it is in heaven." Both traditions invoke the ancient biblical image of God as king to reaffirm God's rule over the earth. Behind these liturgical traditions stand the Psalms of God as King—texts that rivet our attention on the divine ruler who stands above all other gods and rulers. These psalms set out in sharp relief one of the fundamental tenets of the Psalter: When developing a political vision, it is not enough to speak of kings and city walls; the worshiping community's political and social vision must arise out of a profound sense of the reign of the creator God over the world. As seen in these psalms, this deeper awareness of the political implications of the reign of God engenders in the community an abiding concern for justice and for *laws* that embody divine justice. Likewise, this consciousness of the rule of God transforms worship: God's creative power and holiness forge a liturgy that regularly celebrates and renews God's enthronement over the world.

DIVINE JUSTICE

The Psalms of God as King present to us a God who is the effective ruler over *all divine beings*:

129

For the Lord is the great God,
The great king over all other gods (Ps. 95:3).

May all who worship idols feel shame,
Those who boast in worthless [gods].
[For] all gods bow before God! . . .
For you, Lord, are removed above the earth.
You are exalted far above the gods (Ps. 97:7, 9).

As a result of God's exaltation above all other celestial powers and beings, God's rule overshadows *all earthly rule*:

The Lord reigns, clothed in majesty.
The Lord is clothed — girt with strength.
Thus is the world established.
It cannot be moved.
Your throne was established long ago.
You are ancient (Ps. 93:1–2).

For the psalmist, this exalted ruler does not remain aloof
from the world. The primordial deity acts to shape the course
of earthly politics through the people of Israel:

For the Lord is most high, awe-inspiring.
The great king over the whole earth.
God subjects peoples to us,
And nations beneath our feet (Ps. 47:3–4).

To sing of God as king, then, is to sing of a cosmic and celestial ruler. It is to sing of God's reign over divine beings. It is to
praise a ruler who stands above all other earthly rulers.

Is there a direction to God's rule? In what way does this rule
touch and transform the world? For the psalmists, one of the
primary features of God's rule, accented in a number of passages, is *justice*. Beyond all earthly decrees there are divine
decrees:

Your decrees are quite dependable.
Holiness befits your house, Lord, forevermore
     (Ps. 93:5).

Zion heard and was glad;
The daughters [suburbs] of Judah rejoiced
    at your legal decisions, LORD (Ps. 97:8).

According to the psalmists, it is inauthentic to affirm that God is king without coming to terms with God's demands for justice. Divine rule cannot be legitimately celebrated without invoking justice as the basis of that rule:

The LORD *reigns.*
Let the earth rejoice!
May the many isles be glad!
Clouds and thick darkness surround God.
Right conduct and justice are the base of God's throne
    (Ps. 97:1–2).

The notion of an eternal justice emanating from the gods is not unique to ancient Israel. In fact, the earliest Near Eastern law codes look to the gods as the wellspring of justice. The ancients believed that the demands of justice were fulfilled in their numerous law codes—a belief that likewise undergirds the biblical law codes found in Exodus 21–23 and Deuteronomy 12–26.[1] For the compilers of the Pentateuch, the pursuit of law was not an end in itself, but flowed from an overarching sense of divine intention for society. Yet the attempts to realize this intention never led to a static conception of law, either in the biblical record or in later rabbinic tradition as exemplified by the Mishnah and the talmudic commentaries. Just laws are, in other words, the product of a divine-human partnership, the realization of divine decrees in human society through the efforts of human will, intellect, imagination, and a yearning for justice.[2] A lofty sense of justice, in other words, inspired, but did not displace, the hard work that gave rise to the biblical and rabbinic legal traditions. Careful study will reveal particular juridical developments that occur between the time of the framing of Exodus 21–23 and the recasting of the law in Deuteronomy 12–26.[3] Even more pronounced are the many legal debates present in the later rabbinic materials. Yet, underlying this entire legal tradition is a deep sense of the divine call for social justice and equitable decision making (cf. Exod. 22:26; Deut. 24:14–15).

The psalmists' concern for justice is complemented and nourished by an *awareness of divine holiness.*[4] In the Bible, holiness is not an abstract quality but is enmeshed in the pursuit of divine justice. This linkage between holiness and justice comes out most eloquently in Psalm 99:

> *May they praise your great and awe-inspiring name.*
> *God is holy—the strength of the king who loves justice.*
> *You established equity.*
> *You have acted justly and rightly toward Jacob.*
> *Exalt the LORD our God!*
> *Bow at God's footstool!*
> *God is holy.*
> *Moses and Aaron among God's priests,*
> *And Samuel among those who call on God's name—*
> *They called on the LORD and God answered them.*
> *From the cloud pillar God spoke.*
> *They kept God's decrees and the rule that God gave*
>   *them.*
> *LORD our God, you answered them.*
> *To them you became the forgiving God,*
> *Though you exacted retribution for their [wrong]*
>   *actions.*
> *Exalt the LORD our God!*
> *Bow to God's holy mountain.*
> *For the LORD our God is holy* (Ps. 99:3–9).

God's holiness stands back of God's decrees. As the community seeks to carry out these decrees, it *brings God's holiness out of the sanctuary and into the world.* The act of justice is, therefore, a sanctifying vocation: Through deeds of justice, the world is transformed. Through a holiness that knows how to apportion both forgiveness and retribution, justice is established (cf. Ps. 99:8). Conversely, however, *the march of justice leads from the world back to the place of worship.* The psalmist calls on the people to bow down, that is, to worship. The act of justice stirs in the worshiper a return to the posture of worship. In the discovery of God's holiness the worshiper learns that God answers prayer (see Ps. 99:6).

The references to Moses, Aaron, and Samuel in Psalm 99, though rare in the Psalter, serve to highlight the psalmist's awareness of the pivotal figures in Israel's legal tradition. The psalmist hereby tacitly acknowledges and affirms the juridical framework of much of ancient Israelite religion, doing so in a context that emphasizes Israel's pursuit of law and justice as a product of the people's relationship with the holy God. By binding Moses the prophet, Aaron the priest, and Samuel the king-maker together, the psalmist acknowledges the complex theological chords that underlie the Psalter's presentation of God's rule and God's justice. Through Moses we hear of a justice that is rooted in divine decrees. Through Aaron we are reminded of a way of life that is rooted in holiness and worship. The mention of Samuel calls to mind Samuel's quest for just rule in Israel — one in which God alone is acknowledged as king and human kingship is forthrightly critiqued (see 1 Samuel 8; 12). The challenge inherent in this reference to Moses, Aaron, and Samuel is the challenge of concretely realizing divine justice in the interplay among law, worship, holiness, and political power.

CREATION AND LIBERATION

The God who is king is the creator God. The biblical god creates, unlike idols which are deemed impotent: "While all the gods of the peoples are worthless, the LORD made the heavens" (Ps. 96:5). Throughout the Psalms of God as King there are impressive descriptions of God's creative power unleashed in the world. The ancient storm-god motif is adapted to the Israelite context:

> *The LORD's voice is above the water.*
> *The God of glory thunders.*
> *The LORD is above the vast water.*
> *The voice of the LORD in its power,*
> *The voice of the LORD in its majesty,*

The voice of the LORD breaks the cedars.
The LORD shatters the cedars of Lebanon.
God makes them run along like a calf—
Lebanon and Sirion like a young wild ox.
The voice of the LORD hews fiery flames (Ps. 29:3–7).[5]

The Israelites continued to find the power of God in the mighty forces of nature. Yet Psalm 29:10 also links God's creative power to God's kingship: "The LORD sits [enthroned] at/over the flood. The LORD sits [enthroned] as king forever." Similarly, in Psalm 97 God's creative power is said to undergird God's justice:

God's lightning illuminated the earth.
The earth saw it and shook [in anguish].
The mountains melted like wax before the LORD,
Before the Lord of all the earth.
The heavens have announced God's justice,
And all the peoples have seen God's glory
    (Ps. 97:4–6).

God's work in the storms confirms and mirrors God's enduring kingship and reign of justice.[6] It is this intertwining of God's creative power and God's justice that yields God's effective reign. God's creative power displays itself not simply in a one-time act of creation in the past, but in the ongoing recreative processes of a natural order touched by God—a recreation that is exemplified most powerfully through a divine justice that touches the nations of the world.

If this link between God's creative work and God's reign is accepted, we have further support for the view developed by the Peruvian liberation theologian Gustavo Gutiérrez, who holds that God's act of creation is the first salvific act in God's continuing work of world liberation.[7] Gutiérrez refuses to read the Exodus text apart from the story of creation:

The creation of the world initiates history, the human struggle, and the salvific adventure of Yahweh. Faith in creation does away with its mythical and supernatural character. It is the work of a God who saves and acts in history.[8]

The God at work in the history of Israel's liberation is the God at work in creation. History, creation, and salvation are one. Our knowledge of this intimate tie between creation and liberation/justice can stir in us a commitment toward works that bring justice into the world:

> *Say to the nations:*
> *The LORD reigns.*
> *The world is also established.*
> *It will not be moved.*
> *God judges the peoples fairly.*
> *May the heavens be glad.*
> *May the earth exult.*
> *May the sea roar and all that fills it.*
> *May the field rejoice and all that is in it.*
> *Then let all the trees of the forest shout for joy,*
> *Before the LORD.*
> *Because God is coming,*
> *Because God is coming to judge the earth* (Ps. 96:10–
>   13; cf. 93:1).[9]

God's kingship and God's creative power are to be unleashed in our world and our worship, so that we may discover in nature's exultation God's emerging rule. As creation continues to rejoice, the reign of God is realized (cf. Pss. 96:11–12; 98:7–8). This creation-justice perspective liberates us from thinking that the world is ours:

> *The depths of the earth are in God's hands.*
> *The heights of the mountains are God's.*
> *The sea is God's, God made it.*
> *God's hands fashioned the dry earth* (Ps. 95:4–5).

If the world is not ours, then neither are salvation nor liberation intended to be hoarded commodities. We have the burden to seek justice for all. We have the challenge to renew creation for all. We have the duty to include all in our lifeboat.

ENTHRONING GOD

Much of the scholarly discussion of the Psalms of God as King has focused on the notion of the enthronement of God found in several of the texts. Scholars have been particularly interested to know if, standing behind the texts, there was a dramatic ritual reenactment of the enthronment of God that took place at the temple in the autumn during the Feast of Tabernacles (Sukkoth).[10] If so, perhaps this ritualized drama procession served to confirm God's rule, much as the reading of the Babylonian creation epic and the performance of numerous other rituals during the Babylonian New Year's festival established the reign of the god Marduk.[11] Mowinckel's approach to the Psalms of God as King enables us to see that worship cannot be satisfied with the mere affirmation of God's reign. At a deeper level, worship must continually participate in the establishment of that sovereignty.

Critical to this scholarly debate has been the interpretation of the Hebrew verb *mālak*, which appears several times in these psalms (Pss. 93:1; 96:10; 97:1; 99:1; cf. 47:9). Does this word mean "God *is* king/reigns," simply affirming God's reign and therefore signifying nothing of the enthronement motif? Or does the verb mean "God *has become* king"—a phrasing that invites the enthronement analysis?[12] My own view is that while this debate is technically interesting, it actually overlooks the transchronological character of worship and therefore fails to grasp the multiple layers of meaning inherent in the act of worship. Ritual breaks open the possibility of looking at and experiencing all moments of time at once.[13] Worshipers can view creation and death, the history of the nation, and their own personal story at one moment in the act of worship. Those who would dissect sacramental time, to decide whether the psalmists meant God "was," "is," "is becoming," or "will be" king, actually misunderstand the subtle freezing of time that occurs in worship. For the psalmists, all moments blend to affirm and confirm God's rule. God's throne is "ancient" (Ps. 93:2), reminding us that in one sense *God has always been king*, which is to say, God's kingship is rooted in acts of power and creation that long precede our attempts to express in song and prayer the meaning of God's rule. And yet, in another quite radical sense, *God becomes king, in the present, through our worship*:

> *God has ascended amidst joyful shouting,*
> *The* LORD *[has ascended] at the sound of the horn.*
> *Sing to God, sing!*
> *Sing to our king, sing!*
> *For God is the king of the entire earth.*
> *Sing a song!*
> *God reigns over the nations.*
> *God is seated on God's sacred throne* (Ps. 47:6–9).

This is not simply to say that the ancient God reigns in the world now; rather, the writer in Psalm 47 appears to take the deeper view that in its act of worship the community continues to create the reign of God over a world of restless kings and nations (cf. Pss. 47:4; 29:10; 95:7b–11).[14] In addition to these past and present senses of God's reign, *we must also reckon with the eschatological character of God's rule.* God is coming to rule; God's rule has not yet been established:

> *May the rivers clap their hands.*
> *May the mountains together shout for joy,*
> *Before the* LORD *who comes to judge the earth.*
> *May God judge the world justly,*
> *[May God judge] the peoples fairly* (Ps. 98:8–9; cf.
>   96:13 quoted above).

God's reign of justice is in a continual state of becoming.[15] It is a rule that has yet to be achieved, a rule that must be renewed daily through acts of worship in the face of evil, a rule rooted in the primordial reign of God.

WORSHIPERS OF THE GREAT KING

The worshiping community is a community of gesture given over to the establishment of the reign of God in the world: "All peoples, clap your hands. Shout to God in a joyous voice" (Ps. 47:2). The enthronement and reign of God demand not only acts of justice but postures of praise:

> *Come, let us bow and kneel,*
> *Bending our knees before the LORD our maker.*
> *For this one is our God,*
> *And we are the people in God's pasture,*
> *The flock in God's hand.*
> *If only you would listen to God today* (Ps. 95:6–7; cf.
>   29:11; 98:7–8).

God's rule from of old must be renewed in every generation. Worship continues to define the enthronement of God for a community that is poised to return to the world to extend God's reign of justice. Therefore, praise and concrete action cannot be artificially separated in the overall quest for world peace, equity, or the giving of life to those who stand in great need. The great vision of the psalmists reminds us that the establishment of God's throne of justice comes about, in part, through the deep and sustained communion of God's worshipers:

> *Sing to the LORD a new song!*
> *For God has done marvelous things.*
> *God's right hand and holy arm have brought God vic-*
>   *tory. . . .*
> *Shout to the LORD, all the earth!*
> *Break forth, shout for joy, and sing!*
> *Sing to the LORD with the lyre,*
> *With the lyre and a voice of song,*
> *With trumpets and the sound of the horn.*
> *Shout before the king, the LORD* (Ps. 98:1, 4–6).

Through worship we are given to understand that songs of joy and love for God can guide us in our work of justice, not because we have used the correct justice jargon, but because through these songs we are helping to define God's rule of justice in the world (cf. Pss. 95:1–2; 97:10–12).

Yet, in a world racked with pain and injustice, we must ask with Gutiérrez, "How can we thank God for the gift of life when the reality around us is one of premature and unjustly inflicted death?"[16] How is God enthroned in this world? Songs of joy ought not blind us to our "stubbornness in the wilderness":

> *Do not harden your hearts as you did at Meribah,*
> *Or at Massah in the desert,*
> *Where your ancestors tested me,*
> *And tried me, even though they saw what I had done.*
> *For forty years I was disgusted by that generation.*
> *I said: "They are a misguided people.*
> *They do not know my ways."*
> *That is why I swore in my anger,*
> *"They will not enter my place of rest"* (Ps. 95:8–11; cf.
>   Exod. 17:1–7; Num. 20:1–13).

We must acknowledge our contribution to the multiplication of pain and suffering in the world. Elie Wiesel — burdened prophet, survivor of the Holocaust — guides us in this recognition of responsibility when he writes:

> Somebody will have to explain why so many killers were intellectuals, academicians, college professors, lawyers, engineers, physicians, theologians. The *Einsatzkommandos*, those who did the killing directly, not in the gas chambers, were led by intellectuals. They were not shielded by their culture.[17]

Just as all "civilized" society was implicated in the Holocaust, so are all complicit today who share in the benefits of a world built on the backs of the poor, the economically straitjacketed, the disenfranchised peasant, laborer, or farmer. Our "stubbornness in the wilderness" must be acknowledged. If we do not define our contemporary collective guilt, we run the risk of celebrating the reign of God without making sure that the throne retains its base of justice. We must be careful, however, not to let this critique of our complicity paralyze us in the work of justice. The psalmist intends for us to engage in this self–critique of our "stubbornness" in order that our hearts remain open to the reign of God.

How, then, can we achieve this vital openness to the rule of God without collapsing under the weight of guilt, suffering, or a sense of futility in the face of injustice? As Gutiérrez reminds us, the integral bond between our praise and our actions is sustained through our "effort to be faithful, in both prayer and concrete commitments, to the will of the Lord in the midst of the poor."[18] Defining the reign of God in our world cannot be done apart from work with those in need. Our acclamation of the reign of God requires that we wrestle with the concrete issues of our day. The hermeneutical circle roots us in the world of injustice and suffering, but drives us back to the realm of worship and faith. Worship and action clarify and energize each other. Our determined effort to link worship and deed is central to the task of enthroning God as the just ruler of this world.

PART III

HISTORY, WISDOM,
PROPHECY

10

"So That a Later Generation Might Know"

Historical Psalms

Liberation theology has sought to recover the place of the poor in history and to discover the God who acts within the concrete, oppressive historical circumstances of those who suffer injustice. To say, as Gutiérrez does, that the poor have "historical power" is to say that "the poor know that history is theirs."[1] By becoming actors in their own liberation, the poor "know they are on the road to their exodus."[2] Along with this unfolding of the dynamic role of the oppressed in the act of liberation has come a reevaluation of the history writing done by academics and theologians of the first world or dominant classes. The very moment the oppressed and marginalized arise as actors in history, their histories emerge—histories that challenge and frequently overturn long-held beliefs, often stereotypical, about "vanquished" cultures and communities.[3] Reclaiming their past, they refuse to leave the telling of that history to the pens of colonizers or oppressors.[4] By recovering this history, a community can forcefully reassess current social arrangements and imbalances, paving the way for an alternate future of concrete liberation.[5]

To these considerations about history, Gutiérrez adds the theological claim that the biblical faith is a remembering faith, a faith rooted in history. This historical grounding is not an act of nostalgia that lacks transformative power for the present. Rather, proclamation of God's past liberating deeds—in particular, the Exodus event—permits the community to reread the present in light of the past. Gutiérrez describes this past as a "memory" that can create an "openness" to "new paths of liberation."[6] The goal of this present chapter is to study the historical psalms from this theological vantage point.[7] Do we find in the historical psalms a reading of history that opens the worshiping community to a future of freedom?

HISTORY: REMEMBERING REBELLION

For the biblical psalmists, every act of communal remembering has a present significance. History, in other words, grants an understanding of one's current experience. Psalms 78 and 106 contain powerful memories that detail a history of the people's rebellion, yet these two "histories" of sin diverge from each other, pointing to differing readings of God's work in the present moment.

In Psalm 106, the history of rebellion serves as a window into the people's present situation of distress in exile (Ps. 106:47). By invoking the "mighty deeds of the LORD" at the beginning of the psalm, the poet immediately opens the community to the hope that in the recounting of events from the past, the history will lead to deliverance (Ps. 106:4–5). The psalmist then proceeds to briefly recount events that are familiar to us from the books of Exodus and Numbers. Couched under the rubric "we have sinned along with our ancestors," the psalmist speaks of the ancestors' rebellion at the Red Sea (Ps. 106:6–7). God's victory over Pharaoh was hailed by the people but soon "forgot" by a people who "tested God in the desert" (Ps. 106:13–14), leading to punishment by earthquake and fire (Ps. 106:17–18). Mention of the worship of the image of the calf/bull leads the writer to again say of the people, "they forgot God, their deliverer" (Ps. 106:19–21). The anger of God, barely averted through Moses and Aaron, is said to have brought about the deaths of the people in the desert (Ps. 106:23–26). A final series of provocations against God concern idol worship (Ps. 106:28–39)—

deeds which are said to have led God to "place them under the control of the nations; their enemies ruled over them" (Ps. 106:41) — referencing, most likely, the time of the judges or, perhaps, the exile (or both through double entendre).[8] This psalm, while focusing extensively on the people's history of rebellion and forgetfulness, nevertheless returns to the theme invoked at the beginning of the psalm, namely the hope of deliverance (Ps. 106:43–48).

By contrast, the history of rebellion in Psalm 78 is used to reinforce the Davidic royal covenant. This psalm is historical in the sense that the poet is quite consciously grappling with "riddles from ancient times," that is "so that a later generation might know" the theological meaning of the nation's past (Ps. 78:2, 6). To inculcate obedience to God's "instruction" (Ps. 78:5), the poet recounts a history of the people's rebellion against God. God's marvelous actions in the exodus and provision of water in the wilderness (Ps. 78:12–16) were ungratefully met, the poet says, by the rather defiant question, "Can God arrange a table in the desert?" (Ps. 78:19). Even the added provision of bread and meat are not enough, leading to further defiance and an outbreak of the wrath of God (Ps. 78:21–33). There follows a brief passage, arguably the central section of the poem (within an extensive chiastic or mirrored structure) in which the "compassion" of God is emphasized.[9] To this point in the psalm, at least, the history of rebellion leads to an opening toward the God of mercy. A history of forgetfulness does not produce a God who forgets: "God remembered that they were human/flesh — a wind that passes and does not return" (Ps. 78:39).

The second half of Psalm 78 — concerned also with forgetfulness, rebellion, and punishment — balances the subject matter of the first half of the poem. However, significant differences between the two halves do appear and in noting them we find that the latter part of Psalm 78 supplies critical perspectives for the poem's hour of distress (some time prior to the exile). The pivotal event for Psalm 78:65–67 is the rejection of Joseph. Presumably what the psalmist has in mind here is the Assyrian invasion and subsequent collapse of the northern kingdom of Israel in 721 B.C.E. (cf. 2 Kgs. 17:1–6).[10] This decisive event constitutes a paradigmatic warning of destruction for Ezekiel

(Ezek. 16:45–58).[11] The poet's history of rebellion is used here to gain perspective on the national political fortunes of Judah. Is destruction necessarily on the horizon? Does a history of rebellion, forgetfulness, and disobedience lead inexorably to divine wrath? Discerning within that history the power of the merciful God, the poet finds reason to hope, in spite of repeated rebellion. Yet there is another anchor to this history beyond God's mercy, namely God's choice of Zion, the building of the temple, and the establishment of the Davidic covenant (Ps. 78:68–72). These elements balance the references to the instruction, commands, and covenant mentioned in Psalm 78:5–11. The people are called to discern God's mercy not only in God's provision and the forestalling of God's anger, but also in the establishment of the covenant as expressed through the temple and the kingship. The poet's encounter with hope is rooted firmly in the longevity of the temple and the kingship.

Through their theological reflection on rebellion, Psalms 78 and 106 give us variant agendas for the act of remembering. Each text opens the people to futures that peer beyond a past of disobedience. For the writer of Psalm 78, the Davidic covenant is stronger than the history of the people's forgetfulness. The community may continue to have defiant questions to ask of God in time of war and national suffering, but the covenant has been shown to endure beyond repeated eras of rebellion. According to Psalm 78, in every historical moment the people's confidence in God's ability to sustain is rooted in God's covenantal commitment—a commitment that is not thwarted by the people's defiance or forgetfulness. Similarly the writer in Psalm 106 discerns through the history of the people's rebellion that God may continue to deliver and regather the people. Past rebellion does not close the door to future liberation where the compassionate God is concerned. To the extent that the community connects its experience of political uncertainty (Psalm 78) and exile (Psalm 106) to its history of rebellion, it *may* discover in that history a God of compassion. Through a creative reading of the past, the history of rebellion, though negative, is recovered as a source of transformation. Unfortunately the negative and limiting aspects of these psalms tends to overwhelm the psalmists' message of God's compassion.

HISTORY: REMEMBERING GOD'S CARE

The theological interpretation of history expressed in Psalms 78 and 106 is akin to the view adopted by the Deuteronomistic Historian (Deuteronomy–Kings).[12] Martin Noth characterized the story of the Deuteronomist as the history of Israel's rebellion and inevitable demise:

> Dtr. [the Deuteronomist] did not write his history to provide entertainment in hours of leisure or to satisfy a curiosity about national history, but intended it to teach the true meaning of the history of Israel from the occupation to the destruction of the old order. The meaning which he discovered was that God was recognizably at work in this history, continuously meeting the accelerating moral decline with warnings and punishments and, finally, when these proved fruitless, with total annihilation.[13]

Some scholars have attempted to uncover notes of hopefulness in this rather depressing history of Israel's and Judah's rebellion and destruction, but the overall characterization developed by Noth is difficult to deny.[14] Since the notion of history as rebellion dominates the analysis of the Deuteronomistic History, theologians have tended to regard this as the essential biblical understanding of God's action in history. However, Psalms 105 and 136 offer far more positive readings of the history of Israel than do either the Deuteronomistic History or Psalms 78 and 106. In mining these texts, we uncover a history of God's protective care—a history with profound political implications.

Psalm 105 uses a history of the promise to Abraham and the story of God's protection through the exodus as a way to discover the people's vocation in the present. As with Psalms 78 and 106, the poet looks back to God's "wondrous deeds" (Ps. 105:5). God is motivated, the psalmist says, by the covenant made with Abraham (Ps. 105:8–9). God acts, not after a long series of rebellions as in the previous psalms. Rather, God acts at every step of Israel's history to exhibit faithful protection. Thus, when they were wandering, God "did not permit anyone to oppress them, even rebuking kings on their behalf" (Ps. 105:14). When famine stalked the land, God made Joseph "ruler" to lead Egypt in providing the food assistance required by the people (Ps. 105:16–23). In this passage, when God is made the author of the famine (Ps. 105:16), the emphasis is not on divine wrath or punishment but on empowerment and provision. When the Egyptians turned against the Israelites, the psalmist writes, then God sent Moses and Aaron and the plagues (Ps. 105:24–36). Divine protection ultimately brought about the people's release from Egypt.[15] There is no hint of rebellion in the desert; rather, the emphasis again is on God's material provision of God's people. The people's request is granted by God (Ps. 105:40–42) and is not depicted as a test of God (contrast 78:15–31). Food, bread, and water are the practical benefits of the divine promise to Abraham (Ps. 105:39–42).

Political empowerment in Egypt and material provision in the desert find their final fulfillment in another aspect of this covenant mentioned twice in the psalm, namely the giving of land to the Israelites (Ps. 105:11, 44). Theological reflection on divine provision throughout the course of Israel's history opens the hearer to the political ramifications of that protection in terms of socioeconomic power, land ownership, and the redistribution of wealth into the hands of those who are disenfranchised. Beyond this, there is a profound ethical side to political empowerment:

> God gave them the lands of nations,
> They took possession of the wealth of the peoples,
> So that they might adhere to God's laws,
> And keep God's instruction, hallelujah (Ps. 105:44–
>   45).

Psalm 105, therefore, underscores its historical reflection with the affirmation that the people have inherited the land for a purpose, namely to have a place in which they may carry out and adhere to God's laws. Moral *and* material empowerment are the twin dimensions of a biblically grounded understanding of liberation.[16]

Psalm 136 constructs a history of God's care through the

exodus, wilderness wanderings, and conquest of Canaan, in an attempt to discover and affirm the enduring character of God's love for the community. The refrain that pulses throughout the psalm is, "For God's kindness is eternal." This history of divine compassion goes all the way back to creation to see God's love grounded in the fashioning of the sky and the earth, the stars, moon, and sun (Ps. 136:5–9). That creative power was also at work in the exodus events, during which the people were led forth, the waters were split, and Pharaoh's army was drowned (Ps. 105:10–15). God's power finds political fulfillment in the defeat of the kings of Canaan—defeats that pave the way for the people to take over the land (Ps. 136:17–22).[17] As with Psalm 105, there is no hint of Israel's history as one of rebellion; rather, this history of divine kindness ends with the recognition that God has once again "taken note of us in our humiliation"—presumably the distress of the exile—and "snatched us away from our adversaries" (Ps. 136:23–24). For the psalmist, God's creative care is seen in the defeat of kings who would thwart the thriving of the people of Israel. This history of kindness remained alive for the psalmist, who saw in the enemy's defeat yet another example of God's "great wonders" (Ps. 136:4). Again, as in Psalm 105, we discern within this history of divine protection a message of political empowerment.

Setting the lens of the Deuteronomistic Historian aside, we discover in Psalms 105 and 136 radically different assessments of Israel's past—positive assessments which create liberating readings for the present. These psalms also raise questions about the writing of a theology of history that bases itself primarily on the more negative biblical texts. As histories of provision, care, and divine love, Psalms 105 and 136 are far removed from the histories of sin or rebellion found in Psalms 78 and 106. Through a bold reassessment of the past, the community was empowered by a renewed vision of God's action in history—a vision that opened the community to a future of compassion and political liberation.

HISTORY: COMPETING MEMORIES

Taken together, the contrasting interpretations of the history of Israel found in these historical psalms could not be more marked. The psalms that I have termed "histories of God's care" remind us that the "rebellion" interpretation of Israel's history, though dominant because of the Deuteronomistic History, is by no means the only theologically possible or credible interpretation. As Brueggemann reminds us, "History in Israel is a very particular linguistic practice which is a vehicle for a specific conversation about social power and social possibility."[18] And we might add that there were obviously *several* conversations in process concerning social arrangements and liberating futures. Rhetoric about the past opens up particular futures. Debates or variant readings about the past can lead to competing visions about the work of God in the world. One of Brueggemann's observations regarding the constructed character of the historical psalms is pertinent here. He writes, "almost no one assumes . . . that the Psalms are 'records' of what happened. They are rather, as all historical remembering is, rhetorical acts which shape the past in a certain way, and which deny or exclude other shapings of the past."[19] As we confront issues of liberation and story/history telling, we should take comfort in the fact that the biblical text itself offers us variant readings of Israel's past, encouraging us *not* to posit only one understanding of how God works in history.

A bit of reflection on the alternate reading of Israel's history as related in the Book of Chronicles is instructive here. The Chronicler's History, though often neglected by historians and theologians, has been argued by a number of scholars to be much more than a degenerate version of the Deuteronomistic History.[20] It is now clear that this work offers a theological vision that deliberately departs from the guiding motifs of the Deuteronomistic History.[21] Perhaps the most stark example of the historiographic difference between the Deuteronomistic History and Chronicles is found in their competing assessments of David's census:

God was again angered at Israel. So God put David in charge of them, saying, "Number Israel and Judah" (2 Sam. 24:1).

The Adversary (Satan) stood up against Israel and made David count Israel (1 Chr. 21:1).

Of course, the difference in the ascription of the census to God and the Adversary could not be more striking, yet there is more at work here than simply a difference in their evaluations of David. These conflicting statements about God and Satan reflect two different understandings of the movement of history. By the time of the Chronicler, the days were long gone when Israel's sages could posit a single divine hand operant behind all historical events. Consequently, the Chronicler offers an updated theological reading of Israel's history, departing radically from the received Deuteronomistic History.

Perhaps the most important contrast for our study of the historical psalms is found in the constructive reform and *hope* that can be discerned in Chronicles—a hope not apparent in the Deuteronomistic History. The Chronicler achieves this sense of a positive future transformation by deliberately constructing a history that: emphasizes ritually minded reformist kings (David, Solomon, Asa, Jehoshaphat, Joash, Hezekiah, and Josiah); downplays the destruction of Samaria; and ends with the auspicious rise of Cyrus the Persian to power, ushering in the era of restoration after the Babylonian exile.[22] While Chronicles is by no means as singularly positive as Psalms 105 and 136, nevertheless, through the Chronicler's reexamination of the past, the community was empowered through a *historiography of hope*, fostering national unity amid exilic disunity and dislocation.[23] The presence of Chronicles and Psalms 105 and 136 in the canon invites us, therefore, not to be satisfied with a theology that simply replicates the rather negative reading of Israel's history found in the Deuteronomistic History and Psalms 78 and 106. A hopeful historiography stirs us to place in check the "history of rebellion" model as an explanation of God's work in the world. The evidence of these contrasting narrative histories and historical psalms forces open the discussion of divine action and liberation, reminding us that we are not captive to one theology of history.

It may be that the theological interpretation of the Deuteronomistic History has for too long trapped us into a particular reading of the biblical message and hence warped our view of God as an actor in the political realm.[24] Visions of history that make God responsible for all manner of human suffering, war-

fare, and earthly tragedy are inadequate, if not terribly mis-
guided. It is time to discover alternate visions of divine action
in history.[25] Perhaps a more fruitful approach would be to grapple with the more positive empowering theology that flows from
the history of God's protection, love, and hope fostered by texts
such as Psalms 105 and 136. The God of justice discovered in
this divergent history is a God of favor and compassion. A history of divine care can guide us into new paths of liberation.

BEYOND HISTORY: REALIZING THE DIVINE PRESENCE

The beauty of the psalms discussed so far is found in their
straightforward reading of the past. Yet we know that history—
our collective experience of the tumultuous past—cannot be
simply reduced to a single positive or negative thread which ties
events together into a meaningful whole. The chaotic ebb and
flow of historical experience compels us to call into question any
theology that says that history runs according to a simple scheme
of divine punishments or protections. If this is not a history that
we experience, how then can we develop a theology of history
that is truly liberating without having to force the past into a
preconceived mold regarding God's action in history?

The destruction of the northern kingdom created tension and
dissonance for the covenantal/royal theologies of history which
taught that behind history there is a divine hand that acts in
accord with ancient promises—a fact wrestled with in Psalm 78.
The subsequent exile of Judah would create still further difficulties for this dominant theological outlook (see e.g., Jeremiah
7). If we are not content with the rather simple and straightforward theologies of history found in the previous psalms (whether
positive or negative) or in the Deuteronomistic History or the
Books of Chronicles, we can perhaps turn to the radically sub-
versive readings of divine action in history found in the Book of
Job and reflected in Psalm 114. Both texts help us raise relevant
questions about simplistic views concerning God's action in the
world and in history.[26]

The Book of Job offers the most serious challenge to the
interpretation of history I have termed the "history of rebellion."

Unlike the Deuteronomistic History and Psalms 78 and 106, the Book of Job argues that there is no deft divine hand behind the scenes, meting out clear rewards and punishments.[27] In fact, there are many who suffer without cause. Perhaps this explains why the Book of Job seems to be so much truer to human experience than the interpretation that tries to ascribe guilt and blame to those who suffer. This too is a biblical vision of divine action in history, but one that runs counter to views we often consider standard as found in the Deuteronomistic History. Parallels with Psalm 114 may suggest a biblical view that moves beyond the narrow parameters of the psalms of rebellion.

The Book of Job and Psalm 114 point us to the untamed God whose creative power inspires awe:

> *When Israel went forth from Egypt,*
> *The house of Jacob from a people of foreign speech,*
> *Judah became God's sanctuary,*
> *Israel [became] God's dominion.*
> *The sea saw it and fled.*
> *The Jordan turned back.*
> *The mountains scurried like rams.*
> *The hills [ran] like sheep* (Ps. 114:1–4; cf. Job 38:1–
>   39:30).

Both Psalm 114 and the Book of Job rise above the standard understanding of God's work in history to discover God as an unrivaled, fearsome presence:

> *What does it mean, sea, that you flee?*
> *Jordan, that you turn back?*
> *Mountains, that you scurry like rams?*
> *Hills, [that you run] like sheep?*
> *Writhe, earth, because of the presence of the Lord,*
> *Because of the presence of the God of Jacob,*
> *Who transforms rock into a pool of water,*
> *Flint rock into a fountain* (Ps. 114:5–8; cf. Job 40:7–
>   41:26).[28]

According to Psalm 114, the exodus event is not explained by simple historicist schemes of rebellion or protection, but can only be understood as an earthquake that ruptured history—a convulsion in which the unfettered Presence of God was at work fashioning a newly liberated people into God's holy domain.

As we evaluate the biblical interpretation of the people's history, we must remember that these texts are an integral part of the biblical record. Their radically different perspective on Israel's history must not be overlooked in the construction of a theology of divine action/liberation in the world. The Book of Job and even the very brief Psalm 114 can generate a historical discourse that takes seriously the complex severing of history that we are experiencing in the modern world—a history of intense suffering in which it is not at all easy to discern precisely where God is *demonstrably* engaged in the work of personal and national liberation.[29] The discourse engendered by Psalm 114 and the Book of Job is not content to offer simple explanations or shallow theological understandings of history. Taking seriously the complexities behind the historical roots of injustice or liberation provides a necessary corrective to the limited views of divine action encountered in the Deuteronomistic History, the Books of Chronicles, and their imitators in the Psalter.

CONCLUSION: INTO THE FUTURE

Into what future is our history telling propelling us? It may depend on whose story we are telling or whose story we are refusing to tell. It may also depend on telling stories that do indeed unlock the possibilities for compassion and justice in the present. Women, in their discrimination and liberation, have a vital history that urgently needs to be reclaimed.[30] The story of the poor, the suffering, and the marginalized deserves to be given a hearing. In response to disenfranchisement and abuse, the Church needs to discern when to bring to us stories of rebellion so that we may hear, repent, and correct the wrongs that have generated so much injustice. But as its cornerstone of liberation, the Church must offer stories of God's love, care, and transformative presence, so that the community can shape a future wherein new stories of God's liberating work may be written.

11

"Forever at Ease, They Increase Their Wealth"

Wisdom and Torah Psalms

In the modern world, we have become very self-conscious about educational theory and praxis. Liberation education, especially through the writings of Paulo Freire, has directed us to rethink the standard teacher/lecturer centered mode of education, urging us toward a critical, reflective, transformative, problem-solving model of education. As Freire explains,

> Teachers and students (leadership and people), co-intent on reality, are both Subjects, not only in the task of unveiling that reality, and thereby coming to know it critically, but in the task of re-creating that knowledge. As they attain this knowledge of reality through common reflection and action, they discover themselves as its permanent re–creators. In this way, the presence of the oppressed in the struggle for their liberation will be what it should be: not pseudo-participation, but committed involvement.[1]

Liberating education, like liberation theology, has asked us to take seriously our "historicity" as the "starting point" for our theological/educational theory and praxis.[2] For educators and theologians, the common endeavor is to discover a *humanizing*

155

education and catechesis—that is, to develop modes of educational and theological reflection that engage and empower us to transform the world into a place of credible justice and realized freedom.

When we attempt to grapple with the Wisdom and Torah Psalms in light of a concern for contemporary social justice and worship issues, we must bear in mind that we are entering a very ancient educational debate. A proper discussion of "wisdom" (ḥokmâ) and "instruction" (tôrâ) in the Psalter cannot be seriously undertaken without the awareness that the time-honored educational tradition and values of Mesopotamia and Egypt—the wisdom tradition—stand behind the biblical pursuit of ḥokmâ and tôrâ.[3] The wider Near Eastern tradition finds its biblical counterpart in texts such as Proverbs, Job, and Ecclesiastes.[4] Through the many Near Eastern wisdom collections we are brought into contact with an instructional tradition sponsored by the royal courts—a mode of education that elevated the counsel of kings and bureaucrats regarding behavior and success.[5] Study of the Book of Proverbs, in particular, makes it clear that the ancient Israelites shared with their Near Eastern counterparts the common wisdom views concerning poverty and laziness, hard work and wealth, success and rewards, obedience and loyalty, generosity and wickedness. Some of these views find their way into the Wisdom and Torah Psalms (with the notable absence of the notion that poverty is the result of laziness). In the modern worship and catechetical context, we will not find the Wisdom and Torah Psalms terribly liberating to the extent that they perpetuate the common ancient Near Eastern educational notions regarding success, wealth, and obedience. Certainly there is nothing in the Wisdom and Torah Psalms that compares to the radical connection drawn between solidarity with the poor and social justice as found in the text of Job—a wisdom text that diverges sharply from Proverbs in its social analysis.[6] Nevertheless, there are liberating aspects to these psalms, especially at those junctures where we find the poets choosing to depart from the "common wisdom" of the received instructional tradition of Israel and the ancient Near East. At those junctures, the pursuit of ḥokmâ and tôrâ is discerned as an educational end that is personally reconstructive and socially transformative.

DISCIPLINE, OBEDIENCE, AND SUCCESS

Emerging from the wisdom tradition is a conscious social philosophy and public etiquette which breeds individuals who are adept at bureaucratic maneuvering and skillful discourse. This is made clear in the introduction to Proverbs, which states:

> *To know wisdom and discipline,*
> *To gain insight into considered opinions.*
> *To receive the discipline for success,*
> *Right action, justice, and equity.*
> *To bring cunning to the simple,*
> *To bring knowledge and purpose to the young person.*
> *May the wise listen and add to their learning.*
> *May the intellectual acquire counsel.*
> *To understand proverb and phrase,*
> *The words of the wise and their difficult sayings*
>   (Prov. 1:2–6).[7]

Behind the many sentences stands a compelling vision of human reflection and action. In particular, the wisdom teachers show a great concern for diligence and offer strong warnings against laziness (cf. Prov. 10:4; 19:15, 24; 21:5). Hard work is the overriding virtue in this educational tradition:

> *I went through the field of the lazy person,*
> *Through the vineyard of the senseless person.*
> *There were thistles everywhere.*
> *Nettles covered its surface.*
> *The stone wall had collapsed.*
> *I looked carefully and reflected on it.*
> *As I watched, I was disciplined.*
> *"A little sleep, a little rest,*
> *a little folding of hands to lie down,*
> *and your poverty will run everywhere,*

> *your lack [will run] like a prowler"* (Prov. 24:30–34;
> cf. 6:4–11).

Poverty, the wisdom instructions warn, results from too much sleep. The industrious ant becomes wisdom's model of success and prosperity (Prov. 6:6–11). Such a work ethic and ascription of poverty to laziness is cultivated throughout the text of Proverbs.[8]

In addition to hard work, knowing one's place on the social ladder is essential to wisdom teaching.[9] In particular, obedience and loyalty to the king is critical to the worldview of Proverbs.[10] As Bryce says, the king "is to be feared as God."[11] This attitude extends to all behavior in royal circles. Conduct at dinner with a "ruler," for example, is to be circumscribed with respect and austerity (Prov. 23:1–3; cf. 25:15; 28:2). Likewise, God is also to be feared.[12]

If hard work and obedience are the twin pillars of the wisdom philosophy, to what extent are these ideals represented in the Wisdom and Torah Psalms? In the conscious pursuit of *tôrâ* (instruction), the psalmists stand squarely within the wisdom tradition when they affirm that loyalty and obedience yield rewards.[13] Primary obedience is shown to the decrees and judgments of the Lord: "Your servant is warned by them. In observing them there is great reward" (Ps. 19:12). The issue of obedience is dealt with most fully in Psalms 37 and 119.

In Psalm 119, the fact of the speaker's commitment to education and diligent study is used by the speaker as the basis of an appeal to God to bring relief from persecution:

> *I am burdened with a longing for your laws at all times.*
> *You rebuked the accursed arrogant ones,*
> *Who stray from your commandments.*
> *Roll away disgrace and contempt from me,*
> *For I guard your decrees.*
> *Even if princes sit [in judgment] against me and speak,*
> *Your servant will meditate on your rules* (Ps. 119:20–
>   23; cf. 119:58).

By rooting the self in God's decrees and truth, the psalmist seeks to find a way to face the persecutor:

> *How many are the days of your servant?*
> *When will you make a judgment against my persecutors?*
> *The arrogant ones have dug pits for me,*
> *Against your instruction [tôrâ].*
> *All your commandments are trustworthy.*
> *I am pursued for no reason.*
> *Help me!*
> *They nearly wiped me off the earth,*
> *But I did not abandon your injunctions* (Ps. 119:84–
>   87).

Furthermore, the hard work of worship, rooted in love for and obedience to God's decrees, produces prosperity, according to the psalmist:

> *I praise you seven times a day,*
> *For your just judgments.*
> *There is great peace for those who love your instruction*
>   *[tôrâ].*
> *They encounter no obstacle* (Ps. 119:164–165).

How concrete is this well-being engendered by obedience to God's decrees? In Psalm 37, such obedience becomes a precondition for dwelling and remaining in the land:

> *Trust in the LORD and do good.*
> *Live in the land and graze in faithfulness* (Ps. 37:3).

> *Those who cause harm will be cut off,*
> *But those who wait for the LORD will inherit the land*
>   (Ps. 37:9; cf. 37:22).

> *The just will inherit the land and live forever in it*
>   (Ps. 37:29).

> *Wait for the LORD. Adhere to God's way.*
> *And God will elevate you to inherit the land.*
> *When the wicked are cut off, you will see it* (Ps. 37:34).

Success against the wicked is grounded in a steady loyalty toward God and in right action. Continued enjoyment of the land is predicated on the just conduct of the individual that arises from a life rooted in God. Human labor within the land is given renewed focus in Psalm 127:

> *If the* LORD *does not build the house,*
> *Those who build it are laboring without purpose.*
> *If the* LORD *does not guard the city,*
> *The guard keeps watch without purpose* (Ps. 127:1).

One significant reward, says this psalmist, is God's provision of children (Ps. 127:3–5). Psalm 128 points to the additional concrete benefits of loyalty to God:

> *Happy are all who revere the* LORD,
> *Those who walk in God's ways.*
> *When you eat what your hands have produced,*
> *You will be happy and well.*
> *Your spouse will be a fruitful vine within the recesses of*
>   *your house.*
> *Your children will be like olive shoots round your table.*
> *Thus is the person blessed who reveres the* LORD.
> *May the* LORD *bless you from Zion!*
> *Look at the goodness of Jerusalem all the days of your*
>   *life!* (Ps. 128:1–5).

The well-being of obedience to God finds expression in a peaceful, prosperous life in Jerusalem and its environs in the land.

In looking at these passages, we can sense a connection between the larger wisdom tradition and the Wisdom and Torah Psalms on the question of obedience, self-discipline, and loyalty. However, we must also note a significant point of divergence: The Wisdom and Torah Psalms are not concerned about hard work in general — only diligence in studying and adhering to the *tôrâ*. Loyalty and obedience, then, are categories invoked in these psalms to explicate one's relation to God. Here standard wisdom categories receive adaptation and refinement. In contrast to Proverbs, therefore, we find that the Wisdom and Torah Psalms contain nothing about obedience to earthly superiors, in particular the king.

Notably, the Wisdom and Torah Psalms omit discussing the standard wisdom views of hard work and indigence, in particular the view that poverty's main cause is laziness. In the modern context, there is every danger that we might slavishly or unthinkingly perpetuate the value structures of a text like Proverbs. Diligence is certainly a laudable virtue. It is significant, therefore, that the Wisdom and Torah Psalms focus the concept of diligence around the following of God's decrees. The writers thereby avoid promoting Proverb's typical understanding of the origins of poverty, while preserving the dignity of human labor.[14] Certainly the more substantive *challenges* to the prevailing wisdom notions connecting work and rewards are found in Job, Ecclesiastes, and the prophets. Yet, in kernel form, the Wisdom and Torah Psalms potentially open worship and catechesis to an alternate understanding of obedience and success than is generated by Proverbs. These psalmists capitalize on this opening in their discussions of poverty and wealth, where it is not always assumed that abundance is the result of honest labor.

POVERTY AND WEALTH

What are the attitudes toward poverty and wealth in the wisdom tradition?[15] Again, the Book of Proverbs serves as our guide. Poverty, according to the wise, consigns the poor to a miserable, beggarly condition—an existence that is not to be sought or cherished (Prov. 18:23). It is a condition that leaves the poor at the mercy of the whims of the rich and in slavery to lenders (Prov. 18:23; 22:7). It is a friendless, abusive situation (Prov. 14:20; 19:4, 7; 28:3). Socially and economically brutalizing, poverty is also physically destructive. Drunkenness, for example, is connected with poverty (Prov. 31:7). These observations that the wise make are stark and educationally instructive. Through striking images of poverty, the wise develop a picture that serves to steer the student away from a life-style that leads to indigence. These images further strengthen Proverb's view, noted above, that poverty is essentially "a punishment that one brings upon oneself."[16] The student of wisdom has been effectively warned in this regard.

The topic of wealth likewise finds a prominent place in Proverbs. The extended sections of instruction in Proverbs 1–9 take up such issues as the use of wealth (3:9–10) and the problem of unjust gain (1:10–19). Elsewhere in the sentence literature of Proverbs we find wealth and poverty contrasted as two separate domains (Prov. 10:15; 13:7–8; 19:4). To have wealth is to have friends, observe the wise (Prov. 14:20; 19:4), unlike the condition of poverty. Wealth creates security and stability for those who possess it (Prov. 10:15; 18:11). Wealth places one in a position of authority or domination over the poor (Prov. 18:23; 22:7). The contrast between the rich and poor is frequently made in Proverbs 28.[17] Overall, we find three attitudes toward wealth in Proverbs: a respect for wealth; an urging to enjoy abundance; and the suggestion that the rich deserve their wealth.[18]

This does not mean that the wise promoted a hedonistic lifestyle. They understood the transitory character of wealth.[19] They acknowledged the need to exercise restraint in the use of one's wealth, noting that an excessive concern for wealth or the squandering of it can enslave and even lead to poverty.[20] Furthermore, the wise counseled using wealth in charity toward the poor.[21] However, while the wisdom literature dwells on the limits of wealth and refrains from thoroughly despising the poor (cf. Prov. 22:22; 30:14; 31:9), the tradition can still affirm: "The crown of the wise is their wealth, but the stupidity of fools remains stupidity" (Prov. 14:24).

The contemporary appropriation of these texts becomes problematic if we adopt the view that Proverbs' understanding of wealth and poverty is the product of the educational reflection of the ruling elite—a grouping that, in Gordis's words, "had little in common with the poorer peasants clinging desperately to their holdings, or with the petty tradesmen and artisans in the cities, who suffered their own discontents and were evolving new values in their religious tradition."[22] Certainly only those who are well off consistently instruct:

> *Better to be depressed among the oppressed,*
> *Than to share spoil with the arrogant* (Prov. 16:19).

A poor person is better than a liar (Prov. 19:22b).

Better to be a poor person acting with integrity,
Than one who is rich yet crooked in actions
   (Prov. 28:6).[23]

Furthermore and most significantly, only the well-to-do could repeatedly maintain (as we saw earlier) that poverty is largely the result of negligence. We find, therefore, that while Proverbs treats poverty as a harsh reality to be avoided, the writers sought *neither to protest* against that reality, as does the Book of Job, *nor to investigate* the possible connections between the wealth of the rich and the exploitation of the poor, as did many of the Hebrew prophets.[24] The view that poverty is the result of laziness or even of fate — and not exploitation — is a view that is congenial to the mind-set of the economic and political power holders in society.[25] Only they could teach that by simply following the right advice one could avoid poverty.

What are we to make of such views in the contemporary catechetical and worship context? Fortunately, the Wisdom and Torah Psalms offer us some refreshing points of departure from the standard wisdom views about poverty and wealth. Bearing in mind that there are passages that root prosperity in obedience and other passages that use the wisdom comparative style to state, for example, "Better the just person's scarcity than the abundant wealth of the wicked" (Ps. 37:16), nevertheless some of these psalms, in particular Psalms 49 and 73, provide striking critical statements regarding the vanity of wealth — statements that outstrip any of the discussions of the fleeting character of wealth found in Proverbs.

Consciously addressing the world — rich and poor alike — in a song concerning wisdom, the psalmist asks:

Why should I fear in evil times,
When the wrongdoing of those who grab at me sur-
   rounds me —
Those who trust in their wealth,
Those who boast in their material abundance?
One person cannot buy back another,

> *Nor give to God that person's ransom payment.*
> *Their redemption is costly* (Ps. 49:6–9a).

With sentiments that approach Ecclesiastes's sense that death levels the differences between rich and poor, the wise and the ignorant, this psalmist states:

> *Will they live forever and not see the grave?*
> *But one sees that the wise die together with the foolish*
>   *and stupid,*
> *Leaving their wealth to others* (Ps. 49:10–11; cf. Eccl.
>   2:11–12, 18, 21).

Reflection on the ultimate fate of the rich is mined to counter the fear that the rich instill in those who live beneath them:

> *Do not fear when people get richer,*
> *When they increase the wealth of their house.*
> *For they cannot take it all away with them in death.*
> *Their wealth does not descend with them.*
> *While alive, they intoned the blessing:*
> *"May they praise you, for you have done well for your-*
>   *self."*
> *But they shall join their ancestors [in the grave],*
> *Never again seeing light* (Ps. 49:17–20).

This text, although not without parallel to Proverb's acknowledgment of the fleeting character of wealth, powerfully moves beyond Proverbs in the direction of Ecclesiastes's skepticism.

The most strident critique of wealth appears in Psalm 73, a text that rather sharply considers the dangers of amassing wealth. The poet begins by acknowledging a feeling of envy at the ease of the life-style of the wealthy and the health they enjoy:

> *But as for me, my feet nearly turned aside.*
> *My steps almost slipped.*
> *For I envied the arrogant,*

When I saw the well-being of the wicked.
They know no pain at their death.
Their bodies are fat.
They do not experience human toil.
They are not afflicted as other people (Ps. 73:2–5).

The poet proceeds to draw a clear connection between this way of life and injustice, to a degree not found in Proverbs:

Therefore, arrogance acts as their neck-chain.
The garment that covers them is violence.
Their eyes stick out even more than their fat.
Their minds traverse their imaginations.
They mock, speaking harmfully about oppression.
They speak from on high.
They put their mouths in the sky,
And their tongues roam the earth. . . .
They say, "How could God know?
Does the Most High have knowledge?"
These are the wicked:
Forever at ease, they increase their wealth (Ps. 73:6–9;
   11–12).

The last verse is perhaps the most striking. The term *wicked* contains no element of ambiguity in this poet's writing. Sociologically speaking, the text draws the connection, known more clearly from the prophets, that the amassing of wealth was dangerously bound up with social injustices in ancient Israel.[26] In order to come to terms with wealth and the consequent attitudes the author saw it engender, the psalmist turns, like Ecclesiastes, to conscious reflection on the fate of the rich as a source of equalizing and comfort:

I sought to think through what I knew.
It was burdensome in my eyes,
Until I went to the sanctuary of God.
I came to understand their end.
Surely, [God], you have put them in slippery places.
You have flung them into deceptions.

Oh, how they become desolate in a moment!
Snatched away, they are benumbed by terrors
    (Ps. 73:16–19; cf. Eccl. 1:2–3; 2:1, 3–9; 4:7–8;
    5:9–12; 6:2).

In the end, the poet affirms a commitment to the God who is a refuge to those who lack wealth, resources, and health (Ps. 73:23–28). Psalm 73 is outstanding among the Wisdom and Torah Psalms for its critique of the amassing of wealth. While the text's language has some parallels to discussions of the fleeting character of wealth in Proverbs, this psalm's critique of wealth, like that of Psalm 49, closely parallels the skepticism of Ecclesiastes. Indeed, the psalmist's stridency anticipates our consideration of the prophetic voice — a topic reserved for the final chapter of this book.

As we consider Psalms 49 and 73, their lesson for the modern worship and catechetical context becomes clear: Education for peace and justice in the context of worship and prayer must spring from a critical *reassessment* of the received values and beliefs of our educational, religious, and philosophic traditions. The Wisdom and Torah Psalms find their strength not in a simple echoing of the proverbial philosophy, but in a reevaluation of the accepted views of wealth and poverty. Our worship and our instruction must carefully inspect traditional views of poverty, especially since we know that laziness is not the major cause of poverty in the modern world. If the prophets are our guide, neither was it the major cause of poverty in the ancient world.[27] The Wisdom and Torah Psalms serve as a model, compelling worship and catechesis to be proactive in challenging prevailing views of poverty and wealth. This vision of worship is consistent with the U. S. Catholic Bishops' pastoral on the economy, where they state:

Challenging U. S. economic life with the Christian vision calls for a deeper awareness of the integral connection between worship and the world of work. Worship and common prayer are the wellsprings that give life to any reflection on economic problems and that continually call the participants to greater fidelity to discipleship. To worship and pray to the God of the universe is to acknowledge that the healing love of God extends to all persons and to every part of existence, including work, leisure, money, economic and political power and their use, and to all those practical policies that either lead to justice or impede it.[28]

Worship cannot remain content with a status quo that leaves the economic underpinnings of society unexamined. Psalms 49 and 73 begin to probe the problematic character of the amassing of wealth and its attendant effects on both rich and poor. Modern worship and catechesis will likewise endeavor to raise these thorny questions for all who perpetuate or are troubled by economic injustice.

While Psalms 49 and 73 raise fundamental questions about wealth, the Wisdom and Torah Psalms nevertheless do adopt the common wisdom convention of elevating charity as the solution to the problem of poverty. Psalm 112 speaks of acts of giving to those in need and invokes the wisdom motivation of reward as the basis for such generosity:

> *Happy are they who revere the LORD,*
> *Who delight very much in God's commandments.*
> *Their descendants will be strong in the land —*
> *An upright generation that is blessed.*
> *Wealth and riches will be in their house.*
> *Their good works last forever.*
> *The light of the just rises over the darkness —*
> *Graciousness, compassion, and justice.*
> *It is well for those who act compassionately and lend,*
> *Those who arrange their affairs rightly.*
> *They will not ever be moved.*
> *The just person will be remembered always. . . .*
> *They have distributed, given to the poor.*
> *Their good works last forever.*
> *Their horn is raised in honor* (Ps. 112:1–6, 9).[29]

Generosity, that is, charity, is an example of right conduct we have noted already from Proverbs — an act that also finds affirmation in this psalm, with its rewards clearly noted. Nevertheless, Psalm 37 does offer a perspective that rises above mere charity, namely the view that God takes action to vindicate those innocents who are in need:

> *God will lead your justice forth like light,*
> *Your right as the noontime.*
> *Quietly wait for the LORD.*
> *Do not get anxious about those who prosper from their*
>   *actions —*
> *About those who enact wicked plans. . . .*
> *The oppressed will inherit the land.*
> *They shall enjoy great peace. . . .*
> *The LORD understands the days of those who act with*
>   *integrity.*
> *Their inheritance will be everlasting.*
> *They will not be ashamed in a time of disaster.*
> *In times of famine they will find satisfaction. . . .*
> *I was young; now I am old.*
> *I have not seen the just abandoned,*
> *Or their descendants seeking bread.*
> *Every day there is compassion and lending.*
> *Their descendants receive a gift* (Ps. 37:6–7, 11, 18–19,
>   25–26; cf. Prov. 22:22–29).

This text does not mean, as some translations seem to imply, that if one is righteous, then one will always prosper; rather, the psalmist is convinced that in a just society, both God and those who are in a position to give will see to it that the innocent who are in need will be sustained with all life's necessities in their time of affliction. Of course, the Book of Job offers an even stronger statement of solidarity with those who are innocent yet suffering.[30] Yet, in Psalm 37, we have some of the seeds of the line of thought carried out in Job. It is fair to say that the writer in Psalm 37 offers a mediating position somewhere between the standard wisdom line and the critique of Job. The psalmist's words carry something of the conviction of the speaker Elihu in Job 32–37, who argues that God does indeed act in the world on behalf of those who are in need.[31]

Insofar as we take seriously the more strident passages of the

Book of Job, the Wisdom and Torah Psalms offer only a partial foundation for a critical discussion of wealth and poverty. Nevertheless, for us today, Psalms 37, 49, and 73 do create a context and precedent for a worship that seriously grapples with economic disparities and the aspirations of the poor. In this regard, the Wisdom and Torah Psalms depart from the received wisdom of Proverbs in constructive ways. It is the burden of modern worship and catechesis to continue to open up the social justice question through a challenge to the values and beliefs that are nurtured in the centers of education, power, and wealth in our society—namely its academic halls, legislative chambers, and corporate board rooms.

WHO ARE THE WICKED?

In a number of sections of Proverbs, the boundary line between those pursuing wisdom and those who are not is drawn by marking off the "just" and "wise" from the "wicked" and "fool."[32] Contrasts such as the following abound in the text of Proverbs:

> *The LORD will not make the throat of the just suffer hunger,*
> *But [the LORD] casts aside the desire of the wicked* (Prov. 10:3).

> *Through their mouths the impious ruin their neighbors,*
> *But through knowledge the just are able to remove themselves* (Prov. 11:9).[33]

By means of this rhetoric about the "wicked," the wisdom creed's social vision is clarified and reinforced. Unfortunately the vocabulary of the wisdom tradition, as represented by Proverbs, is often sociologically vague and philosophically generalized with respect to the "wicked" and the "fool."

When we turn to the Wisdom and Torah Psalms, we find that similar views prevail concerning the wicked. Psalm 1, speaking in good wisdom fashion, contrasts the folly of the path trodden

by the wicked and sinner with the way taken by those who pursue
tôrâ instruction (Ps. 1:1–2). The wicked are the ones who are
not acquitted and therefore will perish (Ps. 1:5–6). Without
ascribing particular content to the meaning of "wicked," the
poet draws a typical wisdom-like contrast between the two categories, the wicked/sinner and the just (cf. Ps. 1:6). Similar to
the contrasts between the wicked and the just found in Proverbs
is this statement in Psalm 112, a text which contrasts those who
fear the LORD (Ps. 112:1) with those who are wicked:

> *The wicked will see [how well the upright are blessed]*
> *   and be annoyed.*
> *They will grind their teeth and weaken.*
> *The desire of the wicked will vanish* (Ps. 112:10).

Among the most involved of the discussions of the wicked in
the Wisdom and Torah Psalms are several passages in Psalm
119. In this psalm, the poet confesses, "The cords of the wicked
enclosed me, but I did not forget your instruction [*tôrâ*]" (Ps.
119:61). This sense that the wicked are attacking and entrapping
the speaker is found in other places in this psalm (cf. Ps. 119:95,
110). Elsewhere, the text says that the wicked forsake God's *tôrâ*
(Ps. 119:53). The fact that the wicked perish in the end is noted
in passing by the psalmist (Ps. 119:119).

Apart from a few examples, we can say that, in general, the
Wisdom and Torah Psalms rarely take up the topic of the
wicked, and that, when the texts do speak of the wicked, the
language of the poetry is quite vague about who the wicked
are — much as one discovers in Proverbs. Yet there is one significant text, Psalm 37, where the language concerning "those
who cause harm" and "those who do wrong" is given more def-
inite sociological content. Concretely, those so designated are
the ones in society who are "prospering" (Ps. 37:7, 16; cf. 73:3,
12). Their greed is such that they borrow and do not bother to
repay (Ps. 37:21). They are the power holders in society (Ps.
37:35), who seek through their weapons — their "sword" and
"bow" (Ps. 37:14) — to attack and murder the just or innocent
(Ps. 37:14–15, 32–33; cf. Ps. 49:6). The fact that the psalmist
states that the "oppressed will inherit the land" (Ps. 37:11) may

imply that the wicked are the present landowners (Ps. 37:9–11). If so, then the firm conviction that the wicked will eventually fall from power (Ps. 37:35–36) gives strong sociological content to the psalmist's hope that "people of peace have a future" (Ps. 37:37).[34]

Earlier we found the more thoroughgoing critique of wealth in the Wisdom and Torah Psalms to be instructive for the modern worship context. The psalmist's perspective regarding the wicked in Psalm 37 pushes well beyond the characterization of Proverbs, offering us the model for a worship and catechesis that would wish to probe the societal roots of economic injustice. The critique of the wicked found in the Wisdom and Torah Psalms — though certainly not as developed as that of Job, Ecclesiastes, or the prophetic literature — nevertheless opens worship and meditation to a deeper reflection on the question of the connections between wealth, poverty, and social inequity.

CONCLUSION

A closer look at the topics of wealth and the wicked as they arise in the Wisdom and Torah Psalms sustains the view that at some level, these psalms are not exactly at home in the wisdom tradition represented by Proverbs. Sensing the dangers of the unbridled amassing of wealth, hearing the cries of the poor who are oppressed by the wicked, the writers of the Wisdom and Torah Psalms are forced beyond the parochial endeavors of the wisdom tradition represented by Proverbs. Where the Wisdom and Torah Psalms depart from the standard wisdom view of wealth, poverty, and the wicked — and those passages are significant in range and depth — in those places we discover an alternate agenda for the pursuit of wisdom and instruction. Through the psalmists, the pursuit of *ḥokmâ* and *tôrâ* comes to be directed toward a transformative end for education and worship — an end that is open to the plight of the poor in their oppression. Consequently, the Wisdom and Torah Psalms consciously refuse to perpetuate the veritable attack on the poor that infuses Proverbs. The class motives that made the elite think it necessary to launch such an attack in order to establish its proverbial views on work, wealth, authority, poverty, and charity were fundamentally undermined in the context of the Wisdom and Torah Psalms. Where the Wisdom and Torah Psalms capitalize on wisdom's ambiguousness about poverty and wickedness, we catch glimpses of a liberating vision that comes to be more fully enshrined in Job, in Ecclesiastes, and in parts of the prophetic tradition.

Yet, instead of launching a full-scale protest against poverty and social injustice on the order of the prophets, the Wisdom and Torah Psalms offer the posture of patient waiting and a longing for deliverance (Pss. 37:7; 119:81–84, 123). On the positive side, this waiting and longing can foster a reflection that is deeply critical of the injustices that attend the amassing of wealth. However, when the poor are asked to wait for change, being left to the charity of the rich for their salvation, such waiting can lead to despair, alcoholism, laziness, hopelessness, friendlessness—all the conditions that the wise would prefer to blame on the poor when, in fact, the poor are the victims of injustice. Waiting can only be meaningful if it is cultivated in an atmosphere of commitment to social action within the confines of social protest. The needed companion to the emergent critical voice of the Wisdom and Torah Psalms, therefore, is the more dynamic prophetic voice—the focus of the next chapter.

12

"Arise, God! Judge the Earth!"

Prophetic Oracles of Judgment

If we think of the prophetic voice as the voice that is critical of political institutions and social injustice, then we have already met such a voice throughout the Psalter. The settled social arrangements of the status quo are thoroughly probed as the community lifts up its words of lament, trust, thanksgiving, praise, and its psalms of kings, both earthly and divine. There is, however, another dimension to our notion of the prophetic, namely the call for God to judge the world's present disorder. This voice finds consistent expression in a block of psalms termed Prophetic Oracles of Judgment. H. W. Wolff sees two sides to this prophetic voice of judgment—what he terms the "irresistible word"—as found in Amos: "(1) the guilt of the present cannot be refused, and (2) the judgment of the future cannot be escaped."[1] Even a cursory reading of the canonical prophetic texts will reveal that the notion of divine judgment is a primary category in prophetic thought: Out of a present marred by the twin evils of idolatry and social injustice emerges a disturbing vision of God's judgment of oppression.[2] We look to the psalms designated Prophetic Oracles of Judgment to define the moment in worship when the cry is no longer, as in the laments, "God hear us!" nor even "God is king!" as in the psalms of enthronement; rather, having heard the words of lamentation and divine enthronement, the yearning of the

173

oppressed is transformed into the increasingly urgent cry, "Arise, God! Judge the earth!" (Ps. 82:8).

WHO DEVOUR MY PEOPLE

As Gutiérrez has cogently observed, the starting point for theology in the North American and European settings has differed markedly from that of Latin American liberation thought. In particular, the North American and European theological discussions have been driven by the competing forces of rationalism, secularism, and democracy.[3] The theological question in the North American and European realm has become, in Gutiérrez's words, "how to speak of God in an adult world."[4] Using atheism as the background bogeyman, for example, a person attempting to retain the strains of the old faith in the North American and European context will discern great philosophic significance in the psalmist's statement: "The fool thinks that there is no God" (Pss. 14:1; 53:2). If we adopt this approach, the question of belief is central, secularism is the chief error, and political questions are appendages to the theological system.

What happens, however, to Psalms 14 and 53 if we shift the basic questions we bring to the text, as Gutiérrez asks us to do?[5] What insights arise when we ground our reflection in a critical wrestling with oppression rather than the philosophic problems posed by modernity? Immediately our attention is drawn to the psalmist's statement: "Don't all those who do wrong know? — Those who devour my people as if eating bread" (Pss. 14:4; 53:5). The question of belief gives way to the question of oppression. To what, specifically, is the psalmist referring? This phrasing is strikingly reminiscent of Micah's graphic castigation of the ruling elite: "They have devoured the flesh of my people" (Mic. 3:3).[6] In Micah the theological context for the prophet's call for judgment was the concrete situation of oppression and social victimization. The elite amassed its wealth through exploitation and fraud (Mic. 2:1–9; 3:9–10; 6:11). Corrupt business and legal practices formed the matrix of the oppression the prophet condemned (3:10–12; 7:3). Surprisingly, Micah never uses any of the Hebrew words for poor when describing those so exploited;

rather, the prophet selects the very wording found in this psalm to speak of the exploitation of "my people" (Mic. 2:8–9; 3:3). Following Micah, the central question is justice, not belief, the chief error is oppression, not secularism, and political questions are the essential ground to a "prophetic" theological reflection.

To shift the basic theological question to that of exploitation and injustice alters markedly our reading of Psalms 14 and 53. To speak of a time "when God restores the fortunes of God's people" (14:7; 53:7), is to concretize the meaning of "salvation/ victory." Furthermore, to concretize the meaning of salvation is to contextualize the "atheism" combatted by the text. Rereading Psalms 14 and 53 against the backdrop of the language of Micah, we find that the psalmist(s) are not engaged in an abstract, philosophic debate against rationalism, but in a life-and-death struggle on behalf of poor villagers whose "political wisdom" has been scorned (Ps. 14:6).[7] The poor know God as the final "refuge" against exploitation, and it is on their behalf that the psalmist makes the call to God for "salvation/victory" to emerge out of Zion (Pss. 14:7; 53:7). By altering our fundamental theological starting point and rethinking the psalm within its context of oppression, we find that we can give new definition to the "folly" attacked by the psalmist—it is the folly of the social injustice that cuts the oppressor off from God.

THE PROPHETIC VOICE OF JUDGMENT

The prophet Jeremiah was burdened with the task of announcing the voice of judgment. The Book of Jeremiah succinctly defines the prophetic task in these words:

> *See, I give you this charge today,*
> *Over nations and over kingdoms:*
> *To uproot and to tear down,*
> *To destroy and to wreck,*
> *To build and to plant* (Jer. 1:10).

Many chapters, with words of judgment that usher in the Babylonian exile, must follow this charge before the prophet can hold out the balancing hope of replanting and rebuilding (Jer. 24:6; 29:5; 31:28; 42:10). The bulk of the first half of the book, however, is given over to the immediacy of divine judgment—to tearing down and uprooting. Jeremiah agonized over Judah's impending doom and witnessed the destructive expulsion of his people's leadership. The prophet's words offer insightful perspectives on the plight of the poor at the time of the exile, attesting to the keen awareness among the prophets of the close connection that existed between state ideology, exploitation, and divine judgment.[8]

Here I want to single out several of Jeremiah's concerns to serve as background for reexamining the Prophetic Oracles of Judgment:

Wealth

The prophet spoke out against the economic corruption of the bureaucrats and merchants, contending that the rich acquired their wealth through fraud (Jer. 5:27–28). These and other abuses lead to the prophetic word of judgment:

> *Will I not exact punishment for these things?,*
> *Says the LORD.*
> *I must vindicate myself against a nation such as this*
> (Jer. 5:29).

The prophet pursues the economic question directly to King Jehoiakim, who is criticized for exploiting the workers in royal construction projects (Jer. 22:13–14). Several royal figures receive criticism from Jeremiah (Jer. 21:11–23:8). The prophet's uprooting words tear at the complacent sensibilities of a monarchy that operates with complete disregard for the society's unjust economic arrangements.

Justice

Jeremiah underscores his critique of Jehoiakim with an appeal to the reformist tradition of Josiah, whom Jeremiah credits with taking up the "case of the oppressed and impoverished"

(Jer. 22:15–16). The prophet discerns that the existing economic and legal structures are not forever given. The political will to alter history for justice's sake is essential to a rule that God need not uproot.

Idolatry

The prophet's social criticism was riveted with a critique of the ideological base—the religion—of the monarchic establishment.[9] In the prophetic analysis, the exploitation of the poor went hand in hand with the nation's idolatry; a false consciousness drove royal domination and oppression in ancient Israel. Yet, knowing the bankruptcy of the state's god(s), Jeremiah felt free to mock the religion that was used to legitimize the existing social order (cf., e.g., Jer. 2:28).[10]

THE ACTS THAT BRING JUDGMENT

Not surprisingly, these particular concerns—the prophetic task of uprooting, wealth through fraud, justice for the disenfranchised, and idolatry—find their place in the Prophetic Oracles of Judgment:

Uprooting and Wealth

As Psalm 52 begins, we are not clear who is this evil boaster whose "tongue plots ruin" (Ps. 52:3). Yet the linkage between the uprooting task of the prophet found in Jeremiah and verse 7 of the psalm is striking:

> *God will tear you down forever.*
> *God will snatch you away, pulling you out of the tent.*
> *God will root you out of the land of the living* (Ps. 52:7).

In verse 9, the text identifies the person uprooted as the one who "trusted in abundant wealth." For the prophetic voice, it is not enough to point out that wealth is slippery and fleeting, as the voice of wisdom was inclined to do; rather, the prophetic word envisions a God who acts to bring judgment on those who amass wealth through deception and crime.

We should note, however, that, as with Jeremiah, the balancing word of *hope after judgment* is also present in Psalm 52. The poet exclaims:

> *I am a luxurious olive-tree in the house of God.*
> *I trusted in the kindness of God always and forever.*
> *I will give thanks to you for ever, for you have acted.*
> *I await your name,*
> *For it is best to be in the presence of your holy ones*
>   (Ps. 52:10–11).

Ever seeking God's judgment, the prophetic voice yearns for an era of human and social transformation. The vision that led Jeremiah from uprooting to planting or that guided the community to join the judgments of First Isaiah to the hopes of Second and Third Isaiah also led the psalmist to end with expectant hope and not simply a word of judgment. Uprooting and planting, each in its season, are the twin pillars of the prophetic response to economic injustice.

Justice for the Disenfranchised

The profound concern of prophets like Jeremiah for the oppressed is matched by the critique of Psalm 82. For Jeremiah, the rich consistently violated the poor in legal contexts:

> *They have become rich and sleek,*
> *They have gone beyond evil talk,*
> *They do not judge the case,*
> *The case of the orphan,*
> *They have prospered,*
> *They do not render judgment for the impoverished*
>   (Jer. 5:28).

Similarly, the psalmist makes injustices in the legal realm a central concern for all who worship:

> *How long will all of you judge unjustly,*
> *Honoring the wicked?*
> *Render judgments for the poor and orphan!*
> *The oppressed and beggars—declare not guilty!*
> *Rescue the poor and impoverished!*
> *Liberate them from the grasp of the wicked!*
>   (Ps. 82:2–4).

Jeremiah's word of judgment against such abuses (Jer. 5:29), finds its counterpart in the psalmist's caustic statement:

> *They do not know.*
> *They do not understand.*
> *They are walking about in darkness.*
> *All the foundations of the earth are shaking.*
> *I thought, "You are gods.*
> *All of you are the children of the Most High."*
> *But you will die as mortals.*
> *You will fall like any prince.*
> *Arise, God! Judge the earth!*
> *You possess all the nations* (Ps. 82:5–8).

The psalmist's call for judgment emerges out of the failure of the society to adhere to its stated ideals. This call for justice represents, in part, the continued expression of ancient Canaan's expectation for its rulers, as is made clear from the Ugaritic tale of Keret:

> Hear, I beseech you, o noble Keret,
> hearken and let (your) ear be attentive ...
> You have been brought down by your failing power.
> You do not judge the cause of the widow,
> you do not try the case of the importunate.
> You do not banish the extortioners of the poor,
> you do not feed the orphan before your face
> (nor) the widow behind your back.[11]

These primordial yearnings for justice, embodied likewise in the biblical and ancient Near Eastern law codes, became, in

Psalm 82, the fulcrum for the psalmist's critique of the social order. That same concern for the widow and orphan occurs frequently in the prophetic literature.[12]

Lest we should miss the contemporary significance of this language, we would do well to remember that the orphan and the widow were universally recognized in the ancient Near East as the politically and economically disenfranchised elements of society. Modern worship, therefore, must speak up when the most basic ideals of our political and social institutions are being violated. We may use different language—speaking in terms of human rights, democracy, or empowerment—but we must dare to employ such language in worship to call society to a greater sense of compassion for and solidarity with the disenfranchised. When worship makes room for the cause of those violated by the legal system, the community will risk challenging society's power holders. Psalm 82 makes such a challenge critical to a worship that wishes to root itself in a prophetic vision of justice and judgment.

Idolatry

The prophetic denunciation of idolatry likewise makes its way into the Prophetic Oracles of Judgment. Psalm 81 calls for a music—a worship—that not only recounts the past glories of God's victory over Pharaoh but which also confronts the demands that result on every generation that would enjoy freedom from Pharaoh's oppressive hand:

> *It is a rule for Israel,*
> *A law of the God of Jacob.*
> *God made it an obligation for Joseph,*
> *When they went forth from Egypt.*
> *I heard a language that I did not know:*
> *I freed their shoulders from the burden.*
> *Their hands were removed from the basket.*
> *You called from your distress and I rescued you.*
> *I answered you from thunder's hiding place.*
> *I tested you by the waters of Meribah.*
> *Listen, my people. I am admonishing you.*

Israel, you must listen to me!
Let there be no foreign god among you.
Do not worship an alien god.
I, the LORD, am your God,
The one who brought you out of Egypt.
Open your mouths and I will fill them (Ps. 81:5–11).

The worship of the liberating God is to be handed on, but
this text also acknowledges that there will be resistance to that
story of freedom: "My people did not listen to me; Israel did
not accede to me" (Ps. 81:12). Surprisingly, the text does not
seek out divine wrath against Israel—only against Israel's enemies—thereby granting the people time to return to a God who
has "freed them to pursue their stubborn way of thinking and
pieces of advice" (Ps. 81:13). Perhaps sensing the harshness of
such a time of judgment, the psalmist puts off the call for the
judgment of the people so that they can discover the compassion
of God.[13] Proceeding along these hesitant lines, the psalmist
tacitly acknowledges that there is a gap between sin and judg-
ment/punishment. The latter is not necessarily as automatic as
we would often like.

BUT DOES GOD BRING JUDGMENT?

When we see rampant social and international injustice, we
can readily sympathize with the urgent call of the prophets and
psalmists for God to do away with the evildoers. The strong
conviction that it is God's task to judge infuses Psalm 75:

"For I [God] will set the appointed time,
I will judge equitably.." . . .
I [the psalmist] say to the boasters, "Do not boast!"
To the wicked, "Do not act vainly!" . . .
Not from the east or the west,
Nor from the desert or the mountains—
God [alone] is judge.
This one God humiliates and that one God honors.
For there is a cup [of wrath] in the LORD's hand—

Foaming wine, mixed thoroughly.
God pours it out on this one.
Surely all the wicked of the earth will drain and drink
    its dregs (Ps. 75:3, 5, 7–9).

The psalmist's conviction is firm: God is the judge of the
world. There is no escape for the arrogant and the wicked.

Yet the persistence of structural evil in the world, the longevity of dictators, the continued presence of death squads, force
us to ask if God does indeed bring judgment. If there is room
in worship to issue the call for God's judgment against oppression and exploitation, is there not room for worship to wrestle
with God's *inaction* in the face of evil? The Prophetic Oracles
of Judgment by themselves cannot serve as our guide here.
These psalms focus too narrowly on God's ability and determi-
nation to judge the world. To reach this definitive horizon in
worship, we must look outside the Psalter to more probing texts
such as Job and Habakkuk, where the notion of God's judgment
is more critically assessed.

The prophet Habakkuk presents us with a prophetic voice
that dares to wrestle deeply over the darker side of the call for
divine judgment. The text prefaces its compelling poem concerning the judging God (Habakkuk 3) with a series of questions
about a God who supposedly uses the military superpowers to
effect divine judgment in the world. In the face of the injustices
Habakkuk witnessed in his own homeland, the prophet raised
the question: "How long, LORD, must I cry out to you, without
you listening? [How long] must I speak out concerning violence,
without you bringing liberation?" (Hab. 1:2). God's response is
to send the Babylonians in to judge the people. Yet, recognizing
the atrocities that will ensue in the military encounter, the
prophet probes further, to ask if God can really achieve justice
in this fashion (Hab. 1:12–17). God responds with a powerful
speech that indicates that an empire built on plunder and blood-
shed, unjust gain and ruinous plotting, murder and deception,
violence and idolatry, will not stand forever (Hab. 2:6–20). Our
rash calls for God's judgment must not blind us to the horren-
dous terrors unleashed by the armies that bring "judgment."[14]

In Job, we have compelling questions raised against a simplistic view of God as judge—questions raised by the reality of the continued prospering of the wicked (Job 21:7–34; 24:2–25). Job turns, like the psalmist, to the points of the compass—east, west, north, south—but fails to find the judging God so confidently discovered by the writer of Psalm 75 (Job 23:8–9; cf. Ps. 75:7). Job's vain search yields the resounding question: "Why are times [of judgment] not stored up by Shaddai; those who know God never see such days" (Job 24:1). If we follow this logic of Job to the conclusion, then we will not expect that our urgent calls for judgment will always be answered.

Both Job and Habakkuk radically qualify the confidence in God's judgment mustered by the Prophetic Oracles of Judgment. We are reminded by these texts that while worship needs to make room for the urgent call for divine judgment, we must also openly grapple with God's failure to set aside times for judgment.

WORSHIP IN A TIME OF TROUBLE

Through the prophetic voice we are brought face to face with the scandal of poverty, oppression, and human suffering. The Prophetic Oracles of Judgment bring this voice into our worship. Once the prophetic voice has entered the worship arena, however, the question of judgment no longer remains one of finger-pointing at an unjust world *out there*. The justice question forces us to hold up a mirror to our worship and reexamine ourselves.

Psalm 50, in particular, radically redefines the issue of divine judgment by having God put God's own people on trial (Ps. 50:3–6). The pursuit of justice and the call for judgment are pointless without a brutal assessment of the injustices perpetuated by our institutional and liturgical life:

Listen, my people! Let me speak.
Israel! Let me admonish you.
I am God, your God.
I am not reproving you because of your sacrifices,
Nor for your burnt offerings that are ever before me.
I do not take from your house a young bull,

Nor rams from your folds.
For every animal of the forest is mine —
The untamed creatures on a thousand hills.
I know every bird in the mountains.
The rodents of the field are with me.
If I hungered, I would not tell you,
For the world in its entirety is mine.
Do I eat the meat of bulls?
Do I drink the blood of rams?
Sacrifice to God a thanksgiving offering.
Pay your vows to the Most High.
Call on me in the time of trouble,
I will free you and you will honor me.

But God says to the wicked,
What does it mean to you to enumerate my rules,
Paying lip-service to my covenant.
You despise my instruction.
You toss my words behind you.
When you see thieves, you show them favor.
You place your bets on the adulterers.
You have destined your mouths for disaster.
You are binding your tongue to fraud.
When sitting you speak against your own sibling.
You fault your mother's child.
You did these things and I was silent,
So you thought I must be like you.
I will reprove you and set it out before you.
Think about this, you who choose to forget God,
So that I do not tear you apart with no one to save you.

Those who offer a thanksgiving offering honor me.
To those who ready the path — I will reveal the salvation
    of God (Ps. 50:7–23).

The call for a divine judgment of the world gains substance
only insofar as the worshiping community has probed the inner
workings of its worship. The call for justice in the world is a
double-edged sword that demands of us a response to the ques-

tion: Are we pursuing justice within the worshiping community? Our laments, our songs of trust and thanksgiving, our hymns of praise, our embrace of God's reign, all this worship rooted in the Psalter finds direction and purpose to the extent that we let the Psalms uproot and tear down our comfortable visions of the God whom we ask to "come and do not remain silent" (Ps. 50:3). A worship rooted in justice must cross-examine all our homilies, our eucharists, our readings, our petitions, our hymns, and our delegation of institutional power.[15] Only when we, as a community, have been sifted by such a worship will we be ready to take into the world the Psalter's expressions of suffering, words of personal hope, and vision of social transformation.

The Psalms Arranged
by Literary Genre

Laments of the Individual: 3, 4, 5, 6, 7, 10, 13, 17, 22, 25, 26, 28, 31, 35, 38, 39, 40:12–18, 42, 43, 51, 54, 55, 56, 57, 59, 61, 64, 69, 70, 71, 77, 86, 88, 102, 109, 120, 130, 139, 140, 141, 142, 143.

Community Laments: 12, 44, 58, 60, 74, 79, 80, 83, 85, 90, 94, 108, 123, 126, 129, 137.

Psalms of Trust: 11, 16, 23, 27, 62, 63, 91, 115, 121, 125, 131. Two of these are community psalms of trust, namely 115 and 125.

Psalms of Thanksgiving (Individual): 9, 30, 32, 34, 40:1–11, 41, 92, 116, 138.

Psalms of Thanksgiving (Community): 65, 66, 67, 107, 118, 124.

Hymns of Praise: 8, 19:1–7, 33, 100, 103, 104, 111, 113, 117, 135, 145, 146, 147, 148, 149, 150.

Liturgical (Processional) Psalms: 15, 24, 68, 134.

Psalms of the Earthly King (Royal Psalms): 2, 18, 20, 21, 45, 72, 89, 101, 110, 132, 144.

Hymns of Zion: 46, 48, 76, 84, 87, 122.

Psalms of God as King: 29, 47, 93, 95, 96, 97, 98, 99.

187

Historical Psalms: 78, 105, 106, 114, 136.

Wisdom and Torah Psalms: 1, 19:8–15, 36, 37, 49, 73, 112, 119, 127, 128, 133.

Prophetic Oracles of Judgment: 14, 50, 52, 53, 75, 81, 82.

Notes

Introduction

1. H. Gunkel and J. Begrich, *Einleitung in die Psalmen*, 4th Edition (Göttingen: Vandenhoeck and Ruprecht, 1985). Important aspects of Gunkel's analysis are presented in H. Gunkel, *The Psalms: A Form-Critical Introduction*, trans. T. M. Horner, with an introduction by J. Muilenburg (Philadelphia: Fortress, 1967). Studies on the psalms are numerous. Surveys of psalms research and bibliographic data can be found in the following: P. van den Berghe, "ʿānî et ʿānāw dans les Psaumes," pp. 273–95 in *Le Psautier* (Orientalia et Biblica Lovaniensia IV), ed. R. de Langhe (Louvain: Publications Universitaires, 1962); B. Childs, *Introduction to the Old Testament as Scripture* (Philadelphia: Fortress, 1979), ch. 33; D. J. A. Clines, "Psalms Research Since 1955: I. The Psalms and the Cult," *Tyndale Bulletin* 18 (1967): 103–25; "Psalms Research Since 1955: II. The Literary Genres," *Tyndale Bulletin* 20 (1969): 105–25; J. Day, *Psalms* (Sheffield: *JSOT*, 1990); B. Feininger, "A Decade of German Psalm-Criticism," *Journal for the Study of the Old Testament* 20 (1981): 91–103; A. R. Johnson, "The Psalms," pp. 162–209 in H. H. Rowley, ed., *The Old Testament and Modern Study* (Oxford: Clarendon, 1951); A. S. Kapelrud, "Scandinavian Research in the Psalms After Mowinckel," *Annual of the Swedish Theological Institute* 4 (1965): 74–90; J. J. Stamm, "Ein Vierteljahrhundert Psalmenforschung," *Theologische Rundschau*, Tübingen 23 (1955): 1–68.

2. S. Mowinckel, *The Psalms in Israel's Worship*, trans. D. R. Ap-Thomas (Nashville: Abingdon, 1962), 2 vols.

3. For a useful justification of the form-critical approach, see C. C. Broyles, *The Conflict of Faith and Experience in the Psalms: A Form-Critical and Theological Study* (Sheffield: *JSOT*, 1989), pp. 23–34. For criticisms of Gunkel and an alternative schema for the psalms, see H.-J. Kraus, *Psalms: A Commentary*, vol. 1 (Minneapolis: Augsburg), pp. 38–62.

4. Essential perspectives on the historical development of the Psal-

ter are lined out by Gunkel, *Die Einleitung in die Psalmen*, pp. 433–55.
A useful overview of the issues is provided by K. Seybold, *Introducing
the Psalms*, trans. R. G. Dunphy (Edinburgh: T. and T. Clark, 1990),
ch. 1, on which this present discussion relies. See also C. Westermann,
Praise and Lament in the Psalms, trans. K. R. Crim and R. N. Soulen
(Atlanta: John Knox, 1981), ch. 6.

    5. The evolving character of the Psalter is evidenced, in part, by
the superscriptions of many of the psalms where attributions of authorship, musical instructions, and pseudohistorical information can be
found. While scholars today do not suppose that the Psalms were written by David (73 psalms), Moses (Ps. 90), Solomon (Pss. 72; 127),
Asaph (12 psalms), Heman (Ps. 88), and Ethan (Ps. 89), nevertheless,
it is difficult to know precisely by what date the Psalter stabilized into
the form we now possess. Seybold terms the view that the psalms were
written by David and others the "autobiographisation of the Psalter,"
a process he sees reflected in Psalm 151 (Greek) and in the Qumran
document 11QPs[a]. See Seybold, *Introducing the Psalms*, p. 36. Tractate
b. Baba Bathra 14b.15a presents David as the author of the Psalter; cf.
Midrash Tehillim on Ps. 1:1; 2 Macc 2:13. On the instability of the final
stages of the Psalter's development, Seybold comments, "while in content and order the central core of the Psalms already existed in Qumran
at that time, neither the final selection nor the final order of the texts,
particularly of the texts in the last third of the Psalter, had been determined." See Seybold, *Introducing the Psalms*, p. 6. See also J. A. Sand-
ers, *The Dead Sea Psalms Scroll* (Ithaca, N.Y.: Cornell, 1967); E. M.
Schuller, *Non-Canonical Psalms from Qumran: A Pseudepigraphic Collection*, Harvard Semitic Studies 28 (Atlanta: Scholars Press, 1986); P.
W. Skehan, "Qumran and the Old Testament Criticism," pp. 163–82
in M. Delcor, ed., *Qumrân: Sa piété, sa théologie et son milieu*, Biblio-
theca Ephemeridum Theologicarum Lovaniensium, 46 (Paris–Gem-
bloux: Duculot, and Leuven: Leuven University, 1978); G. H. Wilson,
The E ʲiting of the Hebrew Psalter, Society of Biblical Literature Dissertation Series 76 (Chico, Calif.: Scholars Press, 1985).

    6. See M. Goulder, *The Prayers of David (Psalms 51–72): Studies
in the Psalter, II*, pp. 20–24, although his view that the preponderance
of *'ĕlohîm* in Pss. 51–72 results from "common authorship" is debata-
ble. The evidence at best supports the view that Pss. 51–72 constitute
a definable *collection* and nothing more.

    7. Seybold, *Introducing the Psalms*, p. 20.

    8. C. Westermann, *Praise and Lament in the Psalms* (Atlanta: John
Knox, 1981), p. 257. See also B. Childs, *Introduction to the Old Testament as Scripture* (Philadelphia: Fortress, 1979), pp. 513–14.

9. D. Bonhoeffer, *Das Gebetbuch der Bibel: Eine Einführung in die Psalmen* (Neuhausen-Stuttgart: Hänssler, 1978); available in English as D. Bonhoeffer, *Psalms: The Prayer Book of the Bible*, trans. J. H. Burtness (Minneapolis: Augsburg, 1970). The theses that laments have their origins in asylum seeking, L. Delekat, *Asylie und Schutzorakel am Zionheiligtum: Eine Untersuchung zu den Privaten Feindpsalmen* (Leiden: E. J. Brill, 1967), or in legal procedures at the temple, H. Schmidt, *Das Gebet des Angeklagten im Alten Testament*, Beihefte zur *Zeitschrift für die alttestamentliche Wissenschaft* 49 (Giessen: Töpelmann, 1928), are suggestive but lack substantive support.

10. Seybold, *Introducing the Psalms*, p. 39.

11. Ibid., p. 2, emphasis added. Postbiblical evidence for the musical use of the psalms in worship is found in Mishnah *Tamid* 7,4; 1 Macc. 4:54; 2 Macc. 1:30. See Seybold, p. 11.

12. Ibid., p. 27.

13. In an interesting twist concerning the development from individual to community, Seybold suggests that the prayers of individuals were preserved on scrolls for the edification of the community. Ibid., p. 42.

14. Childs, *Introduction to the Old Testament*, pp. 510, 517.

15. The path-breaking book in this regard is N. K. Gottwald, *The Tribes of Yahweh: A Sociology of Liberated Israel 1250–1050 B.C.E.* (Maryknoll, N.Y.: Orbis, 1979). Less theoretical but useful are works such as E. W. Davies, *Prophecy and Ethics: Isaiah and the Ethical Tradition of Israel*, *JSOT* Supp. 16 (Sheffield: *JSOT*, 1981); J. A. Dearman, *Property Rights in the Eighth-Century Prophets*, Society of Biblical Literature Dissertation Series 106 (Atlanta: Scholars Press, 1988); and M. E. Polley, *Amos and the Davidic Empire: A Socio-Historical Approach* (New York: Oxford, 1989). These books show the enduring and decisive importance of a biblical hermeneutic that takes seriously matters emanating from a sociohistorical analysis of biblical texts.

16. Childs, *Introduction to the Old Testament*, pp. 513, 515–17.

17. See P. D. Miller, *Interpreting the Psalms* (Philadelphia: Fortress, 1986), ch. 2.

18. For other ways of appropriating the Psalms, see W. Brueggemann, "Psalms and the Life of Faith: A Suggested Typology of Function," *Journal for the Study of the Old Testament* 17 (1980): 3–32.

19. In general, I make reference to English-language scholarly sources when directing readers to additional background discussions or alternate interpretations. However, in some cases it has been necessary to direct readers to works that remain untranslated.

20. Seybold, *Introducing the Psalms*, p. 46.

21. Here I adapt the categories of W. G. E. Watson, *Classical Hebrew Poetry: A Guide To Its Techniques, JSOT* Supp. 26 (Sheffield: *JSOT* Press, 1986). Watson's analysis retains something of the flavor of the older parallelism scheme but is sufficiently nuanced to capture the varied character of biblical poetry in terms of form, content, and literary style. The debate over parallelism has increased in recent years. See R. Alter, *The Art of Biblical Poetry* (New York: Basic Books, 1985); A. Berlin, *The Dynamics of Biblical Parallelism* (Bloomington: Indiana University Press, 1985); T. Collins, *Line Forms in Hebrew Poetry: A Grammatical Approach to the Stylistic Study of the Hebrew Prophets*, Studia Pohl: Series Maior 7 (Rome: Pontifical Biblical Institute, 1978); R. Follis, ed., *Directions in Biblical Hebrew Poetry, JSOT* Supplement 40 (Sheffield: *JSOT* Press, 1987), esp. chs. 3 and 4; S. A. Geller, *Parallelism in Early Biblical Poetry*, Harvard Semitic Monographs 20 (Missoula, Mont.: Scholars Press, 1979); J. Kugel, *The Idea of Biblical Poetry: Parallelism and Its History* (New Haven, Conn.: Yale, 1981); M. O'Connor, *Hebrew Verse Structure* (Winona Lake: Eisenbrauns, 1980). Important comparative studies with Ugaritic poetry are provided by D. Pardee, *Ugaritic and Hebrew Poetic Parallelism: A Trial Cut (ᶜnt I and Proverbs 2)*, Supplements to Vetus Testamentum 39 (Leiden: E. J. Brill, 1988); and M. C. A. Korpel and J. C. de Moor, "Fundamentals of Ugaritic and Hebrew Poetry," pp. 1–61 in *The Structural Analysis of Biblical and Canaanite Poetry*, eds. W. van der Meer and J. C. de Moor, *JSOT* Supplement 74 (Sheffield: *JSOT* Press, 1988).

22. See Alter, *Biblical Poetry*, p. 29.

23. Some have tried to argue that Hebrew poetic meter is rooted in accent and stress patterns; see Watson, *Classical Hebrew Poetry*, ch. 5. A convenient summary of the essential features of biblical Hebrew poetry can be found in Miller, *Interpreting the Psalms*, ch. 3. See also D. L. Petersen and K. H. Richards, *Interpreting Hebrew Poetry* (Minneapolis: Fortress, 1992); and L. A. Schökel, *A Manual of Hebrew Poetics, Subsidia Biblica* 11 (Rome: Pontifical Biblical Institute, 1988).

24. Bonhoeffer, *Psalms: the Prayerbook of the Bible*, p. 24.

1. Laments of the Individual

1. See O. Keel, *The Symbolism of the Biblical World: Ancient Near Eastern Iconography and the Book of Psalms*, trans. T. J. Hallett (New York: Seabury, 1978), ch. 6.

2. For a comparative pictorial representation of postures of lament and petition, see *ibid.*, pp. 319–23.

3. For a convenient summary of the hermeneutic questions related

to the "suffering servant" songs in Deutero-Isaiah, see R. N. Whybray, *The Second Isaiah* (Sheffield: *JSOT*, 1983), ch. 5.

4. In this section I tend to concur with, but would also broaden (to include domestic oppressors), H. Birkeland's much-disputed analysis that, sociologically speaking, the enemies alluded to in the psalms of lament are Israel's foreign enemies. See H. Birkeland, *The Evildoers in the Book of Psalms* (Oslo: J. Dybwad, 1955). T. R. Hobbs and P. K. Jackson, "The Enemy in the Psalms," *Biblical Theology Bulletin* 21/1 (1991): 22–29, tend to support Birkeland's interpretation but read the psalms as products of the sort of propaganda that is commonly devised to foster distrust of foreign opponents. G. T. Sheppard, " 'Enemies' and the Politics of Prayer in the Book of Psalms," pp. 61–82 in *The Bible and the Politics of Exegesis: Essays in Honor of Norman K. Gottwald on His Sixty-Fifth Birthday*, ed. D. Jobling, P. L. Day, and G. T. Sheppard (Cleveland: Pilgrim, 1991), supports Gottwald's sociological readings of the psalms, thereby rescuing the Psalter's references to the enemies from the oblivion of "stylized forms" and placing them back into a social matrix that knows economic and political oppression. However, Sheppard's view that these texts were intended for the hearing of the enemy far too narrowly construes the function of such cultic/worship prayer texts. Cf. N. K. Gottwald, *The Hebrew Bible: A Socio-Literary Introduction* (Philadelphia: Fortress, 1985), pp. 537–41.

5. For a compelling contrary analysis, see C. Westermann, *Praise and Lament in the Psalms*, trans. K. R. Crim and R. N. Soulen (Atlanta: John Knox, 1981), pp. 193–94, where he argues for a clear distinction between the enemies found in the individual laments and the communal laments. In the case of the latter texts, the enemies are Israel's national opponents, but Westermann contends that in the individual laments the speaker suffers alone and in nonpolitical terms. See also the criticisms of G. W. Anderson, "Enemies and Evildoers in the Book of Psalms," *Bulletin of the John Rylands Library* 48 (1965/6): 18–29. My added considerations lead me to an alternate analysis.

6. See J. D. Pleins, "Poverty in the Social World of the Wise," *Journal for the Study of the Old Testament* 37 (1987): 61–78.

7. C. Westermann, *Praise and Lament in the Psalms*, trans. K. R. Crim and R. N. Soulen (Atlanta: John Knox, 1981), pp. 273–74.

8. Cf. P. D. Miller, *Interpreting the Psalms* (Philadelphia: Fortress, 1986), p. 10, who emphasizes this point.

9. See W. Brueggemann, "Psalms and the Life of Faith: A Suggested Typology of Function," *Journal for the Study of the Old Testament* 17 (1980): 3–32; and *The Message of the Psalms: A Theological Commentary* (Minneapolis: Augsburg, 1984).

10. Cf. C. Westermann, *Praise and Lament in the Psalms*, pp. 266–67. Walter Brueggemann has pointed out to me that perhaps the bleakest exception to this general observation is Psalm 88. The psalmist's confidence in the efficacy of prayer (Ps. 88:14) emerges rather weakly out of a text immersed in affliction and dark depression. Even the psalmist's sense that prayer reaches God is qualified in the very next verse by the statement: "Why, LORD, do you reject me?" (Ps. 88:15). In the words of T. Fretheim, *The Suffering of God: An Old Testament Perspective* (Philadelphia: Fortress, 1984), p. 118, this psalm is one of the "few instances where the complaint is that God does not seem to answer." Is there a suffering that admits only despair as its mode of worship? Thus, Westermann's analysis is correct if we treat Psalm 88 as a faithful statement of the poet's longing for the removal of suffering. In this sense, the text is not simply an expression of self-pity.

2. Community Laments

1. B. Childs, *Introduction to the Old Testament as Scripture* (Philadelphia: Fortress, 1979), pp. 519–20, emphasizes this dimension for the canonical interpretation of the Psalter. By contrast, Westermann, *Praise and Lament in the Psalms*, trans. K. R. Crim and R. N. Soulen (Atlanta: John Knox, 1981), p. 167, argues for a clear distinction between the individual and national laments, based on content differences. I do not adhere to his distinction, although his view is strongly argued. Others, such as J. Eaton, *Kingship and the Psalms*, Second Edition (Sheffield: *JSOT*, 1986), pp. 20–26, treat many of the individual laments as royal laments, thereby broadening the political and national significance of the "I." The royal analysis of the individual laments appears to me to confuse the genuinely royal motifs found elsewhere in the Psalter. On this, compare the considered comments of W. H. Bellinger, *Psalmody and Prophecy* (Sheffield: *JSOT*, 1984), pp. 28–31, who supports a non-royal reading of the laments. See also S. J. L. Croft, *The Identity of the Individual in the Psalms* (Sheffield: *JSOT*, 1987), who develops a mediating position but nevertheless reads a number of the individual laments as royal texts. Thus, where Eaton treats 64 psalms as royal, Croft identifies 48 as royal. See Croft, p. 80.

2. See S. Mowinckel, *The Psalms in Israel's Worship*, trans. D. R. Ap–Thomas (Nashville: Abingdon, 1962), vol. 1, ch. 7.

3. For references to the scholarly discussion of the enemy question, see endnotes 4 and 5 from chapter 1. Westermann is clear that the enemies of the communal laments are Israel's national opponents. See Westermann, *Praise and Lament*, pp. 174, 180–81, 188–94.

4. Of all the psalms that we would label community laments, only Psalms 85 and 126 fall short of this characterization, and yet even these psalms touch on the economic and agricultural sphere by calling for the restoration of the fortunes of Zion (Ps. 126:1, 4–6) and Jacob (Ps. 85:5). Arguably, these psalms can be included with the rest of the community laments that seek the righting of the wrongs that have occurred because of Israel's destruction at Babylonian hands.

3. Psalms of Trust

1. Quoted in Krishna Kripalani, *Mahatma Gandhi: All Men are Brothers: Autobiographical Reflections* (New York: Continuum, 1990), p. 3.

2. Westermann, *Praise and Lament in the Psalms*, trans. K. R. Crim and R. N. Soulen (Atlanta: John Knox, 1981), p. 34, sees lament and praise as opposite poles that define the human response to God in worship. If this is the case, I would also add two mediating stages that move from lament to praise, namely trust and thanksgiving. I read this as a continuum—lament, trust, thanksgiving, praise—and have structured the book accordingly. This modifies the location and function of psalms of thanksgiving in contrast to Westermann's scheme and creates an integral role for the psalms of trust. See Westermann, pp. 31–32. In Brueggemann's terminology, the psalms of "disorientation" and "dislocation," i.e., the laments, balance those of "orientation" and "new orientation," e.g., songs of thanksgiving and hymns of praise. See W. Brueggemann, *The Message of the Psalms: A Theological Commentary* (Minneapolis: Augsburg, 1984), pp. 15–28, 51–58, 123–25; and "Psalms and the Life of Faith: A Suggested Typology of Function," *JSOT* 17 (1980): 3–32, where he uses slightly different terminology. My own analysis is somewhat different than Brueggemann's, since I suggest that lament is a basic datum at one end of a spectrum, whereas for Brueggemann, "disorientation" stands in between "orientation" and "new orientation." See Brueggemann, *The Message of the Psalms*, p. 21. However, this difference in emphasis should not obscure our shared belief in the cruciality of the justice question for the Psalter.

3. Christopher Walker, "Like a Child Rests," *Out of Darkness* (Portland, Ore.: OCP Publications, 1990).

4. See G. Gutiérrez, *On Job: God-Talk and the Suffering of the Innocent* (Maryknoll, N.Y.: Orbis, 1987), ch. 9. According to Beyerlin's masterful analysis of Psalm 115, trust in this Creator-God is the critical response (expected of all people, not only of Israel) to God's gift of the earth to humankind. See W. Beyerlin, *Im Licht der Traditionen:*

Psalm LXVII und CXV—Ein Entwicklungszusammenhang. Supplements to *Vetus Testamentum,* 45 (Leiden: Brill, 1992), chs. 4-6.

5. Elie Wiesel, *Night* (New York: Bantam, 1982), pp. 61–62. On the complications of using this text for moral analysis, see M. Sarot, "Auschwitz, Morality and the Suffering of God," *Modern Theology* 7/2 (1991): 135–52. E. Fackenheim, *What is Judaism?: An Interpretation for the Present Age* (New York: Collier, 1987), finds profound insight in this story: "The God that hangs with that boy on the Auschwitz gallows, however, does lack power. He lacks it absolutely, and this because He persists in His intimacy with His people" (p. 289).

6. See José Míguez Bonino, *Toward a Christian Political Ethics* (Philadelphia: Fortress, 1983), ch. 5.

7. Cf. Westermann, *Praise and Lament,* p. 266.

4. Psalms of Thanksgiving

1. Westermann's terminology, though cumbersome, helps to bring out the connection between psalms of thanksgiving and psalms of praise. He refers to psalms of thanksgiving as "descriptive praise," i.e., praise of God for God's actions (in general) and God's character. He terms psalms of praise "declarative praise," i.e., praise of God for a "specific deed." See Westermann, *Praise and Lament in the Psalms,* trans. K. R. Crim and R. N. Soulen (Atlanta: John Knox, 1981), p. 30. The underlying distinction between the Hebrew *ydh* in the Hiphᶜil stem, generally rendered "give thanks," and *hll,* "praise," lends support to Westermann's characterization, although Westermann would prefer to render the Hiphᶜil of *ydh* as "confess, affirm." This translation is adopted by G. Mayer, *"ydh, tôdâ,"* pp. 427–43 in *Theological Dictionary of the Old Testament,* eds. G. J. Botterweck and H. Ringgren, trans. D. E. Green (Grand Rapids: Eerdmans, 1986), who is heavily influenced by Westermann's interpretation. I employ the more traditional translation for this term, since "thanks" speaks more directly to the notion of a human *response* to God's saving action that goes beyond mere declaration. This response is different than praise, particularly what Westermann defines as "descriptive praise."

2. Positive reflections on this theme are offered by M. L. King, Jr., *Strength to Love* (Philadelphia: Fortress, 1963), ch. 8.

3. Helpful in this regard are F. M. Lappé and J. Collins, with C. Fowler, *Food First: Beyond the Myth of Scarcity,* revised and updated (New York: Ballantine, 1979); F. M. Lappé and J. Collins, *World Hunger: Twelve Myths* (New York: Grove, 1986); and F. M. Lappé, R. Schurman, and K. Danaher, *Betraying the National Interest* (New York: Grove, 1987).

4. F. M. Lappé mines the moral tools for such political change in *Rediscovering America's Values* (New York: Ballantine, 1989).

5. See, e.g., D. Ussishkin, *The Conquest of Lachish by Sennacherib* (Tel Aviv: Tel Aviv University, Institute of Archaeology, 1982).

6. M. L. King, Jr., *The Trumpet of Conscience* (New York: Harper and Row, 1967), p. 17.

7. Westermann, *Praise and Lament*, p. 112.

8. S. Mowinckel, *The Psalms in Israel's Worship*, trans. D. R. Ap-Thomas (Nashville: Abingdon, 1962), vol. 2, p. 32, notes the communal aspect of personal thanksgiving when he writes, "From one point of view it [the thanksgiving psalm] is meant for the fellow countrymen present; it is being sung for them and in their hearing, and has the character of a laudatory and narrative *testimony* before them to the saving work God has performed upon the worshipper."

9. M. Fox, *Creation Spirituality: Liberating Gifts for the Peoples of the Earth* (San Francisco: Harper, 1991), pp. 13–16, 31, expands the ritual horizon by suggesting that a celebration of native cosmologies can lead to a deeper ecumenism rooted in a common experience of awe at creation.

10. This is the path delineated by the Bishops' Committee on the Liturgy, *Environment and Art in Catholic Worship* (Washington, D. C.: United States Catholic Conference, 1978), which in III, 42–3, stresses that the community's worship building—its "skin" for "liturgical action"—"does not have to 'look like' anything else, past or present." They proceed to stipulate, "In the renovation of these spaces for contemporary use, there is no substitute for an ecclesiology that is both ancient and modern in the fullest sense." Elsewhere the document emphasizes, "Contemporary art forms belong to the liturgical expressions of the assembly as surely as the art forms of the past. . . . If liturgy were to incorporate only the acceptable art of the past, conversion, commitment and tradition would have ceased to live" (sec. II, 33). For a thoughtful consideration of existing examples, see J. Buscemi, *Places for Devotion*, Meeting House Essays 4 (Chicago, Ill.: Liturgy Training Publications, 1993).

11. H. M. Barstad, *The Religious Polemics of Amos*, Vetus Testamentum Supplement 34 (Leiden: E. J. Brill, 1984), pp. 111–18, offers a balanced assessment of the various prophetic statements concerning the sacrificial cult. He concludes, "The prophets reacted to what they *saw* in society, they reacted to particular occasions, under various circumstances. It is hardly *fair* to ask them for a reflective view on the nature of the cult" (p. 117).

12. A detailed study of this text is offered by W. Beyerlin, *Werden*

und Wesen des 107. Psalms. Beihefte zur *Zeitschrift für die alttestamentliche Wissenschaft* 153 (Berlin: Walter de Gruyter, 1979). Beyerlin argues that the text developed in several stages, most importantly suggesting that the first three sections constituted the original poem and that the fourth section was written by a later poet under wisdom influence (cf. pp. 29–31, 76–80, 110–12).

5. Hymns of Praise

1. N. S. Ateek, *Justice, and Only Justice: A Palestinian Theology of Liberation* (Maryknoll, N.Y.: Orbis, 1989); I. J. Mosala, *Biblical Hermeneutics and Black Theology in South Africa* (Grand Rapids: Eerdmans, 1989).

2. For a comprehensive treatment of the issue of poverty in the Hebrew Bible, see J. D. Pleins, "Poor, Poverty (Old Testament)," *The Anchor Bible Dictionary*, ed. D. N. Freedman (New York: Doubleday, 1992), vol. 5, pp. 402–14. Concerning poverty in the Psalter, see S. J. L. Croft, *The Identity of the Individual in the Psalms* (Sheffield: JSOT, 1987), ch. 2.

3. G. von Rad, *God at Work in Israel* (Nashville: Abingdon, 1980), p. 116.

4. M. Fox, *Creation Spirituality: Liberating Gifts for the Peoples of the Earth* (San Francisco: Harper, 1991), p. x.

5. Ibid., p. 39.

6. For a comprehensive discussion of this divine name, see T. N. D. Mettinger, *In Search of God: The Meaning and Message of the Everlasting Names*, trans. F. H. Cryer (Philadelphia: Fortress, 1988), ch. 2.

7. C. Westermann, *Praise and Lament in the Psalms*, trans. K. R. Crim and R. N. Soulen (Atlanta: John Knox, 1981), p. 121, draws an intimate link between God's kindness and the concept of grace: "*Hesed* [steadfast love] is thus a way in which God is related in community. Precisely in this is it grace in the proper sense of the word. The O. T. [Old Testament] does not know any grace except this. God's grace is both a free expression and a relationship determined by a community. It never becomes God's 'duty', but it also never was and never is merely arbitrary. Freedom and restriction are one in God's grace."

8. An additional indicator for the meaning of the Hebrew verb *hll*, "to praise," may be provided by several texts in which the word is used in scenes from daily life. In Gen. 12:15, Pharaoh's courtiers are said to "*hll*" Sarai to Pharaoh, meaning that they rave about or offer comments in admiration of her beauty. Similarly, in 2 Sam. 14:25, where the handsome character of Absalom is under consideration, the text says that

"there was no handsome person in all Israel to so *hll*" as Absalom. Again, *hll* is used to express an admiring response to physical beauty. This meaning provides a context for a reinterpretation of the frequently misunderstood passage in Psalm 78:63. Set in the time of war, the text states that, "its [Israel's] young men have been devoured by fire; its young women remain without admiration." Accordingly, to praise God is to offer a vivid verbal response to the character of God and God's creation.

6. Liturgical Psalms

1. This chapter does not take up the "psalms of ascent" (Pss. 120–34), texts that were presumably used in connection with pilgrimage. These psalms are treated under their respective genres. On the psalms of ascent see C. C. Keet, *A Study of the Psalms of Ascents* (London: Mitre, 1969).

2. See J. D. Levenson, *Sinai and Zion: An Entry into the Jewish Bible* (San Francisco: Harper and Row, 1985), pp. 169–76, whose reading of Psalms 15 and 24 demonstrates the intimate link between ethics and cult. See also J. T. Willis, "Ethics in a Cultic Setting," pp. 147–69 in J. L. Crenshaw and J. T. Willis, eds., *Essays in Old Testament Ethics* (New York: KTAV, 1974), who questions whether Psalms 15 and 24 are indeed "entrance liturgies."

3. For inclusive language resources, consult N. Mitchell, "Inclusive Language: References and Resources," *Today's Liturgy* 13/4 (1991): 14–15. Useful resources specific to the psalms include: *Inclusive Language Psalms: From an Inclusive-Language Lectionary* (New York: Pilgrim Press, 1987); *The Psalms: An Inclusive Language Version Based on the Grail Translation from the Hebrew* (Chicago: G. I. A. Publications, 1986).

4. See, e.g., the U.S. Bishop's Meeting statement entitled "Inclusive Language in Liturgy: Scriptural Texts," published in *Origins* 20/25 (November 29, 1990), pp. 405–8. The quoted material appears on page 407.

5. The question of women's experience in Israel and its possible impact on the interpretation of the Psalter deserves further exploration. Insightful hermeneutical approaches to the Hebrew Bible can be found in the following: P. Bird, "The Place of Women in the Israelite Cultus," pp. 397–419 in *Ancient Israelite Religion: Essays in Honor of Frank M. Cross*, eds. P. D. Hanson, P. D. Miller, and S. D. McBride (Philadelphia: Fortress, 1987); P. Day, ed., *Gender and Difference in Ancient Israel* (Minneapolis: Augsburg Fortress, 1989); C. Meyers, *Discovering Eve: Ancient Israelite Women in Context* (New York: Oxford, 1988); R. Rad-

ford Ruether, *Sexism and God Talk: Toward a Feminist Theology* (Boston: Beacon, 1983); L. M. Russell, ed., *Feminist Interpretation of the Bible* (Philadelphia: Westminster, 1985).

6. On this image of God in its ancient Near Eastern context, see M. Weinfeld, " 'Rider of the Clouds' and 'Gatherer of the Clouds'," *The Journal of the Ancient Near Eastern Society of Columbia University* 5 (1973): 421–26; see especially pp. 422–25, where Weinfeld stresses the martial aspect of this image. Cf. also M. Smith, *The Early History of God: Yahweh and the Other Deities in Ancient Israel* (New York: Harper and Row, 1990), pp. 48, 53–55, 101.

7. The extent to which earthly kingship shaped (or failed to shape) thinking about God's rule as king is delineated by M. Zvi Brettler, *God is King: Understanding an Israelite Metaphor, JSOT* Supplement 76 (Sheffield: *JSOT*, 1989).

7. Psalms of the Earthly King

1. I do not find in these psalms any evidence to support the view propounded by some that these texts emerge out of a ritual of royal humiliation/vindication during Israel's autumn festival. Concerning arguments in favor of this theory see, e.g., A. R. Johnson, *Sacral Kingship in Ancient Israel*, 2nd ed. (Cardiff: University of Wales, 1967), pp. 102–28.

2. See, e.g., Bertil Albrektson, *History and the Gods: An Essay on the Idea of Historical Events as Divine Manifestations in the Ancient Near East and in Israel* (Lund: C. W. K. Gleerup, 1967); H. W. F. Saggs, *The Encounter with the Divine in Mesopotamia and Israel* (London: University of London, the Athlone Press, 1978).

3. Day contends that such "battle psalms" were "repeatedly used in war situations and probably do not reflect particular historical events." He cites the deliverance prayer in 2 Chronicles 20:6–12 as a clear example of such a setting for this type of psalm. See J. Day, *Psalms* (Sheffield: *JSOT*, 1990), p. 94.

4. See W. Brueggemann, *David's Truth: In Israel's Imagination and Memory* (Philadelphia: Fortress, 1985), pp. 99–109.

5. Although the term *king* is not explicitly mentioned, commentators generally treat this psalm as a royal psalm. Cf., e.g., H. A. Kenik, "Code of Conduct for a King: Psalm 101," *Journal of Biblical Literature* 95 (1976): 391–403, who regards the text as "the king's statement before Yahweh about fidelity to his kingly obligations" (p. 395). Kenik offers a number of suggestive links between Psalm 101 and the text of Proverbs—considerations which lend added support to my thesis that

kingship, in part, is a question of "wisdom" (see Kenik, pp. 399–402); cf. also J. S. Kselman, "Psalm 101: Royal Confession and Divine Oracle," *Journal for the Study of the Old Testament* 33 (1985): 45–62.

6. A. R. Johnson, *Sacral Kingship*, p. 137.

7. Some will find precedent in the Levant for the notion of the divine sonship of the king in the Ugaritic legend of King Keret, where the god El is treated as the "father" (*'ab*) of King Keret. See, e.g., "Keret," in John Gibson, *Canaanite Myths and Legends* (Edinburgh: T. & T. Clark, 1978), col. i, line 41; col. ii, lines 59, 77; col. iv, line 169. I. Engnell, *Studies in Divine Kingship in the Ancient Near East* (Oxford: Blackwell, 1967), ch. 4, lines out the west-semitic background for viewing the king both as son of god and as a god (p. 80). He finds this pattern throughout the ancient Near East and suggests the notion applies to the Hebrew Bible as well (cf. pp. 174–77). In point of fact, there is little evidence for such a view in the psalms. A substantive critique is offered by M. Noth, "God, King, and Nation in the Old Testament," pp. 145–78 in *The Laws in the Pentateuch and Other Studies*, trans. D. R. Ap–Thomas (Philadelphia: Fortress, 1967). Noth argues that for ancient Israel, "the king was not by nature a 'son' of God, nor did he by natural necessity enter the sphere of divinity through his enthronement, but was *declared* to be a 'son' by a deliberate decision of Israel's God at his accession" (p. 172). The argument that sonship language is metaphorical or adoptive language is also made by G. Cooke, "The Israelite King as Son of God," *Zeitschrift für die alttestamentliche Wissenschaft* 73 (1961): 202–25. Cf. also the more cautious assessment of G. von Rad, "The Royal Ritual in Judah," pp. 222–31 in *The Problem of the Hexateuch and Other Essays*, trans. E. W. Trueman Dicken (New York: McGraw–Hill, 1966).

8. On the difficulties in translating Psalm 45:7, see J. A. Emerton, "The Syntactical Problem of Psalm XLV.7," *Journal of Semitic Studies* 13 (1968): 58–63. Emerton supports the translation: "Thy throne is like unto God's throne that endureth for ever" (p. 63). An important critical analysis countering Emerton is offered by A. M. Harman, "The Syntax and Interpretation of Psalm 45:7," pp. 337–47 in *The Law and the Prophets: Old Testament Studies Prepared in Honor of Oswald Thompson Allis*, ed. J. H. Skilton (Presbyterian and Reformed, 1974), who defends the traditional translation, "Thy throne, O God, is for ever and ever." However, his messianic interpretation of this psalm is less than convincing.

9. For an alternate interpretation see C. Brekelmans, "Psalm 132: Unity and Structure," *Bijdragen, Tijdschrift voor filosofie en theologie* 44 (1983): 262–65, who sees in the text a reaffirmation of God's enduring promises.

10. W. Brueggemann, *Hopeful Imagination: Prophetic Voices in Exile* (Philadelphia: Fortress, 1986), p. 66.

11. R. J. Clifford, "Psalm 89: A Lament Over the Davidic Ruler's Continued Failure," *Harvard Theological Review* 73 (1980): 35–47, convincingly argues for the unity of this psalm. He maintains that the creation/cosmogonic elements are integral to community laments and provide an internal logic to the creation-lament structure of Psalm 89: "the lamenting vocabulary is matched to the founding event, cosmogonic victory. Appropriately, what is mourned exclusively is military powerlessness" (p. 46).

12. This reading of the Hebrew text is somewhat uncertain.

13. Contrast Brekelmans, "Psalm 132," p. 264.

14. Cf. W. Brueggemann, *David's Truth: In Israel's Imagination and Memory*, pp. 91–94, 96–99, where he argues that whereas Psalm 89 expresses a dynastic hope of renewal, Psalm 132 builds on the moral/critical dimensions of the Mosaic covenantal tradition.

8. Hymns of Zion

1. For a series of creative reflections on Jerusalem today, see D. Burrell and Y. Landau, *Voices from Jerusalem: Jews and Christians Reflect on the Holy Land* (Mahwah, N.J.: Paulist, 1992).

2. B. C. Ollenburger, *Zion, The City of the Great King: A Theological Symbol of the Jerusalem Cult, JSOT* Supplement 41 (Sheffield: *JSOT*, 1987), concludes from his thorough study of the Zion hymns, "What we have found in the Zion symbolism of the Jerusalem cult tradition is a constant pervasive concern for justice, a consistent and radical criticism of royal attempts to pervert justice, a theologically motivated attempt to ground this justice in the action and character of God and a sustained emphasis on the poor as the particular concern not only of Yahweh himself but also of the very symbolism of the Jerusalem cult ... " (p. 154).

3. Ibid., pp. 33–35, emphasizes reading the Zion hymns within the larger context of God's kingship.

4. Ibid., pp. 66–80.

5. Ibid., pp. 87–100, who speaks of this activity as God's "exclusive prerogative."

6. See M. Weinfeld, "Zion and Jerusalem as Religious and Political Capital: Ideology and Utopia," pp. 75–115 in *The Poet and the Historian: Essays in Literary and Historical Biblical Criticism*, ed. R. E. Friedman (Chico, Calif.: Scholars Press, 1983). See specifically pp. 93–114. Cf. Ollenburger, *Zion*, pp. 136–40. There is no need here to separate

ancient Israel from its environment, as was once common among some biblical scholars who, for apologetic purposes, tried to portray early Israel as a thoroughly unique religious tradition. See, e.g., G. E. Wright, *The Old Testament Against Its Environment* (London: SCM, 1950) and the criticisms of B. Childs, *Biblical Theology in Crisis* (Philadelphia: Westminster, 1976), ch. 4.

7. On mountain imagery, see R. J. Clifford, *The Cosmic Mountain in Canaan and the Old Testament*, Harvard Semitic Monographs, vol. 4 (Cambridge: Harvard, 1972), esp. pp. 131–60; R. L. Cohn, *The Shape of Sacred Space: Four Biblical Studies* (Chico, Calif.: Scholars Press, 1981), ch. 3; J. D. Levenson, *Sinai and Zion: An Entry into the Jewish Bible* (San Francisco: Harper and Row, 1985), ch. 2; and M. S. Smith, *The Early History of God: Yahweh and the Other Deities in Ancient Israel* (New York: Harper and Row, 1990), pp. 53–55.

8. See A. L. Oppenheim, *Ancient Mesopotamia: Portrait of a Dead Civilization*, revised ed. (Chicago: University of Chicago, 1977), pp. 95–109. W. Brueggemann, *Israel's Praise: Doxology Against Idolatry and Ideology* (Philadelphia: Fortress, 1988), ch. 3, wrestles with the extent to which the monarchic context redefined Israel's liturgy.

9. Toward a sociological/historical definition of the prophetic, consult H. B. Huffmon, "The Origin of Prophecy," pp. 171–92 in *Magnalia Dei: The Mighty Acts of God. Essays on the Bible and Archaeology in Memory of G. Ernest Wright* (New York: Doubleday, 1976), eds. F. M. Cross, W. E. Lemke, and P. D. Miller; and R. R. Wilson, *Prophecy and Society in Ancient Israel* (Philadelphia: Fortress, 1980), ch. 3.

10. Cf. Ollenburger's discussion of Pss. 20, 33, and 44 in Ollenburger, *Zion*, pp. 90–100. These psalms, though not Hymns of Zion, provide comparable perspectives on the effectiveness of human weaponry.

11. N. Waldman, "The Breaking of the Bow," *Jewish Quarterly Review* 69 (1978): 82–88, in a comparative study of biblical and Mesopotamian sources, observes that, "In Biblical passages the two themes of breaking the weapons and the ending of war, with God as ruler of the world, are combined, while they are kept distinct in the Akkadian sources" (p. 84).

12. On the language of these verses see Ollenburger, *Zion*, pp. 142–44. The theme of ending war appears several times in the section of the Ugaritic Baal cycle devoted to the war making of the goddess Anat and her efforts to secure a proper "house" for the god Baal. In that tale, the war goddess is summoned into the presence of Baal by messengers who call on her to cease making war in the world. Here I take the mention of *mlhmt* in these texts to refer to war, as does H. L. Ginsberg, "Ugaritic Myths, Epics, and Legends," *Ancient Near Eastern*

Texts: Relating to the Old Testament, 3rd Edition with Supplement, ed. J. B. Pritchard (Princeton: Princeton University, 1969), pp. 136–37. This is the primary meaning offered in J. C. de Moor, *An Anthology of Religious Texts from Ugarit* (Leiden: E. J. Brill, 1987), p. 9; cf. J. C. de Moor, *The Seasonal Pattern in the Ugaritic Myth of Baʿlu: According to the Version of Ilimilku*, Alter Orient und Altes Testament 16 (Neukirchen–Vluyn: Neukirchener Verlag, 1971), p. 157–8, from which it is clear that autumn provided a regular season of cessation from war. The alternative translation of *mlḥmt* as "offering of bread" is noted by de Moor, *Anthology*, p. 9, n. 43; and is actually strongly defended in de Moor, *Seasonal Pattern*, p. 103. J. C. L. Gibson, *Canaanite Myths and Legends* (Edinburgh: T. and T. Clark, 1977), pp. 49–51, likewise translates *mlḥmt* as "loaves." If we take *mlḥmt* to mean "war," this would mean that the Ugaritic mythic poet has chosen to link together the successful enthronement of Baal with the notion of the cessation of war. This mythology provides a cultural precedent for similar motifs in the Zion hymns. We will take up the notion of divine enthronement in the next chapter.

13. Ollenburger, *Zion*, p 142.

14. Psalm 84:10 apparently offers prayer for the king, "Your anointed one." Unfortunately, this statement lacks a clear context, and its precise significance is difficult to determine.

15. Cf. Ollenburger, *Zion*, pp. 66–80, 82–87, who emphasizes that Zion provides security for the poor.

16. J. H. Hayes, "The Tradition of Zion's Inviolability," *Journal of Biblical Literature* 82 (1963): 419–26, ascribes the origins of this theological concept to the "pre-Davidic or non-Israelite traditions concerning the invulnerability of Jerusalem" (p. 426). R. E. Clements, *Isaiah and the Deliverance of Jerusalem*, *JSOT* Supplement 13 (Sheffield: *JSOT*, 1980), ch. 4, though acknowledging the partial contribution of Davidic royal ideology to this concept (and denying any mythic background), firmly roots the belief in Zion's inviolability in the historical events of Jerusalem's escape from destruction by the Assyrian Sennacherib in 701 B.C.E. (p. 84). For additional information on this doctrine, see H. J. Kraus, *Theology of the Psalms* (Minneapolis: Augsburg, 1986), pp. 82–83; and Ollenburger, *Zion*, pp. 16–18. The inviolability thesis is sustained by Levenson, *Sinai and Zion*, pp. 155–65.

17. See, e.g., R. H. Bainton, *Christian Attitudes Toward War and Peace: A Historical Survey and Critical Re-evaluation* (Nashville: Abingdon, 1960). But note the comments of D. G. Hunter, "A Decade of Research on Early Christians and Military Service," *Religious Studies Review* 18/2 (1992): 87–94; and J. B. Hehir, "The Just-War Ethic and

Catholic Theology: Dynamics of Change and Continuity," pp. 15–39 in *War or Peace?: The Search for New Answers*, ed. T. A. Shannon (Maryknoll, N.Y.: Orbis, 1980). See also P. Ramsey, *The Just War: Force and Political Responsibility* (New York: Charles Scribner's Sons, 1968).

18. The complicating factors are detailed in M. Walzer, *Just and Unjust Wars: A Moral Argument with Historical Illustrations* (New York: Basic Books, 1977), who observes, "the world of war is not a fully comprehensible, let alone a morally satisfactory place. And yet it cannot be escaped, short of a universal order in which the existence of nations and peoples could never be threatened. There is every reason to work for such an order. The difficulty is that we sometimes have no choice but to fight for it" (p. 327). See also G. Dyer, *War* (New York: Crown, 1985).

19. A model for this effort is provided in the following document: National Conference of Catholic Bishops, *The Challenge of Peace: God's Promise and Our Response—A Pastoral Letter on War and Peace, May 3, 1983* (Washington, D. C.: United States Catholic Conference, 1983).

20. See, e.g., R. McAfee Brown, *Religion and Violence*, second ed. (Philadelphia: Westminster, 1987), ch. 4.

21. Boesak, for example, seriously grapples with the violence option and thereby builds a stronger case for nonviolence. See A. A. Boesak, *Farewell to Innocence: A Socio-ethical Study on Black Theology and Power* (Maryknoll, N.Y.: Orbis, 1977), chs. 2 and 5.

22. These questions concern the rationale for going to war. Such questions were raised in the months preceding the Gulf war. See, e.g., "Mahony Letter on Just War Affirmed," *Origins* 20/24 (Nov. 22, 1990), pp. 384–86. Just-war theory is also concerned about conduct in war. Cf. J. F. Childress, "Just-War Criteria," pp. 40–58 in T. A. Shannon, *War or Peace?*.

23. "Modern War and Christian Conscience," *Origins* 21/28 (Dec. 19, 1991), pp. 450–55. This essay originally appeared as an editorial in the July 6, 1991, issue of *La Civiltà Cattolica*. For an alternate approach to the concept of "total war," see J. T. Johnson, *Just War Tradition and the Restraint of War: A Moral and Historical Inquiry* (Princeton: Princeton University, 1981), ch. 8.

9. Psalms of God as King

1. See, e.g., H. J. Boecker, *Law and the Administration of Justice in the Old Testament and Ancient East*, trans. J. Moiser (Minneapolis: Augsburg, 1980); and D. Patrick, *Old Testament Law* (Atlanta: John Knox, 1985).

2. See, e.g., J. Neusner, *The Mishnah: An Introduction* (Northvale, N.J.: Jason Aronson, 1989), ch. 5.

3. J. D. Pleins, *Biblical Ethics and the Poor: The Language and Structures of Poverty in the Writings of the Hebrew Prophets*, Ph.D. dissertation (Ann Arbor: University Microfilms, 1986), pp. 240–58.

4. For other references to holiness in these psalms, see 29:2; 47:9; 93:5; 96:9; 97:12; 98:1; 99:9. Cf. J. G. Gammie, *Holiness in Israel* (Philadelphia: Fortress, 1989), pp. 104–6.

5. For the mythological background of this language, see M. Weinfeld, " 'Rider of the Clouds' and 'Gatherer of the Clouds'," *The Journal of the Ancient Near Eastern Society of Columbia University* 5 (1973): 421–26, who observes, "While 'the rider of the clouds' is mostly associated with war activity, 'the gatherer of the clouds' belongs to the cosmic sphere" (p. 425). C. Kloos, *Yhwh's Combat with the Sea: A Canaanite Tradition in the Religion of Ancient Israel* (Leiden: Brill, 1986), analyzes this psalm against the backdrop of Ugaritic Baal mythology, wherein "Baal triumphs over Yam [the sea] and wins thereby his 'eternal kingship' " (p. 93). Cf. M. Smith, *The Early History of God: Yahweh and the Other Deities in Ancient Israel* (New York: Harper and Row, 1990), pp. 48, 101.

6. For a full discussion of the storm theophany in the Bible and the Ugaritic materials, see F. M. Cross, *Canaanite Myth and Hebrew Epic: Essays in the History of the Religion of Israel* (Cambridge, Mass.: Harvard University Press, 1973), pp. 147–86. See also J. Day, *God's Conflict with the Dragon and the Sea: Echoes of a Canaanite Myth in the Old Testament* (Cambridge: Cambridge University Press, 1985), ch. 1.

7. G. Gutiérrez, *A Theology of Liberation: History, Politics and Salvation* (Maryknoll, N.Y.: Orbis, 1973), pp. 154–55. In chapter 5 on the Hymns of Praise, we noted this link between God's creative work and God's liberation of the poor in connection with Psalm 146. The psalms in this present chapter draw out this intimate link between God's creative and liberating actions.

8. Ibid., p. 154.

9. Concerning 96:13, Kraus comments that "cultic and cosmic" are linked, i.e., God's "universal kingship" and God's work of "creation" correspond. In this, Kraus textually infers the sort of linkage between creation and divine rule that Gutiérrez theologically reasoned must exist between the notions of creation and liberation. See H. J. Kraus, *Psalms 60–150: A Commentary*, trans. H. C. Oswald (Minneapolis: Augsburg, 1989), p. 255.

10. Mowinckel's influential view posited the autumn festival as the occasion of God's enthronement, and hence the context for the reading

of these psalms. See S. Mowinckel, *The Psalms in Israel's Worship*, vol. 1 (Nashville: Abingdon, 1962), chap 5. A refined interpretation of the autumn festival and God's kingship is offered by A. R. Johnson, *Sacral Kingship in Ancient Israel*, 2nd ed. (Cardiff: University of Wales Press, 1967). See Johnson, pp. 134–36 for a concise summary of his frequently misconstrued views. H. Gottlieb, "Myth in the Psalms," pp. 62–93 in B. Otzen, H. Gottlieb, and K. Jeppesen, eds., *Myths in the Old Testament* (London: SCM, 1980), in the context of the "Scandinavian school," offers a positive appraisal of the new year festival as "cultic drama." T. N. D. Mettinger, *The Dethronement of Sabaoth: Studies in the Shem and Kabod Theologies* (Lund: CWK Gleerup, 1982), argues that under Josiah, Passover "achieved the status previously accorded to the Autumn Festival" and that after the exilic destruction "the material basis of the Autumn Festival was eliminated" (pp. 67, 74). Criticisms and alternatives to the enthronement thesis can be found in the following: H. J. Kraus, *Psalms 1–59: A Commentary* (Minneapolis: Augsburg, 1988), pp. 86–89; and H. J. Kraus, *Theology of the Psalms* (Minneapolis: Augsburg, 1986), pp. 86–91; N. H. Snaith, *The Jewish New Year Festival* (London: SPCK, 1947), chs. 7 and 8. C. Westermann, *Praise and Lament in the Psalms*, trans. K. R. Crim and R. N. Soulen (Atlanta: John Knox, 1981), pp. 146–51, who likewise disputes the thesis of the enthronement festival, draws attention to significant connections between these psalms and Second Isaiah. Westermann maintains that, "The significance of these enthronement Psalms lies in that a motif which was prophetic in origin, the eschatological exclamation of kingship, was absorbed into the descriptive praise of the Psalms. In its original occurrence, Isa. 52, this exclamation was the glad tidings proclaimed to exiled Israel, 'Your God reigns!' This message was to assure the exiles of their coming deliverance. Since it lived on after the Exile in the worship of the community, the certainty of the coming intervention of God lived in it, Ps. 96:13, 'For he comes to judge the earth,' " (p. 151). For a convenient summary of scholarly positions on the enthronement thesis, see B. C. Ollenburger, *Zion, The City of the Great King: A Theological Symbol of the Jerusalem Cult, JSOT* Supplement 41 (Sheffield: *JSOT*, 1987), pp. 24–28.

   11. On which see J. A. Black, "The New Year Ceremonies in Ancient Babylon: 'Taking Bel by the Hand' and a Cultic Picnic," *Religion* 11 (1981): 39–59, who argues that the Babylonian New Year ceremonies functioned, in part, as "a patronal festival of the city-god, Marduk, including his enthronement" (p. 56). K. van der Toorn, "The Babylonian New Year Festival: New Insights from the Cuneiform Texts and Their Bearing on Old Testament Study," pp. 331–44 in *Congress*

Volume: Leuven 1989, ed. J. A. Emerton (Leiden: E. J. Brill, 1991), refines the points of comparison between the *akitu*-festival and Israel's Autumn Festival. In the Canaanite sphere, J. C. de Moor, *New Year with Canaanites and Israelites, Part One: Description, Part Two: The Canaanite Sources* (Netherlands: Kamper Cahiers, 1972), argues that the Ugaritic data do to some extent support Mowinckel's enthronement thesis (see esp. part one, pp. 25–29). The Canaanite sources are discussed more thoroughly in J. C. de Moor, *The Seasonal Pattern in the Ugaritic Myth of Baʿlu: According to the Version of Ilimilku*, Alter Orient und Altes Testament 16 (Neukirchen–Vluyn: Neukirchener Verlag, 1971), see especially ch. 4.

12. M. Zvi Brettler, *God is King: Understanding an Israelite Metaphor*, *JSOT* Supplement 76 (Sheffield: *JSOT*, 1989), ch. 6, studies this metaphorical language against the backdrop of ancient Israelite coronation patterns. Brettler concludes, "A close examination of the contexts in which the phrase appears uncovered a significant anomaly — it is generally used in contexts where the non-Israelite nations are supposed to acknowledge God's kingship . . . — instead of *celebrating* God the king as *newly enthroned*, the nations are projected as *newly (recognizing and) celebrating* the achievements of God (who has *always* been *enthroned*)" (p. 167).

13. Cf. S. Mowinckel, *The Psalms in Israel's Worship*, trans. D. R. Ap-Thomas. (New York: Abingdon, 1962), vol. 1, pp. 112–13.

14. W. Brueggemann, *Israel's Praise: Doxology Against Idolatry and Ideology* (Philadelphia: Fortress, 1988), chs. 1 and 2, creatively defends the view that praise is a theologically constitutive act of "world" construction done by the community.

15. Martin Luther King, Jr., saw in the biblical certainty of the defeat of evil a source of strength to continue the fight against colonialism and racism. See "The Death of Evil Upon the Seashore," pp. 76–85 in *Strength to Love* (Philadelphia: Fortress, [1963], 1981).

16. G. Gutiérrez, *We Drink from Our Own Wells: The Spiritual Journey of a People* (Maryknoll, N.Y.: Orbis, 1985), p. 7.

17. E. Wiesel et al., *Dimensions of the Holocaust* (Evanston, Ill.: Northwestern University, 1977), p. 17.

18. G. Gutiérrez, *Wells*, p. 18.

10. Historical Psalms

1. G. Gutiérrez, *The Power of the Poor in History*, trans. R. R. Barr (Maryknoll, N.Y.: Orbis, 1983), p. 107.

2. Ibid., p. 106.

3. Ibid., p. 20–21.

4. Perhaps the most forceful, though certainly not final, statement of this view can be found in E. W. Said, *Orientalism* (New York: Vintage, 1978).

5. A provocative rereading of United States history is offered, e.g., by H. Zinn, *A People's History of the United States* (New York: Harper and Row, 1980).

6. G. Gutiérrez, *Power of the Poor*, p. 12.

7. This chapter limits itself to those psalms that are labeled form critically as "historical psalms." For a broader discussion of the topic of history throughout the Psalter, consult E. Haglund, *Historical Motifs in the Psalms*, Coniectanea Biblica, Old Testament Series 23 (Uppsala: CWK Gleerup, 1984); and C. Westermann, *Praise and Lament in the Psalms*, trans. K. R. Crim and R. N. Soulen (Atlanta: John Knox, 1981), ch. 5.

8. Haglund, *Historical Motifs*, reads this text as "a prayer of deliverance from the Exile" (p. 63).

9. This chiastic analysis is suggested by M. C. A. Korpel and J. C. de Moor, "Fundamentals of Ugaritic and Hebrew Poetry," pp. 1–61 in *The Structural Analysis of Biblical and Canaanite Poetry*, eds. W. van der Meer and J. C. de Moor, *JSOT* Supplement 74 (Sheffield: *JSOT* Press, 1988), esp. pp. 55–60.

10. Haglund, *Historical Motifs*, places the composition of Psalm 78 "soon after the fall of the Northern Kingdom, such as the reign of Hezekiah" (p. 100–101).

11. Functioning much as Shiloh does in Jeremiah (7:12–15; 26:6–9), an event mentioned in Psalm 78:60. W. Brueggemann, *Abiding Astonishment: Psalms, Modernity, and the Making of History* (Louisville: Westminster/John Knox, 1991), p. 20, keenly observes, "Whereas the Psalm *contrasts* Jerusalem and northern alienations, the prophetic text proposes a close *parallelism*. In the prophetic rendition of the tradition, the contrast between Shiloh and Jerusalem, which served Jerusalem's interests, is soundly rejected. In this Psalm, however, which is celebrative of the Jerusalem establishment, it is this contrast which is the point of the recital, whereby the Jerusalem establishment gains legitimation."

12. Conveniently described in T. E. Fretheim, *Deuteronomic History* (Nashville: Abingdon, 1983).

13. M. Noth, *The Deuteronomistic History*, 2nd ed., *JSOT* Supplement 15 (Sheffield: *JSOT*, 1991), p. 134.

14. See, e.g., G. von Rad, "The Deuteronomic Theology of History in I and II Kings," pp. 205–21 in *The Problem of the Hexateuch and Other Essays*, trans. E. W. Trueman Dicken (New York: McGraw-Hill,

1966); and H. W. Wolff, "The Kerygma of the Deuteronomic Historical Work," pp. 83–100 in *The Vitality of Old Testament Traditions*, ed. W. Brueggemann and H. W. Wolff (Atlanta: John Knox, 1975), p. 14.

15. A theme studied in the liberation context by J. Severino Croatto, *Exodus: A Hermeneutics of Freedom* (Maryknoll, N.Y.: Orbis, 1981).

16. Cf. G. Gutiérrez, *We Drink From Our Own Wells: The Spiritual Journey of a People* (Maryknoll, N.Y.: Orbis, 1985), ch. 6.

17. Presumably to farm the land in small village communities. See L. E. Stager, "The Archaeology of the Family in Ancient Israel," *Bulletin of the American Schools of Oriental Research* 260 (Fall/November 1985): 1–35.

18. Brueggemann, *Abiding Astonishment*, p. 28.

19. Ibid., p. 13.

20. See S. Japhet, "The Historical Reliability of Chronicles," *Journal for the Study of the Old Testament* 33 (1985): 88–92.

21. Cf. S. L. McKenzie, *The Chronicler's Use of the Deuteronomistic History*, Harvard Semitic Monographs 33 (Atlanta: Scholars Press, 1985), who charts the points of variation and omission between Chronicles and Samuel–Kings in detail. There is a problem knowing to what extent the Chronicler's source text(s) differed from or supplemented our present Samuel–Kings; hence, current analysis finds it difficult to determine precisely in every case the Chronicler's own deviations and hence purpose or ideology, but the overall tendencies of the document are clear (cf. McKenzie, pp. 26–28).

22. J. D. Newsome, "Toward a New Understanding of the Chronicler and His Purposes, *Journal of Biblical Literature* 94 (1975): 201–17, sees the Chronicler's "eschatological hope" grounded in the eternal kingship granted to David (cf. pp. 208–10). On the prophetic dimension of David's rule, see pp. 203–4. Cf. D. N. Freedman, "The Chronicler's Purpose," *Catholic Biblical Quarterly* 23 (1961): 436–42. For additional thoughtful reflection on the Chronicler's portrait of David, see W. Brueggemann, *David's Truth: In Israel's Imagination and Memory* (Philadelphia: Fortress, 1985), pp. 99–109. On the reformist emphasis in the Chronicler's presentation of Judah's kings, see F. L. Moriarty, "The Chronicler's Account of Hezekiah's Reform," *Catholic Biblical Quarterly* 27 (1965): 399–406. Even Manasseh is credited with repentance and ritual reform (cf. 2 Chr. 33:10–17), an account lacking in Kings which makes Manasseh "the worst king of all" (McKenzie, *The Chronicler's Use*, p. 170). This dominant emphasis on ritual reform contrasts markedly with the Deuteronomistic Historian's boundless interest in the transfer of power/kingship from Saul to David to Solomon. W. Johnstone, "Guilt and Atonement: The Theme of 1 and 2 Chronicles,"

pp. 113–38, in *A Word in Season: Essays in Honour of William McKane*, J. D. Martin and P. R. Davies, eds., *JSOT* Supplement 42 (Sheffield: *JSOT*, 1986), argues that whereas the Deuteronomistic History focuses on blessing and curse, "Chronicles constitutes an aggadic midrash on the complementary levitical (including priestly) doctrine of guilt and atonement" (p. 125). His thesis, while provocative, does not do justice to the complexity of the Chronicler's ideology. Concerning the Assyrian seige of Samaria, the Chronicler only alludes to the Assyrian invasion by recounting a letter sent from Hezekiah to *those who remained after the invasion* (2 Chr. 30:6–11); cf. H. G. M. Williamson, *Israel in the Books of Chronicles* (Cambridge: Cambridge University, 1977), pp. 66–67. The letter, although stressing the need for the people's renewed obedience, also places explicit emphasis on the compassion of God. I do not find good reason to sever the Cyrus reference in 2 Chr. 36:22 from the reference to the land's seventy years of desolation found in 2 Chr. 36:21, *contra* H. G. M. Williamson, pp. 7–10. I also see no need to posit several editions of Chronicles as does, for example, F. M. Cross, "A Reconstruction of the Judean Restoration," *Interpretation* 29/2 (1975): 187–203. For other matters concerning the Chronicler's overall "ideology," see H. G. M. Williamson, ch. 5. For an examination of the issues behind the Chronicler's vision for the future, see H. G. M. Williamson, "Eschatology in Chronicles," *Tyndale Bulletin* 28 (1977): 115–54. M. Noth, *The Chronicler's History*, trans. H. G. M. Williamson with an Introduction, *JSOT* Supplement 50 (Sheffield: *JSOT*, 1987), p. 105, depicts the Chronicler's hope in terms of a "hope for a future renewal of the throne of David."

23. Even with respect to passages of prophetic warning and judgment, H. G. M. Williamson, *1 and 2 Chronicles* (Grand Rapids: Eerdmans, 1982) observes: "The Chronicler's doctrine of retribution and repentance thus becomes another of his ways of demonstrating the openness of the future. ... His general policy is to demonstrate from a retelling of the people's history that there is no barrier from that quarter to the hopes for a restoration of one people united under one king around one temple" (p. 33).

24. K. W. Whitelam, "Recreating the History of Israel," *Journal for the Study of the Old Testament* 35 (1986): 45–70, draws attention to the problem of the proliferation of modern textbooks on biblical history which largely replicate the basic biblical storyline and issues, without seriously confronting questions of methodology and social–scientific analysis.

25. E. Fackenheim, *What is Judaism?: An Interpretation for the Present Age* (New York: Collier, 1987), ch. 14, wrestles with notions of divine infinity and intimacy in light of the Holocaust.

26. W. Brueggemann, *Abiding Astonishment: Psalms, Modernity, and the Making of History* (Louisville: Westminster/John Knox, 1991), p. 48, stresses the need for a methodology that moves us beyond "establishment accounts" of Israel's history to the extent that these agendas are reflected in the Historical Psalms.

27. See W. Brueggemann, "Theodicy in a Social Dimension," *Journal for the Study of the Old Testament* 33 (1985): 3–25; J. D. Pleins, " 'Why do you hide your face?': Divine Silence and Speech in the Book of Job," *Interpretation* (forthcoming).

28. On God's freedom, see G. Gutiérrez, *On Job: God-Talk and the Suffering of the Innocent* (Maryknoll, N.Y.: Orbis, 1987), ch. 9.

29. Although I must emphasize that the effort to read the "signs of the times" is a terribly necessary component in a modern theological discourse that seeks to take human rights, warfare, and economic issues seriously, as exemplified in the encyclical *Pacem in Terris* 39–45, 75–79, 126–29, 142–45. Printed in J. Gremillion, ed., *The Gospel of Peace and Justice: Catholic Social Teaching Since Pope John* (Maryknoll, N.Y.: Orbis, 1976), pp. 201–41.

30. Instructive here is the approach taken by P. Trible, *Texts of Terror: Literary–Feminist Readings of Biblical Narratives* (Philadelphia: Fortress, 1984), who studies some of the most disturbing biblical tales concerning women in Genesis, Judges, and 2 Samuel—stories of rejection, violence, rape, and murder. Trible reclaims these narratives *in memoriam*. This approach, Trible writes, "interprets stories of outrage on behalf of their female victims in order to recover a neglected history, to remember a past that the present embodies, and to pray that these terrors shall not come to pass again" (p. 3).

11. Wisdom and Torah Psalms

1. P. Freire, *Pedagogy of the Oppressed*, trans. M. Bergman Ramos (New York: Seabury, 1970), p. 56.

2. Ibid., p. 71.

3. For further discussion of the biblical wisdom writings within the context of the international ancient Near Eastern wisdom tradition, see the following: G. E. Bryce, *A Legacy of Wisdom: The Egyptian Contribution to the Wisdom of Israel* (Lewisburg, Pa.: Bucknell University, 1979); J. L. Crenshaw, "Education in Wisdom," *Journal of Biblical Literature* 104 (1985): 601–15; T. Donald, "The Semantic Field of Rich and Poor in the Wisdom Literature of Hebrew and Accadian," *Oriens antiquus* 2 (1964): 27–41; R. Gordis, *Poets, Prophets, and Sages: Essays in Biblical Interpretation* (Bloomington, Ind.: Indiana University, 1971);

H.-J. Hermisson, *Studien zur israelitischen Spruchweisheit*, Wissenschaftliche Monographien zum Alten und Neuen Testament 28 (Neukirchen-Vluyn: Neukirchener Verlag, 1968); A. Lemaire, "Sagesse et Ecoles," *Vetus Testamentum* 34 (1984): 270–81; T. N. D. Mettinger, *Solomonic State Officials: A Study of the Civil Government Officials of the Israelite Monarchy* (Lund: CWK Gleerup, 1971); J. P. J. Oliver, "Schools and Wisdom Literature," *Journal of Northwest Semitic Languages*, Stellenbosch 4 (1975): 49–60; J. D. Pleins, "Poverty in the Social World of the Wise," *Journal for the Study of the Old Testament* 37 (1987): 61–78. For translations of representative texts, consult W. G. Lambert, *Babylonian Wisdom Literature* (Oxford: Clarendon, 1960), and M. Lichtheim, *Ancient Egyptian Literature, Volume I: The Old and Middle Kingdoms* (Berkeley: University of California, 1973); *Ancient Egyptian Literature, Volume II: The New Kingdom* (Berkeley: University of California, 1976); *Ancient Egyptian Literature, Volume III: The Late Period* (Berkeley: University of California, 1980); *Late Egyptian Wisdom Literature in the International Context: Study of Demotic Instructions*, Orbis Biblicus et Orientalis 52 (Göttingen: Vandenhoeck & Ruprecht, 1983).

4. A useful introduction to the wisdom tradition is provided by R. E. Murphy, *The Tree of Life: An Exploration of Biblical Wisdom Literature* (New York: Doubleday, 1990). On the complex issue of the delimitation of the wisdom genre in the Psalter see: A. Hurvitz, "Wisdom Vocabulary in the Hebrew Psalter: A Contribution to the Study of 'Wisdom Psalms'," *Vetus Testamentum* 38/1 (1988): 41–51; R. E. Murphy, "A Consideration of the Classification 'Wisdom Psalms'," pp. 156–67 in *Congress Volume: Bonn*, Supplements to Vetus Testamentum 9 (Leiden: E. J. Brill, 1963); reprinted as pp. 456–7 in J. L. Crenshaw, ed., *Studies in Ancient Israelite Wisdom* (New York: KTAV, 1976); and L. G. Perdue, *Wisdom and Cult: A Critical Analysis of the Views of Cult in the Wisdom Literatures of Israel and the Ancient Near East*, Society of Biblical Literature Dissertation Series 30 (Missoula, Mont.: Scholars, 1977), ch. 5.

5. Administrative and royal connections abound in the Egyptian texts: The earliest example is from the Old Kingdom (c. 2686–2181 B.C.E.), a text ascribed to crown prince Hardjedef (cf. Lichtheim, *Ancient Egyptian Literature I*, 1973, pp. 58–59). Another text from this period was composed by an unknown vizier, but the son for whom the piece was written, Kagemni, was eventually elevated to a governing post (ibid., pp. 59–60). The Old Kingdom text ascribed to Ptahhotep depicts the author as a crown prince and governing official (ibid., pp. 61–80). The *Instruction to Merikare* from the First Intermediate Period (c. 2181–2040 B.C.E.) is that of an elder king to his son, the heir appar-

ent (ibid., pp. 97–109). Wisdom's royal associations are carried on in the Middle Kingdom (c. 2040–1786 B.C.E.) through *The Instruction of King Amenemhet I for His Son Sesostris I* (ibid., pp. 135–45). The New Kingdom (c. 1558–1085 B.C.E.) text of Any is the writing of a scribe to his son (Lichtheim, *Ancient Eyptian Literature II*, 1976, pp. 135–46). The instruction of Amenemope is the work of a royal overseer (ibid., pp. 146–63). In the Late Period (after 1085 B.C.E.), the writing of Ankhsheshonq is attributed to a priest of the sun god Re at Heliopolis (Lichtheim, *Ancient Egyptian Literature III*, 1980, pp. 159–84; *Late Egyptian Wisdom Literature*, pp. 13–92). In the biblical text, kings Solomon and Hezekiah are expressly connected to the text of Proverbs (1:1; 25:1). Against the royal analysis of the wisdom traditions, some, such as R. E. Clements, *Prophecy and Tradition* (Oxford: Basil Blackwell, 1975), pp. 74, 81, have argued that the materials evidence a "popular, and often rural, background." Cf. J. A. Emerton, "Wisdom," pp. 214–37 in *Tradition and Interpretation*, ed. G. W. Anderson (Oxford: Clarendon Press, 1979), esp. pp. 221–27; P. J. Nel, *The Structure and Ethos of the Wisdom Admonitions in Proverbs*, Beihefte zur *Zeitschrift für die alttestamentliche Wissenschaft* 158 (Berlin: Walter de Gruyter, 1982), pp. 79–81. What I am arguing is *not* that wisdom materials did not have a function (or origin) in the family or village; rather, my view is that *the traditions we possess in Proverbs* represent the educated urban-based wisdom tradition. As Lemaire, "Sagesse et Ecoles," p. 272, incisively observes, "The *written* transmission of *collections* of proverbs presupposes a cultural milieu different than that of the oral transmission of isolated proverbs used occasionally in daily life or in traditional palavers." That setting, I argue, is the urban educational context, i.e., the *bêt midraší*, "my school," of Ben Sirach (Sir. 51:23). The view I develop runs somewhat counter to the analysis offered by R. N. Whybray, *The Intellectual Tradition in the Old Testament. Beihefte zur Zeitschrift für die alttestamentliche Wissenschaft* 135 (Berlin: Walter de Gruyter, 1974), who, while he sustains an intellectual tradition as the ethos for the wisdom texts, does not envision the institutional background suggested here. Whybray's views find additional elaboration in *Wealth and Poverty in the Book of Proverbs, JSOT* Supplement 99 (Sheffield: *JSOT*, 1990), pp. 45–59, 68–72, where he challenges the view that there is a royal ethos to the sentence literature of Proverbs 10:1–22:16 and chs. 25–29. On the other hand, Whybray does place the instruction literature of Proverbs 1–9 and 22:17–24:22 in the urban/royal educational context (Whybray, *Wealth and Poverty*, sections C. and D.).

6. See W. Brueggemann, "Theodicy in a Social Dimension," *Journal for the Study of the Old Testament* 33 (1985): 3–25; G. Gutiérrez,

On Job: God-Talk and the Suffering of the Innocent, trans. M. J. O'Connell (Maryknoll, N.Y.: Orbis, 1987).

7. Cf. the opening to the *Instruction of Amenemope*, which states:

Beginning of the teaching for life,
The instructions for well-being,
Every rule for relations with elders,
For conduct toward magistrates;
Knowing how to answer one who speaks,
To reply to one who sends a message.
So as to direct him on the paths of life,
To make him prosper upon earth,
Steering him clear of evil (I, 1–10).

> Translation of Lichtheim,
> *Ancient Egyptian Literature II,*
> 1976, p. 148.

8. Cf. Prov. 10:4; 14:23; 19:15, 24; 21:5; 24:34.

9. The more skeptical and sociologically observant writer of Ecclesiastes recognizes that the poor are victims of a system of hierarchical control, hence the social ladder is one with power holders and officials dominating and oppressing those who stand below them (Eccl. 5:7–8). The language used in this passage is striking, since the writer adopts the term *rāš* for "poor," the very term that Proverbs uses to speak of the poor as lazy. Kugel, "Qohelet and Money," *Catholic Biblical Quarterly* 51/1 (1989), pp. 35–38, offers the following nonstandard alternate but intriguing translation of Ecclesiastes 5:7: "If you see the oppression of the poor and the perversion of justice and right in the place of judgment, do not be astonished at the matter; for one payment-taker upon another is at watch, and other payment-takers upon them." His argument sustains the view that the writer of Ecclesiastes is brutally clear about the fact of oppression, but Kugel's translation alters the hierarchical dimension of standard translations of the text.

10. Cf. Prov. 16:12, 15; 20:28; 24:21–22; 25:2–6; 30:31.

11. Bryce, *A Legacy of Wisdom*, p. 201. Cf. Prov. 14:35; 16:10, 14; 19:12; 20:2, 8; 24:21.

12. Cf. Prov. 1:7, 29; 2:5; 3:7; 9:10; 10:27; 14:26–27; 15:16, 33; 19:23; 22:4; 23:17; 24:21.

13. On the pursuit of wisdom, see Ps. 1:2; 19:8–9, 11; 37:34; 112:1; 119:1–16. In contrast to W. Soll, *Psalm 119: Matrix, Form, and Setting,* Catholic Biblical Quarterly Monograph Series 23 (Washington, D.C.: Catholic Biblical Association, 1991), esp. ch. 5.

14. Cf. John Paul II, *On Human Work: Encyclical Laborem Exercens* (Washington, D. C.: United States Catholic Conference, 1981), especially sections 9–10, 21–22.

15. For a survey discussion of poverty in the biblical tradition, see J. D. Pleins, "Poor, Poverty (Old Testament)," *The Anchor Bible Dictionary*, ed. D. N. Freedman (New York: Doubleday, 1992), vol. 5, pp. 402–14; and T. Hanks, "Poor, Poverty (New Testament)," ibid., pp. 414–24. For studies specific to the wisdom tradition, see: N. Habel, "Wisdom, Wealth and Poverty Paradigms in the Book of Proverbs," *Bible Bhashayam* 14 (1988): 26–49; J. Kugel, "Qohelet and Money," pp. 32–49; R. N. Whybray, *Wealth and Poverty*, pp. 14–22; G. H. Wittenberg, "The Lexical Context of the Terminology for 'Poor' in the Book of Proverbs," *Scriptura: Tydskrif vir bybelkunde*, Stellenbosch 2 (1986): 40–85.

16. C. Van Leeuwen, *Le développement du sens social en Israël avant l'ère chrétienne*. Studia Semitica Neerlandica 1 (Assen: Van Gorcum, 1955), p. 153.

17. Prov. 28:6, 8, 11, 19, 20, 22, 25, 27. Cf. W. McKane, *Proverbs: A New Approach* (Philadelphia: Westminster, 1970), p. 621. Bryce maintains that Proverbs 28–29 is more favorable to the poor than the rich, thereby indicating a late date for this passage (cf. Bryce, *A Legacy of Wisdom*, p. 118).

18. Following the analysis of B. V. Malchow, "Social Justice in the Wisdom Literature," *Biblical Theology Bulletin* 12 (1982): 121.

19. Cf. Prov. 11:28; 20:17, 21; 23:4–5; 23:23–27; 28:22; 29:3. The Egyptian wisdom writings exhibit a clear awareness of the transitory character of wealth (cf. Ptahhotep §6, 30; Any 8:5–10; Amenemope IX:10–X:5, XVIII:12–13, XIX:11–15, XXIV:15–17; Ankhsheshonq 9:11, 18:17; Papyrus Insinger 18:5).

20. Cf. Prov. 1:19; 10:2; 11:4, 28; 13:8, 11; 16:8; 17:1; 20:17, 21; 21:17; 23:20; 28:20; 29:3; 30:7–10. The Egyptian wisdom literature, likewise, counsels restraint in the use of wealth (cf. Ankhsheshonq 6:10; 7:7; 9:11, 24–25; 12:3; 25:6; Papyrus Insinger 6:17, 24; 15:7; 26:16).

21. Students are expressly told not to despise or mock the poor (Prov. 17:5; 14:31; 22:22). Similar counsel obtains in the Egyptian wisdom materials (Amenemope IV:4–7; XIV:5–8; XV:6–7; XXVI:9; Papyrus Insinger 33:16). Charity toward the poor is enjoined as a virtue in the wisdom tradition (Prov. 21:13; 22:9, 16; 29:7, 14; cf. the Egyptian Any 8; Amenemope XVI:5–10, XXVI:13–14, XXVII:4–5; Ankhsheshonq 15:6; Papyrus Insinger 15:22, 16:12–14, 25:6). I disagree with Malchow, "Social Justice," p. 122, when he argues that wisdom charity is an active posture deserving the label "social justice." In failing to sep-

arate the more "activist" posture of Job from the charity solution of Proverbs, Malchow has overlooked an important debate within the wisdom tradition. Cf. J. D. Pleins, "Poverty in the Social World of the Wise," *Journal for the Study of the Old Testament* 37 (1987): 61–78, esp. 70–71. The motivations provided in Proverbs for charitable giving do not exhibit a sense of social justice. One gives to the poor (1) to avoid falling into poverty (Prov. 22:16), (2) to avoid being mistreated should one become poor (Prov. 21:13; 28:27), or (3) to obtain blessings and rewards from God (Prov. 11:24; 14:21; 19:17).

22. R. Gordis, *Poets, Prophets, and Sages*, p. 162.

23. Cf. Prov. 19:1. Similar views obtain in the Egyptian wisdom writings, where the notion that there are things worse than poverty is used to stress the importance of a life of happiness and integrity (cf. Amenemope VIII:19–20, IX:5–6, IX:7–8; Ankhsheshonq 21:22, 23:8–9; Papyrus Insinger 27:9). Note the calculated reversals in the skeptical Ecclesiastes (Eccl. 6:8; 9:15–16). In the latter text, the possession of wisdom in a context of poverty is recognized to be useless.

24. See J. D. Pleins, "Poverty," p. 67–68. If the prophetic literature offers any insight into the structures of poverty in ancient Israel, it is that the members of the ruling elite were the agents devouring the poor (cf., e.g., Isa. 3:13–14, 5:8; Jer. 2:34, 5:4–5, 5:27–28; 22:13–14; Ezek. 18:12, 18:17, 22:29; Amos 2:6, 4:1, 5:11, 6:1–6; 8:4). Such a view is scarcely entertained in Proverbs, the sole exception being Prov. 31:9, which utilizes terminology for poverty that echoes Jer. 22:16.

25. On poverty as the product of fate or the hand of God, see Prov. 10:22; 22:2; 29:13. For Egyptian comparisons, consider Ptahhotep §10; Amenemope VII:1–6, XXI:15–16; Ankhsheshonq 12:3, 22:25, 26:8, 26:14; Papyrus Insinger 7:18, 17:2, 28:4, 30:15.

26. See J. A. Dearman, *Property Rights in the Eighth-Century Prophets*, Society of Biblical Literature Dissertation Series 106 (Atlanta: Scholars Press, 1988); L. Epsztein, *Social Justice in the Ancient Near East and the People of the Bible*, trans. J. Bowden (London: SCM, 1986), ch. 7.

27. The mid-sixth century A.D./C.E. Byzantine historian Procopius, *Secret History*, trans. R. Atwater (Ann Arbor: University of Michigan, 1961), offers us a similar picture of the economic and social injustices that attended the construction of the empire of Justinian and Theodora—tales that could not be included in official histories of the empire.

28. The U. S. Bishops' Pastoral Message and Letter, "Economic Justice for All: Catholic Social Teaching and the U. S. Economy," *Origins* 16/24 (1986): 409–55, is a document that stands in a long tradition of Catholic efforts to bring religiously grounded convictions to bear on the paramount wealth and poverty issues of our time. The

quote is taken from chapter 5, section 329, p. 444. For the broader background, see J. Gremillion, *The Gospel of Peace and Justice: Catholic Social Teaching since Pope John* (Maryknoll, N.Y.: Orbis, 1976).

29. Contrast this passage with the more complex Deut. 15:4–18 which combines the wisdom notion of rewards for generosity/loyalty with the additional covenantal/historical motivation to act because "you were slaves in the land of Egypt" (Deut. 15:15). In the mind of the Deuteronomist, instruction (*tôrâ*) alone is not a sufficient catalyst for action apart from the recreative reality of the Exodus liberation and the contractual obligations of the Sinaitic covenant. Within the wisdom tradition represented by Proverbs, however, the story of God's dealings with Israel plays no role as a basis for right action.

30. Cf. G. Gutiérrez, *On Job*, chs. 5 and 6.

31. Cf. J. D. Pleins, " 'Why do you hide your face?': Divine Silence and Speech in the Book of Job," *Interpretation* (forthcoming).

32. The Hebrew term *rāšāᶜ*, "wicked," for example, appears 76 times in the book of Proverbs, more than in the entire Psalter (74). The same word occurs regularly in the text of Job (25) and in Ecclesiastes (6), in contrast to its rarity in the Pentateuch and the Deuteronomistic History. Generally the term is rare in the prophetic literature, appearing most frequently in Isaiah, and is concentrated in specific chapters of Ezekiel (chs. 3, 18, 21, 33). Virtually the same comments apply to the distribution of the term *ṣaddîq*, "just," with the exception that this word is noticeably less frequent in Job. With regard to the distinction between wise and fool, consult: J. L. Crenshaw, *Old Testament Wisdom: An Introduction* (Atlanta: John Knox, 1981), p. 80; and W. O. E. Oesterley, *The Book of Proverbs* (London: Methuen, 1929), pp. lxxxiv–lxxxvii.

33. Cf. Prov. 11:4–5; 12:15; 13:6; 14:9; 14:24; 15:5; 16:14; 17:10.

34. The parallels with the rural Micah's social critique are important (Micah 2:1–9; 3:1–4, 9–12; 6:10–12; 7:3). The prophet uses the term *rāšāᶜ*, "wicked," once, but significantly in a context that makes the wicked an owner of a house and granary which are seats of economic injustice (Ps. 6:10). The sociological content is clear and precise. Possibly high officials or even the palace is under consideration here (cf. 6:16). On the rural character of Micah, see H. W. Wolff, "Micah the Moreshite–The Prophet and His Background," pp. 77–85 in *Israelite Wisdom: Theological and Literary Essays in Honor of Samuel Terrien*, eds. J. G. Gammie et al. (Missoula, Mont.: Scholars, 1978); *Micah the Prophet*, trans. R. D. Gehrke (Philadelphia: Fortress, 1981), pp. 17–25.

12. Prophetic Oracles of Judgment

1. H. W. Wolff, *Confrontations with Prophets: Discovering the Old Testament's New and Contemporary Significance* (Philadelphia: Fortress, 1983), p. 20.

2. See the detailed study of P. D. Miller, *Sin and Judgment in the Prophets* (Chico, Calif.: Scholars, 1982). On the intertwining of idolatry and oppression, see T. Hanks, *God So Loved the Third World: The Bible, The Reformation, and Liberation Theologies* (Maryknoll, N.Y.: Orbis, 1983), ch. 2.

3. G. Gutiérrez, *The Power of the Poor in History* (Maryknoll, N.Y.: Orbis, 1984), pp. 169–85.

4. Ibid., p. 193.

5. Psalms 14 and 53 are virtually identical. The relevant differences will be indicated in the course of the discussion.

6. Both texts speak of calling upon God. In the case of the psalm, "They do not call upon the LORD" (Pss. 14:4; 53:5). The accent in Micah is slightly different: "They will cry out to the LORD, who will not answer them" (Mic. 3:4). In both cases, the act of oppression cuts one off from God—a fact that concretely defines the "folly" addressed by the psalmist.

7. Parallel not found in Psalm 53. On the political character of ʿṣh see W. McKane, *Prophets and Wise Men*, Studies in Biblical Theology 44 (Naperville, Ill.: Alec R. Allenson, 1965).

8. A detailed discussion of this topic can be found in L. Wisser, *Jérémie, Critique de la Vie Sociale* (Genève: Labor et Fides, 1982). See also W. Brueggemann, *Jeremiah 1–25: To Pluck Up, To Tear Down* (Grand Rapids: Eerdmans, 1988).

9. See, e.g., Jer. 1:15–19; 2:5–8; 2:20–27; 4:1–9; 5:26–31; 8:8–12.

10. For a study of the socially legitimizing character of Canaanite religion, see G. Mendenhall, "The Worship of Baal and Asherah: A Study in the Social Bonding Functions of Religious Systems," pp. 147–58 in *Biblical and Related Studies Presented to Samuel Iwry*, A. Kort and S. Morschauser, eds. (Winona Lake, Ind.: Eisenbrauns, 1985).

11. Translation of J. C. L. Gibson, *Canaanite Myths and Legends* (Edinburgh: T. and T. Clark, 1977), p. 102.

12. Cf. Isa. 1:17, 23; 10:2; Jer. 7:6; 22:3; Zech. 7:10; Mal. 3:5. Although, as M. Fendler notes in "Zur Sozialkritik des Amos," *Evangelische Theologie*, Munich 33 (1973), p. 36, such language does not appear in all the prophetic books to bolster their social critique. For additional background consult F. C. Fensham, "Widow, Orphan and the Poor in the Ancient Near Eastern Legal and Wisdom Literature," *Journal of Near Eastern Studies* 21 (1962): 129–39.

13. Following the analysis of T. Booij, "The Background of the Oracle in Psalm 81," *Biblica* 65 (1984): 465–75, the distance of the day of judgment argues in favor of a pre-exilic date for this text. On the concern to put off the day of divine wrath in prophetic literature, see Amos 5:18–20.

14. Although the critical voice of Habakkuk does not find a counterpart in the Prophetic Oracles of Judgment, a number of scholarly studies into the nature and character of prophecy have come to blur the boundary line between the prophets and the cult, suggesting that prophetic oracles like those of Habakkuk may have found their way into ancient Israelite worship. See, e.g., M. A. Sweeney, "Structure, Genre, and Intent in the Book of Habakkuk," *Vetus Testamentum* 41 (1991): 63–83; R. Wilson, *Prophecy and Society in Ancient Israel* (Philadelphia: Fortress, 1980), pp. 278–79. The discussion of the social location of the prophets and their relation to the cult has gained substantial depth since P. L. Berger, "Charisma and Religious Innovation: The Social Location of Israelite Prophecy," *American Sociological Review* 28 (1963): 940–50; cf., e.g., J. S. Kselman, "The Social World of the Israelite Prophets: A Review Article," *Religious Studies Review* 11/2 (1985): 120–29. See also A. R. Johnson, *The Cultic Prophet and Israel's Psalmody* (Cardiff: University of Wales, 1979); and S. Mowinckel, "III. Kultprophetie und Prophetische Psalmen," *Psalmenstudien* (Amsterdam: P. Schippers, 1961). Much in this regard remains subject to debate and discussion: Supposing there were indeed cult prophets, to what extent did they shape the Psalter? Were the canonical prophets indebted to the cult and its worship as reflected in the Psalms?

15. I. T. Kaufman, "Undercut By Joy: The Sunday Lectionaries and the Psalms of Lament," pp. 68–78 in *The Psalms and Other Studies on the Old Testament: Presented to Joseph I. Hunt*, ed. J. C. Knight and L. A. Sinclair (Nashotah, Wisc.: Nashotah House Seminary, 1990), critically assesses the psalms selected for the Sunday lectionary readings of several Christian communions, drawing our attention to the notable omissions and serious editing problems that exist throughout these widely used sets of readings. Kaufman makes it clear that it is imperative for us to consciously seek to recover the full depth of the Psalter in Sunday worship, particularly with respect to the psalms of lament.

General Index

Aaron, 132-33, 144, 148
Abandonment, 21
Abraham, 147-48
Acrostic, 8
Adversary, 150-51
Affirmation, 27
Ahab, 110
Amos, 110, 173
Anger, 15
Atheism, 174-75
Baal, 119, 203n12
Babylonian invasion, 35, 37, 41, 176
Bonhoefer, Dietrich, 3, 8-9
Brueggemann, Walter, 27, 111, 150
Bryce, G. E., 158
Bull, 22
Canaan, 81-82, 149, 179
Charitv, 167
Chiasma, 8
Childs, B., 4
Chronicles, 106, 150-51, 210n22, 211n23
City of God, 117-18
Comfort, 19
Community and king, 113-15
Covenant, 88-89, 114, 146
Creator, 81-82, 85-86, 134; and liberation, 133-36
Cyrus, 151
David, 2, 102, 106, 111-12, 126, 150-51, 190n5

Deuteronomist, 110, 147, 149, 151, 153
Diligence, 161
Dog, 22-23
Domination, 84
Doubt, 27
Drunkennness, 161
Ecclesiastes, 161, 164-65, 172, 215n9
Education, liberative, 155
Elohim, 2
Enemies, 21-24, 34, 39, 66, 193nn4,5
Enthronement of God, 136-38, 206n10
Epiphany, 106
Eternity, 87-89
Ethics, 92
Exile, 23, 33, 72
Exodus, 72, 134-35, 144
Exploitation, 38
Ezekiel, 111, 145
Food, 63-64
Forgetfulness, 145-46
Forgiveness, 61-62
Fox, Matthew, 84, 86
Freire, Paulo, 155
Gandhi, Mahatma, 45, 54
God: as conquerer, 102-5; judges nations, 64-68; and judgment, 181-83; of justice, 94-96; of the quest, 50-52; as refuge,

Scripture Index

The verse numbering of the Psalms followed in this book
is that of the Hebrew Bible.